The Cultural Side of Innovation

T0330815

'This book provides us with thrilling ideas about how innovations emerge and survive. Dany Jacobs's discussion about culture and the evolution of innovations touches upon a topic that ought to be more discussed by anyone who wants to understand tomorrow's knowledge economy.'
—*Bertil Rolandsson, University of Gothenberg, Sweden*

In most discussions about the knowledge-based economy, innovation is associated or even equated with technology, whereas culture's influence is ignored. However, innovation is embedded in cultural and social contexts, and neglecting these crucial contexts may impede an innovation's diffusion—and eventual success.

This book places culture at the centre of discussions on innovation, beginning with a comprehensive introduction to innovation's various forms, including the history, sociology and economics of innovation. Insights from marketing and psychology are integrated into a complexity theory framework, which are then utilized to evaluate case studies of organizations experiencing repeated innovation successes. The sometimes-fraught relationship of firms to creativity is discussed, and a new model for to calculating the creativity of an economy is presented.

Dany Jacobs is Professor of Industrial Dynamics and Innovation Policy at the University of Amsterdam, as well as Professor of Art, Culture and Economy at the Universities of Applied Science HAN and ArtEZ in Arnhem, the Netherlands. He is the author of *Mapping Strategic Diversity* (2010).

RIOT! Routledge Studies in Innovation, Organization and Technology

The Cultural Side
of Innovation
Adding Values

Dany Jacobs

Routledge
Taylor & Francis Group

NEW YORK AND LONDON

First published 2014 by Routledge
605 Third Avenue, New York, NY 10017
4 Park Square, Milton Park, Abingdon, Oxon OX14 4RN

Routledge is an imprint of the Taylor & Francis Group, an informa business

First issued in paperback 2018

Library of Congress Cataloging-in-Publication Data

Jacobs, D. (Dany)
   The cultural side of innovation : adding values / by Dany Jacobs.
     pages cm. — (Routledge studies in innovation, organization and
   technology ; 33)
   Includes bibliographical references and index.
  1. New products. 2. Diffusion of innovations. 3. Consumer behavior
I. Title.
   HF5415.153.J332013
   338064—dc23
   2013019497

ISBN 13: 978-0-415-71619-2 (hbk)
ISBN 13: 978-1-138-37748-6 (pbk)

Typeset in Sabon
by Apex CoVantage, LLC

The reasonable man adapts himself to the world;
the unreasonable one persists in trying to adapt the world to himself.
Therefore all progress depends on the unreasonable man.

—George Bernard Shaw, 'Maxims for Revolutionaries,'
appendix to Man and Superman, 1903

Contents

Tables

Figures

BONUS TRACK

Introduction

This is an innovative book about innovation. First, it is more about culture than about technology. In most discussions about the knowledge-based economy, innovation is associated, if not equalized, with technology, whereas culture is only sparingly mentioned. The thesis of this book is that this leads to many problems related to the diffusion and success of innovations, as not enough attention is paid to the necessary cultural and social embeddedness of innovations. As a consequence, taking culture more into account will increase the chances for innovative success.

Second, this book starts from a broad definition of innovation: something new which is realized, hopefully with an added value. Based on this, a fuzzy approach is presented with the help of which a broad range of innovations can be discussed, from marginal style innovations to radically new concepts. Moreover, a third basic category of 'transaction innovations' is introduced, beside the traditionally recognized product and process innovations.

Third, this is a thoroughly cross-disciplinary book. It deals with the history, sociology and economics of innovation from a 'generalized Darwinian' and complexity theory perspective. In addition, insights from marketing and psychology are integrated. More than other books in the field of evolutionary economics, basic Darwinian questions are dealt with, such as how exactly the selection systems in which innovations are chosen are structured, and what the precise units are at different levels of selection.

Regarding my first contention, of course, more than a few authors have written about the culture that is necessary for creativity and performance *within* organizations or societies at large. This book, however, deals with the cultural side of innovation mostly from another, *societal* perspective: its relationship with culture at large and with the culture (norms, values, preferences and expectations) of different customer groups. Innovation is first and foremost a cultural process through which new concepts and meanings are created and new categories developed. Successful innovation means changing people's sets of preferences to a lesser or greater extent, and therefore changing their cultural 'value systems.'[1] Without this, innovations will not make the necessary connections with potential customers and, as a consequence, be rejected. In short, there is no economic value creation without cultural value creation, or at least value change—that is, cultural 'revaluation.' In a 2006 essay on creativity and the economy for the Dutch Ministry of Economic Affairs,[2] I argued that creativity in itself does not lead to economic value but has to be combined with professionalism and focus to become productive (Jacobs 2006b: 23). With this book, I want to provide an analytical basis for this idea of 'productive creativity.'

In this connection, co-evolution is a crucial concept. Innovators are not the sole agents of change. Innovation does not occur in isolation but is related to all kinds of changes at different levels of societies. As a consequence of different sorts of top-down and bottom-up changes in society, our lives are continuously changing—most of the time slowly, sometimes more rapidly. In order to be successful, innovation is being connected more or less consciously with these changes, bringing them forward or maybe hampering them—innovation is indeed not necessarily progressive. This idea was summarized in the title of the original working paper from which this book was developed: 'Innovation and Value Creation as a Co-Evolving Cultural Process.'

In this book, I develop my argument in a systematic way. In the first part, important building blocks are presented separately, which later on are brought together. In Chapter 1, I present and categorize the variety of innovations in a more extensive form than is mostly the case in innovation literature. Compared to other texts, one will find more examples in the realm of fashion, design and services. In addition to product and process innovation, a new basic category of innovation is introduced, 'transaction innovation,' meaning innovations in the field of publicity, marketing, sales and institutions which all stimulate economic transactions. Subsequently I look at more comprehensive forms of innovation, from new business models to system innovations and changes in techno-economic regimes in which these basic forms are combined. In Chapter 2, the difference between the technical and nontechnical (mostly cultural) aspects of innovation is clarified. In Chapter 3, I introduce my fuzzy approach to innovation related to the different degrees of innovativeness or 'radicalness' of innovations. We will see that radicalness of innovations is related to their cognitive distance from the existing cultural framework. Incremental (step-by-step) innovations are easier to understand—to 'place' in existing frameworks—than more radical innovations. The risks related to radical innovations are therefore much higher. Because of this, strategies related to more radical innovations have to take this cultural distance as their point of departure. Moreover, as a consequence of this cultural distance, radical innovations are more open-ended and unpredictable. In the end, in many cases, they are used quite differently from the way their original inventors envisaged them. Certain user groups may appropriate the innovation and use it for their own purposes. This entails co-evolution.

In Chapter 4 the relevance of a Darwinian evolutionary approach towards innovation—with its traditional three steps—(1) variation, (2) selection (of the fittest) and (3) retention (inheritance), multiplication and possibly speciation—is discussed. Evolutionary approaches have been quite common in innovation literature, especially since Nelson and Winter's pioneering book *An Evolutionary Theory of Economic Change* (Nelson & Winter 1982), which has stimulated a whole research programme in this field. At the same time, however, many books on innovation employ rather simplistic evolutionary metaphors—for instance, equating Darwin with surviving on the market. For this reason, some basics in this realm have to be clarified. At the same time, a few common objections against this approach and some simplistic adaptations are addressed.

In the second part, these different building blocks are then combined to discuss innovation success at different levels. Chapter 5 addresses the issue of fitness from an economic point of view. In this book, we look at two levels of selection: one in which organizations (with their innovation routines) are the units of selection and a second one where we look at the possible survival of innovations. Regarding the latter, the distinction between the technical and cultural elements in the valuation of innovations will turn out to be crucial. This is illustrated in a special section on the 'added values' of industrial design.

In Chapter 6, we dig deeper into the different mechanisms of socioeconomic selection. We will see that there is never just one selection system (mostly seen as the market) but always a particular combination of different selection systems, each of them with its own values and institutional setting. We will also look at the structure of networks in various industries, which helps us to understand the concrete and always complex combination of selection systems which determine the relative success of innovations in each case. Moreover, as just said, innovations never take place in isolation. They are part of a social and cultural environment in which all kinds of changes and other innovations—some more bottom-up, others more top-down—interact in what complexity theorists call complex adaptive (or evolving) systems (CAS or CES). Therefore, we will finish by looking at the structure of our clustered network world, with its possible effect on 'information cascades.' Analysing this structure will help us to understand the emergence of hypes on the one hand and tendencies towards globalization *and* remaining diversity on the other hand.

In Chapter 7, the more active, strategic and managerial consequences of the approach presented in this book are further elaborated. Here we will see that 'co-evolution' is a useful concept not only for description but also for prescription. In Chapter 8, we finally move from selection of innovations to selection of organizations. How come some organizations have been systematically more successful with their innovations than others? Here I introduce the concept of innovation routines, which I developed together with Hendrik Snijders in a study we did in 2007–2008 about Dutch firms which have been repeatedly successful with their innovations. This was a practically oriented study in the field of innovation management in which also the Darwinian assumptions of this book were tested. Chapter 9 concludes and summarizes.

This book is an extended and updated version of *Adding Values: The Cultural Side of Innovation,* which was published by two small Dutch publishers in 2007. It was well received and has been used as a textbook by design and business departments in different countries. On the basis of feedback from users—yes, co-evolution—the structure of the book has been changed and simplified. By lecturing, answering questions and discussing the subject with many people, I also learned a lot, all of which has helped me to—I hope—clarify my argument. Finally, the results of new research by myself and others has been integrated, as well as some new interesting literature.

ACKNOWLEDGEMENTS

People that know me well will recognize quite a few themes that have occupied me over the last twenty years in this book: the amazing variety of innovation, the dynamic and co-evolutionary nature of diffusion of innovations, the importance of nontechnical innovations and the emergence of a creative experience economy. Cutting through all of this is the overriding importance of culture (language, values, frames) in incremental innovation (think of fashion and design), but especially in more radical innovation (sensemaking and the creation of concepts) and the necessity of totally new approaches in the fields of innovation, marketing and strategy as a result of all of this.

Also, the importance of process approaches in the field of strategic management and the complexity of co-evolution (and therefore the relevance of emergence, self-organization and the complexity theories which put these at the centre of their attention) have been major themes in my research.

As will emerge from quite a few citations, I am indebted to an important degree to my colleague Nachoem Wijnberg, first at the University of Groningen and now at the University of Amsterdam, for my elaboration of evolutionary selection systems. Despite my long-standing awareness of evolutionary approaches in the field of economics, Nachoem enhanced my understanding of their practical usefulness in the realm of innovation. Nachoem and I share many interests and preferences (especially related to the importance of culture for the economy), but both of us are also more than a little stubborn. As a consequence, in important aspects my elaboration of selection systems diverges from his.

I also wish to thank Jan Brand, Thijs Broekhuizen, Jan Buijs, Paula Buit, Ritzo ten Cate, Jenny Elissen, Marjon Elshof, Lucie Huiskens, Ton Lamers, Otto Lappöhn, Ewan Lentjes, Constantin von Maltzahn, Marco Mossinkoff, Diane Nijs, Theo Postma, Tamara Rookus, Hendrik Snijders, José Teunissen, Jeroen van den Eijnde and Véronique Timmerhuis for stimulating discussions and very useful comments on previous drafts of this text.

Zutphen, March 2013

Part I
Building Blocks

1 The Variety of Innovation

Innovation is at the centre of discussions on what has been called the knowledge-based, the experience or the creative economy. It is, however, striking to observe that the framework for discussions of innovation has not changed a lot during recent decades and, moreover, to a large extent has remained poorly defined. Most approaches, for example, go no further than a simple distinction between product and process innovation. Many authors do not define innovation at all and partly, as a consequence, implicitly assume that innovation is always technological (e.g., Freeman & Soete 1997). This assumption prevents an appreciation of much real-life innovation. Quite a few authors even see success as a defining element of innovation. As such, a positive selection of the innovation is presupposed, even when many of these same authors admit that most innovations fail!

In this chapter, the diversity of innovation is presented with the help of a basic trichotomy: product innovation, process innovation and transaction innovation. We will also see that more-comprehensive innovations combine elements of these three basic forms. However, let us define innovation first.

1.1 DEFINING INNOVATION

Since the time of the famous economist Joseph Schumpeter (1934: 88–89), who put innovation central in his work, a distinction has been made between the original 'invention' of something new and its first commercial application, the 'innovation.' Possibly three different processes are necessary to move from invention to innovation:

- Research and development to think everything through, in many cases to make the invention work technologically. Airbus's new jumbo A380, for example, required a great deal of technological work in order to develop important new aspects of this huge airplane. However, not all inventions require technological research.
- Learning about possible user needs to increase the chances of commercial success.

- Continuous negotiation between these two developing insights: experimentation and translation of possible market requirements into theoretical questions and vice versa.

If we take the Airbus A380 example, we see that nowadays these processes are performed simultaneously and interactively to a greater extent than was the case before. Airbus did not start the technological development of this airplane before it had made sure that enough customers (airlines and airplane-leasing companies) were interested in its new plane and had expressed their related wishes and requirements. Thus, to some extent, we can understand why certain authors have defined innovation as a '*successful* exploitation of new ideas' (UK DTI Innovation Unit, quoted by Tidd et al. 2005: 66; for a similar definition see Dodgson et al. 2002: 54).[1] However, this kind of learning about user needs as a rule does not lead to certainty about commercial success. Airbus did not make the kind of technology-push mistake that a combination of French and British airplane manufacturers did in the 1970s with their futuristic Concorde airplane—of which not more than twenty were built. Nevertheless, no preliminary dealings to influence the launching airlines have been able to guarantee the commercial success of the A380. As a rule, innovation requires at least a certain degree of risk taking.

According to Schumpeter, an innovation is the commercial application of an idea, its introduction into a market. This may be successful or not. As we will see further in this book, from an evolutionary perspective there is always first variety and then selection. In the economy, there are different levels of selection: first innovations are selected within organizations (in Williamsons's (1985) terms: hierarchies), later on outside them: the market or other hierarchies (such as government agencies, juries). An innovation, for instance, may have to be selected by public authorities to receive a subsidy for its further development. For all these reasons, I think Wijnberg's (2004: 1472) definition of innovation as 'something new, which is presented in such a way that the value will be determined by the selectors' is adequate. Even if this definition may sound a bit vague, it has its advantages:

- In principle, all types of innovation, technical or not, within the fields of manufacturing, services or even the arts, can be included.[2]
- Success is not part of the definition. Many innovations fail. When that happens, the relevant selectors determine that the value of the innovation is too low. However, an innovative concept has to be developed at least far enough for its value to be assessed by the relevant selectors.
- Selection is a broader term than 'the market.' Markets provide an important selection system but, as we will see in Chapter 6, certainly not the only one.

I propose, however, a somewhat simpler definition, which implicitly integrates Wijnberg's key elements:

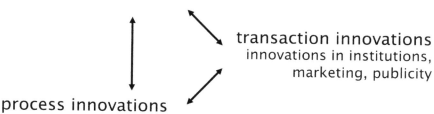

product innovations
from technical improvements and style
innovations to totally new concepts

transaction innovations
innovations in institutions,
marketing, publicity

process innovations
more productive techniques and/or organizational forms
(within organizations or larger parts of value systems)

Figure 1.1   Three basic forms of innovation

An innovation is something new[3] which is realized, hopefully with an added value.[4]

Also in this definition, success is not presupposed. When the relevant selectors do not see any added value to an innovation, compared with existing supply, they will not select it.

In the following sections, the diversity of innovation is presented. First we look at the three basic forms—product innovation, process innovation and transaction innovation (see Figure 1.1) —and then at their possible combinations in more comprehensive forms of innovation such as new business models, system innovations or techno-economic regimes.

1.2   PRODUCT INNOVATION

Ultimately, product innovation, the development of new products and services, is the most important form of innovation. Without product innovations, the two other forms have no purpose in the end. As there are different kinds of products, there are also different kinds of product innovations. In this section, I will discuss consecutively:

- new material products;
- new information products;
- new services (including experiences and transformations).

Material Products

When we think about products, we most easily think about the material products which surround us: our houses, furniture, clothes, food products, toys, cars, books, TVs and mobile phones. Therefore, material products seem the easiest to understand. This may, however, disguise the fact that— expressed in economic value terms—the intangible, nontechnical elements of these products are increasingly more important than their basic material presence and technical functionality. For instance, the value of a car is increased by the knowledge required to build it and increase its quality, the symbolic value of its design and brand and the software integrated in its different parts (Jacobs 1999a). The same dress, sold in a Primark or a Dior shop, will have a quite different value. But without their material presence and functionality, this car or dress wouldn't have any value.

Product innovations may be totally new product concepts (such as the first fax machine or the first video game), they may entail a new *concept* for an existing product (the jet airplane, or IKEA's flat-pack furniture to be assembled by the customers)[5] or only a new *style* or *design* (design or stylistic innovation). In the latter case of small, 'incremental' innovations, selection may be easier, as the product is already well known. However, as a rule, then there will be more competitors, so that such incremental innovations may fail as a consequence of oversupply in the field or because the relevant customers do not appreciate the new varieties. At the other side of the spectrum, new concepts for existing product categories, or totally new products, may be more difficult to sell because the relevant *selectors* do not yet recognize their possible added value, but at the same time they may face a lower level of competition. I come back to the issue of different degrees of radicalness of innovations in Chapter 3.

A bike is not a bike

A mountain bike seems like an odd concept in the Netherlands, which is one of the flattest countries in the world. What would one do with such a bike in this flat country? This was the prevailing idea amongst bicycle producers in the Netherlands at the beginning of the 1980s. At that time, mountain or all-terrain bikes (ATBs) had experienced increasing success in the United States. As a result, some people in the Dutch bicycle industry considered introducing them into the Dutch market. This did occur, especially in the most expensive segment of the market, mainly targeting world bikers who tour various continents, encountering regions where rough road conditions are more the rule than the exception. However, introducing such a bike on a mass scale was thought to be out of the question. The main idea among bicycle producers was 'a bike is a bike,' and who would contradict them?

Well, Giant did. This Taiwanese bicycle producer thought about conquering Western markets, as have many producers in East Asia. To Giant, the Netherlands appeared to be the most attractive market for such an attempt: a small country with the highest density of bicycle use in the world. However, how could they differentiate themselves from Dutch producers, who had maintained a strong cartel for a very long time? Introducing a good, reasonably priced ATB seemed to be a good option. Giant was right, and its mountain bike was a huge success. Why were people in the Netherlands buying such bikes? Apart from the fact that there are actually some hills and dirt roads in the country, the main reason was probably the same as why people drive four-wheel-drive vehicles in the centre of Manhattan. It is the dream, the fantasy of adventure and considering oneself to be different. Increasingly what one is selling is not just a product but also a dream or a fantasy.

Since Giant's introduction of the mountain bike into the Netherlands, the bicycle market has never been the same. In addition to the traditional dark green or black city bike and a few racing bikes, there is now a multitude of bicycle categories: ATBs, hybrid bikes, folding bikes, recumbent bikes. Many people now have two or three bikes: a city bike and one or two more-expensive models. Clearly, this is a good example of product innovation in a mature industry leading to new growth. As a consequence, it should never be said again that 'a bike is just a bike.' This kind of assumption simply kills any inspiration for innovation. Instead, thinking of new categories for a product is a major source of innovation. I shall come back to this when I talk about speciation in the realm of evolutionary approaches further on.

In this respect, the different experience of the recumbent bike (Figure 1.2) in the Netherlands is another interesting case to consider. About the same time as the mountain bike, various small producers tried to make the recumbent bike more popular in the Netherlands. Superficially, one could expect that recumbent bikes would have a high probability of success in a flat, windy country such as the Netherlands. As a consequence of better aerodynamics, the average speed attainable with a recumbent bike is much higher than with a normal one. However, recumbent bikes are not very popular. Why? The main reason is probably that their design is further from the traditional bike design than the mountain bike. In other words, it is a more radical innovation, which is at a larger distance culturally from customers' perceptions of a bike, the dominant design of

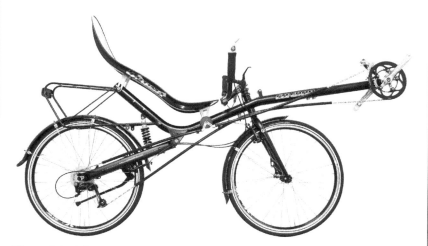

Figure 1.2   The Optima Condor recumbent bicycle

bicycles.[6] For this reason, bikers have no idea whether such a bike is as easy or as safe to ride as a normal one. Moreover, there is quite some variety in the designs of recumbent bikes. So, as well as the question of whether to buy such a bike or not, there is the question of which one to buy. In this sense, a recumbent bicycle is a nice example of an experience good—a product which customers have to try before they buy. Consequently, producers should perhaps give customers more opportunities to try and experience these bikes. In addition, there is probably a need for a daring producer to take the risk of introducing this kind of bicycle on a mass scale, thereby making them cheaper.

Information Products

A second basic kind of products is constituted by *information products or goods* which can be easily reproduced and transported in digital form: music, software, movies, electronic games, magazines, books and other forms of *content*. A special feature of these products is that the cost of producing the first copy (for example, writing a good book or producing a movie) is relatively high compared with the cost of later reproductions. Moreover, in their intangible or digital form, information products are nonrivalrous. This means that one can sell them while keeping them at the same time. This characteristic leads to special considerations in the field of strategy (defending the value of the innovation) and marketing (pricing, or 'versioning')[7] (Shapiro & Varian 1999: 3, 22–26). Especially since the arrival of the Internet, firms producing information goods (newspapers, music firms, encyclopaedia companies)[8] have been struggling to defend their business model because it is very easy to make many copies of their products or because users have become accustomed to free downloads.

Sometimes, it has been argued that more and more products become information products. Cars, for example, contain a lot of software nowadays. This may be true, but this does not change the fundamental character of the car: a car is a tangible and rivalrous product. When you sell your car, you don't have it anymore. Moreover, it cannot be sent through the Internet (just try!). Amazon needs huge warehouses to stock most of its wares and traditional mail services to deliver them. So from the moment that information is included in a material form of hardware, the rules related to the production and transportation of that hardware apply.[9]

Services and Experiences

A service is a kind of product for which the action of a service provider is necessary: the plumber, the consultant, the retailer, the hairdresser. In most cases, this requires the action of real people, but some services may be automated to some extent. Think of ATMs, telecom systems or search engines. So *service innovations* are a third form of product innovation. These can also be ranked from incremental to radical: changes in the design of an existing service (for example, a new shop design, creating a new hairstyle), new concepts for existing products or product categories (new mortgage forms, a new theme park with a new theme, online gambling) and new service concepts (fashion consultancy, call centres, search engines on the Internet). New services may also be based on new processes—and thus process innovation—which produce and deliver the services.

Sometimes it is said that there is a straightforward development in the economy from material products to services. This is not correct. Innovation sometimes means switching between these basic varieties: there may be a development from buying food (a material product) to going to restaurants (a service), but at a certain moment these meals may be sold again in supermarkets and heated by the consumers in their own kitchen. Equally, films have been moving back from cinemas (a service) to DVD boxes (an information product sold in material form) and downloads (pure information products). Of course, these DVDs may be rented in a video shop or library—again a service. These films may also be sold as downloads through the Internet or mobile telecommunication—then the information-product character of movies prevails. As a consequence of these developments, cinemas have improved the experience character of their service offering. Capturing value from innovations increasingly means selling them in different forms through different channels at the same time—multichannel marketing—and competing on ever-new elements.

Technical and nontechnical aspects of service innovation

Pim den Hertog provides an illuminating account of the relationship between technical and nontechnical aspects of service innovation on the basis of his six-dimensional (6-D) model of service innovation (den Hertog 2010: 139–148).

The starting point is the new service concept which as a rule is a new idea about how to organize a solution to a group of customers' problems or needs.

In many cases, this leads to a new way of interaction with customers—for example, by taking over tasks from them. But the opposite may also happen: the innovation may give customers a larger role to play, in this way performing more of the service activities (think for example of e-banking or IKEA's flat-pack furniture).

This leads to a new value system with possibly new business partners. E-business, for example, requires cooperation with web designers, companies handling the payments and a logistics firm specialized in delivering small parcels.

The example just given about e-business also clarifies that service innovations may lead to new revenue models, as each of the new partners has to be able to be profitable.

In many cases, a new service-delivery system has to be designed. This has an organizational (including new human competences) and a technical component: not all service innovations require new technologies, but it is always good to look at different technical options for a new service. Some new services originate from new technological opportunities, such as the Internet, huge databases or new medical technologies, but not all do.[10]

All these changes reflect two developments in innovation literature which den Hertog supports: first the nontechnical elements of innovation increasingly considered to be the more important ones, even when in most cases one takes advantage of new technical opportunities; and second the growing interest in open innovation in which all kinds of customers and business partners play an active role. I will come back to this in the next section where I will discuss process innovation in the realm of innovation processes itself.

Despite all of this, den Hertog still tends to forget two important nontechnical aspects of service innovation. The first one is its aesthetic design, even when in his case study of the hospitality sector the 'serviscape' (the look and feel of the place) appears to be the aspect in which most innovation activity took place (den Hertog 2010: 72). On close reading, it seems that in his 6-D model, this is part of the first dimension, but it doesn't get the attention it deserves. Later in this section, I will come back to this in the box on 'imagineering.' A second neglected nontechnical aspect is external valuation—to which I will come back regularly in this book. A service, just any other product, is never only what it is in the eyes of the supplier. The value of each product is dependent of continuous requalification by a network of outsiders, as a consequence of the continuous dialogues which are taking place in its environment (Callon et al. 2002). Den Hertog's six dimensions hopefully help suppliers to position and if necessary reposition their services as well as possible in these dialogues, but they will never be able to determine the outcome of these.

In general, there are huge differences between service industries relating to economies of scale and their need for investment. Similarly to what has been said about industries in the field of information and content, in some service industries, the original investments to get started (and related fixed costs) may be quite high compared to the variable costs of operation—for example, telecommunications, theme parks or airlines[11] (Shapiro & Varian 1999: 22). But the resulting products are not as easily copied as digitized information products.

Finally, following Pine and Gilmore, in the field of services we can make a distinction between traditional services and the creation and staging of special *experiences*. Theme parks are an obvious example of this, but think also of authentic bakers who do not just make and sell bread but create the ambiance of a traditional bakery in which they have to perform in a special way. As a consequence, in more and more jobs a person becomes a kind of actor.[12] A service or experience in which possibly even more value is created is provided in the realm of *transformations* in which the customers themselves become the product, being processed into better, improved people—healthier, more beautiful, more confident and better educated (Pine & Gilmore 1999: 1–25, 163–183). Pine and Gilmore are certainly correct to state that the more an economy develops, the more economic activities become less tangible, whereas their added value may increase. A normal product or service may be consumed and forgotten rapidly and a nicely packaged product or service already may secure a higher return, whereas a well-designed product catches everyone's attention, will be cherished and as a rule will command a higher price. A special experience is not easily forgotten, whereas because of transformations—consider, for example, education, a more healthy lifestyle, coaching activities, cosmetic surgery—the consumers themselves are transformed and in this way become the product of the process themselves. The result of such a transformation—literally added value—is as a rule not easily taken away.[13]

Pine and Gilmore are, however, less correct when they suggest that plain commodities, products and services will disappear. As long as human beings have a physical nature, they will go on to consume products such as sugar, gas and public transport. It is certainly true that some of these develop into more special products or services such as different kinds of bread or unforgettable travel experiences. But Pine and Gilmore themselves emphasize that features which at a certain moment are special later on may become common again (commodified) and included in what is considered to be normal. Related to this, rationalization of production and delivery take place, so that certain service products are industrialized, standardized and commodified (a process sometimes called McDonaldization; Miles 2007: 437–438). As a result, innovators need to think of ever-new possible sources of value creation for their customers.

From Pine and Gilmore's story, we also learn that not all consumption is passive. In the field of experiences and transformations, consumers in many cases have to take an active role and learn new capabilities and skills. In Pierre Bourdieu's (1979) terms, they have to invest in their 'cultural capital.' This is most obvious when we talk about services in the realm of education and high culture. However, for the consumption of movies, games, food, fashion styles, travel and sports also, people have to acquire at least some new capabilities. The development of the experience economy leads certainly not only to 'Disneyfication' and more spectacle but also to many people thinking about their ideas and values relating to the quality of life. Here we see already that the more an economy develops, the more important the role of culture (including high culture) will be.[14]

Imagineering, the development of strong, 'high emotional involvement' concepts

As the economy develops in the direction of a creative experience economy, in which the attention of customers is also scarce, it increasingly becomes necessary for all organizations to be easily recognizable. For this, they have to develop a strong recognizable identity, based on a strong concept and a strong position in everyone's mind (Ries & Trout 1986), which hopefully leads to a high level of emotional involvement by their main stakeholders. Related to this, in the realm of theme parks, the term 'imagineering'—engineering for imagination—has been coined. The more an economy develops towards an experience economy, the more different firms compete with each other on the basis of strong creative concepts and their realization. This involves more than just creating pleasant experiences, adding a few flags or coloured balloons to your shop window. It's even more than the look and feel of your shop and the quality of your service. Imagineering works best when it starts from a credible, comprehensive vision of a company or brand with which at least a part of the public can identify itself. According to Diane Nijs, imagineering therefore is related to the key values (the soul) of an organization which is translated into concrete, authentic embodiments in the fields of communication, products, services and experiences (Nijs & Peters 2002; Nijs 2003).

Product-Service Combinations

Just as there are combinations of material and information products, there are ever more *product-service combinations*. The traditional example is after-sales services of products in the realm of maintenance: from bicycles, copiers and elevators to all kinds of machinery. Some products are useless without the related service, but this does not mean that they are necessarily bundled. Think of telecommunications or television. Of course, some providers try more or less successfully to tie product-service bundles as strongly as possible—think about Apple's iPod, which is worthless without the related iTunes service—but many customers don't like the inflexibility which comes with this. Competition authorities as a rule like such bundling even less. So in the end, the success of a product-service bundle such as Apple's will depend on the quality (and price-quality performance) of that bundle (including the value of Apple's brand) compared to that of its competitors (Tukker 2004; Shankar et al. 2009). Other examples can be found in the realm of crossmedia concepts: TV programmes combined with a website (the second screen) or televoting or Harry Potter books leading to games, movies and merchandizing (Reynaert & Dijkerman 2011).

1.3   PROCESS INNOVATION, TECHNICAL AND ORGANIZATIONAL

Process innovations are changes in the production processes of products (including services) which in principle should lead to more efficient production, not only within factories and service organizations, but also between them, by organizing efficient forms of outsourcing, co-design, comanufacturing and logistics. Basically, process innovation is about *increasing productivity* in one way or another.

Process innovation as decreasing productivity

Increasing interest for workers' rights in developing countries, food safety and animal welfare may lead to process innovations which actually decrease productivity. This is directly related to product innovation, when quality is put before quantity.

In addition, related to the modernization of society in recent decades, a kind of romantic reaction can be observed in which much value is attached to craft. As a consequence, people are prepared to pay more for handcrafted products.

Like product innovation, process innovation has been viewed as mainly technical for a long time, primarily involving forms of automation which lead to higher levels of productivity. However, more often than not this overemphasizing of technology has led to missed opportunities because new process technologies were not aligned with the organizational processes of firms. A traditional example is the American car industry where in the 1980s expensive flexible manufacturing technologies were used for standardized mass production (Jaikumar 1985). A comparative study at that time revealed that quality was higher in Japanese car factories, which had a lower level of automation than their American counterparts (Womack et al. 1990: 92–95).

As a consequence, it has to be emphasized that process innovation as a rule requires an alignment of investment in process technologies and organizational innovation or, in other words, technical with nontechnical innovation (Hammer & Champy 1993; de Sitter 1994). This is also true in the realm of services. Retail firms may invest in many forms of new technology—electronic cash registers, electronic data interchange with suppliers, huge databases with customer information—but they should not forget their purpose. Translating customer information into value-added services, for example, remains a daunting task which only a few firms appear to be mastering.[15] As a rule, investing in such new technologies is only the beginning of a much more complex innovation process.

Thus, process innovation sometimes may be mainly technical (a new technique for making steel) or mainly organizational[16] (introducing a matrix structure), but in most cases a combination of both will be necessary (the first introduction of the assembly line). Process innovation may concern not only one firm but also different firms in a larger supply chain. Think of 'chain innovations' such as (international) outsourcing, streamlining the supply chain, collocating and comanufacturing with one's main industrial suppliers and co-design together with customers. Quite a few concepts have been launched in the last decade—such as Quick Response, Early Consumer Response, and Collaborative Planning, Forecasting and Replenishment—aiming at the reversal of this chain, feeding back customer information as far and as early as possible, and in this sense converting the supply chain into a kind of 'demand chain.' But, of course, the supply and demand sides of this chain are two faces of the same coin (Jacobs 2006a).

In the realm of services, an important form of process innovation leading to higher productivity is franchising, an organizational innovation that tries to replicate a successful business format as rapidly as possible with the help of individual entrepreneurs. Think of McDonald's fast food restaurants which are mostly run by independent entrepreneurs. Such a system leads not only to efficiencies as a consequence of a larger scale and related higher purchasing power vis-à-vis suppliers but also to more rapid growth of new businesses, tapping into the capital and motivation of individual entrepreneurs (Croonen 2006). Most new franchising systems are based on a new service concept but entail the adoption of specific organizational and technical systems as well (I will return to this topic in Section 1.7 when I will discuss business model innovation).

A final form of process innovation which is discussed quite often nowadays is the development towards greener, more sustainable production using as few new resources as possible, preventing ecologically harmful waste and recycling as much as possible. Design for disassembly or for recycling and cradle-to-cradle design are a few of the concepts which have been developed in this realm. In the short term, such processes may be less productive and more expensive than existing ones. But in the end they should lead to all kinds of cost savings for everybody. As there may be a contradiction between the interests of individual players versus that of the whole society, not to say the planet, as a rule governments have to play a role to create a level playing field in this respect by setting minimum health and environmental standards with which all firms must comply. I will come back to this in Section 1.8 when I will discuss system innovations.

Innovating Innovation Processes

In addition, the process of organizing innovation is continuously innovated itself with the aim of increasing productivity. Technically, the speed of innovation has increased through the development of what Dodgson et al. (2005) call 'Innovation Technologies.' These include new search tools and new tools for modelling, simulating and visualizing new designs (including virtual reality, which make it possible to examine every aspect of a design or, in the realm of fashion, to drape designs onto virtual 3-D mannequins to see the effect on the design when they walk) and rapid prototyping for example with the help of 3-D printers. These innovation technologies also make it easier to involve customers at an earlier stage or even to let them make their own designs (Dodgson et al. 2005: 39–40, 131–133, 152–153; von Hippel 2005: 121–131, 147–164). In Chapter 6 I will dig a bit deeper into forms of co-development with the help of customers which may lead to a higher chance of innovation success.

This brings us to the nontechnical aspects of innovating innovation processes themselves. One important element of this is the routinization of such processes, making sure that there is a continuous flow of innovations within firms which is continuously monitored (Jacobs & Snijders 2008). I will come back to this in Chapter 8.

Another very important change in the last decades has been the 'externalization' of innovation processes, also called 'open innovation' (Chesbrough 2003). Of course, for a long time 'industrial districts' or regional 'clusters' have been recognized in which there is a high level of specialized interaction and knowledge exchanged (Porter 1990; Krugman 1991; Lundvall 1992; Nelson 1993; Edquist 1997). However, during recent decades the awareness that it is nearly impossible to organize more complex innovation processes in isolation has grown. Hence the concepts of co-development and co-design, mentioned previously, also stimulated by the Internet. As a consequence, much more innovation is taking place in formal or informal networks, in strategic alliances and communities of practice, which often include a firm's (lead) customers. This has led to the concept of 'open innovation' (Chesbrough 2003; Von Hippel 2005; AWT 2006a, 2006b; Laursen & Salter 2006). In addition, firms sometimes innovate by setting up new ventures or acquiring those of others, in this sense replacing research and development (R&D) with acquisition and development (A&D). Cisco, in particular, has been a pioneer in this field (Jacobs & Waalkens 2001).

There is, however, still a lot that can be done within firms to increase efficiency and productivity of innovation processes at the firm level. One is to imply one's own workforce to a higher degree in such processes. Many people in production and maintenance functions have very concrete and useful ideas for possible improvements in the products and the production process. Therefore, organizing the collection and selection of those ideas is an important form of process innovation. Sometimes, this integration of the intelligence and creativity of the own workforce in the organization's innovation processes is called 'social innovation.' But of course, social innovation is a much broader concept which shouldn't be restricted to organizations. Open innovation and co-development with customers, to which I will come back in Chapter 6 (Section 6.7), are also forms of it.

1.4 TRANSACTION INNOVATION

A third basic form of innovation, which I call 'transaction innovation,' is mostly neglected in innovation literature. Admittedly, marketing innovation has been recognized by ever more authors in the field, but this is only one part of a broader range of transaction innovations. These latter innovations refer to new ways of facilitating economic transactions. Such innovations may take place not only at the level of individual organizations but also at that of society and government. Organizations have to think of ever-new ways to bring products to the attention of consumers and selling them. They have to position (or reposition, if necessary) their products in the continuous dialogues which are taking place in society about different offerings. They can also develop new markets for existing products. Then we talk of innovations in the realm of publicity, marketing (including branding) and sales. These kinds of innovations have indeed been called 'market innovations' or 'marketing innovations' or even 'trade innovations' (den Butter et al. 2008). Imagineering, discussed in Section 1.2, can also be seen as part of this. Transaction innovation is, however, about more than just marketing or trade. It also encompasses all kinds of institutional innovations at the societal level through which economic transactions are stimulated (North 1990, 1997).

Let me begin the discussion of transaction innovations with institutional innovations, the historical importance of which is difficult to overestimate. Think of the invention of the market itself, of money, of all kinds of credit or regulations in different markets, of recognized titles to ownership, of joint-stock and limited companies and of the establishment of larger free market zones such as the European Union. Each time, it took a long period of trial and error to fine-tune these institutional innovations before they really worked. Most of these we now take for granted, but in large parts of the world they don't exist and as a consequence transactions and thus economic development are hampered (de Soto 2000). However, in the industrialized countries we are continuously experimenting with de- and re-regulations in order to fine-tune which kind of regulatory environment works best. The experience of the credit crisis in 2008–2009 has taught us again that institutions are never perfect.

The coming into being of large steel firms at the end of the 19th century

In most historical accounts, the emergence of large steel firms in Western Europe at the end of the nineteenth century is related to new technological inventions such as the Thomas and Bessemer convertors and the Siemens-Martin process. However, at least as important was the establishment of joint-stock banks. For a long time such banks were not allowed, as governments feared that such limited liability companies couldn't provide enough security in the field of repaying deposits. Permitting joint-stock banks—originally under very strict regulations—led to the rapidly increasing scale of banks. In Germany and France, this only happened in the 1870s. These large banks in turn were able to finance larger companies, in this way leading to the establishment of much larger industrial firms such as the big steel firms which came into being shortly after the establishment of these banks (Jacobs 1988).[17]

The example of credit shows that also at the firm level the development of transaction innovations has been quite important in economic history, from traditional letters of credit to all kinds of loans, mortgages, leasing contracts or credit cards. In addition, innovations in the realm of marketing and publicity are, of course, not that new. So isn't it striking that all of these have received so little attention in innovation literature for such a long time? Their relevance is only increasing. The more the economy develops from a supply-side to a demand-side orientation as a consequence of the increasing variety of products, the more important transaction innovations become. So long as there was relative scarcity in supply, the suppliers ruled. In the previous socialist countries for instance, but also in the years after the World War II in Western countries, innovations were more easily successful. When, for instance, a new radio was brought on the market, people were happy to be able to buy it. In the beginning, there were long waiting times for these. Sometimes, when there is high demand for a successful product—like certain new car models, It bags or tickets for pop concerts—we still see this scarcity effect, but nowadays scarcity is the exception, not the rule. Since the onset of the consumer society, competition has increased tremendously and as a consequence also consumers' choice. When relative scarcity came to an end, companies which traditionally had dominated their home market—such as Philips in the Netherlands, Fiat in Italy or Siemens in Germany—had huge problems adapting to this new situation. Only slowly did they learn to become more customer oriented, and as a consequence, all of them faced major crises in their firms. Quite a few even went bankrupt or were taken over.

Since the 1950s, competition has only increased. For this reason Davenport and Beck (2001) talk about the 'attention economy.' Increasingly, the attention of consumers has become *the* scarce resource for which companies are competing. As a consequence, suppliers wage a competitive battle for a strong and recognisable 'position' in the minds of their customers (Ries & Trout 1986). All kinds of publicity specialists and consultants are racking their brains to find new, surprising ways of catching consumers' attention: guerrilla marketing, buzz marketing, publicity through search engines on the Internet, or providing space on the Internet in which consumers themselves can place their videos and animations. E-business, the use of loyalty cards and the development of new social media may provide firms with detailed information about their customers which allows them to microtarget them better. The consequence of all of this is that, as a rule, costs to launch and market new products now exceed those of developing them.

Listerine: Inventing a new problem

A nice example of increase in sales of a product, without really changing it, is provided by Listerine, a disinfectant, which has been sold since the 1870s. First, it was mainly used as surgical antiseptic. Later on, it was sold, in

distilled form, as floor cleaner and a cure for gonorrhoea. 'But it wasn't a run-
away success until the 1920s, when it was pictured as a solution for 'chronic
halitosis'—a then obscure medical term for bad breath. . . . Until that time,
bad breath was not conventionally considered such a catastrophe. But Listerine changed that. As the advertising scholar James B. Twitchell writes, "Listerine did not make mouthwash as much as it made halitosis." In just seven
years, the company's revenues rose from $115,000 to more than 8 million'
(Levitt & Dubner 2005: 91).

Moreover, in the field of sales and distribution, new ideas are being developed and tested continuously. Think for example of the first supermarkets and department stores, mail order, e-business or guerrilla stores, and
of the increasing importance of shop design and special experiences in the
realm of retail. Think also about the effect on sales the invention of the
fashion outlet store had. We might also consider the establishment of tem-
ping agencies, which have had an important impact on the nature of the
labour market in various countries. In many cases, new intermediaries—for
example, various kinds of brokers—make markets more transparent and in
this way change the nature of competition. Sometimes, new intermediaries
gain a place in the market. In other cases, such intermediaries lose their
position—for instance, when direct Internet sales replace retail shops. As
a consequence, many traditional organizations see such new actors as a
threat, as they try to capture a part of the value in the system. However, in
many cases these new actors actually stimulate the development of these
markets.

Transaction innovations sometimes have a huge impact on an industry. An
important part of the luxury car industry would not have existed without the
invention of leasing. Opportunities for leasing airplanes have made it much
easier to establish new airline companies, with tremendous consequences on
competition in this industry.

Some people may argue that transaction innovations are just a subcat-
egory of service and thus product innovation. This may indeed be the case.
As just mentioned, transaction innovation may entail disintermediation or
re-intermediation—new service providers trying to create a new position in
the supply chain with a new service. But that doesn't matter. Just as product
innovations in the machine industry stimulate process innovation in other
industries using them, product innovations in retail, brokerage or publicity
may lead to transaction innovations in the industries that use them. The essence of such services—introduced by new actors or not—is that they do not
change the products they want to advertise or sell. The same product may
be advertised or sold but only in a different way.

Others may see transaction innovation as a kind of process innovation. It
is certainly true that transaction innovations are a kind of process, be it in
the realm of transactions. As traditionally the term 'process innovation' has

been reserved for all kinds of innovations related to production (including the whole supply chain),[18] I propose to keep it like that, and call the innovations which stimulate transactions 'transaction innovations.' Process innovations are mostly[19] about increasing productivity in producing products and services, transaction innovations are about their marketing and sales. In contrast with process innovations, customers are always the key focal point of transaction innovations.

Of course, transaction innovations may also lead to product and process innovations. As a consequence of new marketing techniques, for example, customer information may be fed back into product and process innovation processes—for instance, in the realm of customization. Equally, endeavours in the realm of presentation, marketing and branding may increase the value of products. Previously I already mentioned the same dress which has a higher value in a Dior than in a Primark shop. However, even then the distinction between the transaction innovation, product and process innovation remains valid. This appears also from the fact that contrary to product and process innovation, investment in transaction innovation generally has not been counted as investment in R&D which is mostly equated with investment in innovation. This leads to an underestimation of investment in innovation. I will come back to this in Section 2.2 when I deal with hidden innovation and the decreasing relevance of R&D statistics.

1.5   A FIRST OVERVIEW

At this stage, I suppose that the discussion of the various forms of innovation appears to be relatively straightforward and familiar to most readers. However, this only makes it more striking that most popular handbooks on innovation (even the more extensive ones by Freeman & Soete 1997 and Tidd et al. 2005) only deal with a specific part of the topic and do not even mention concepts such as stylistic innovation, fashion, industrial design, experiences, leasing, imagineering or franchising. This omission only illustrates to what extent innovation is still mainly understood in technical or technological terms. As a consequence, a large amount of actual innovation has not really been appreciated or understood, thereby also leading to biased discussions about innovation policies. In Table 1.1, an overview is given of the forms of innovation discussed so far, along with a few examples. In this table a distinction is also made between technical and nontechnical forms of innovation. In Chapter 2, I will come back on the precise distinction between these forms.

In this table, the examples relate to the first introduction of an innovation. Moreover, a product innovation in one industry may lead to a process or transaction innovation in another one. In addition, new nontechnical concepts for existing products such as SUVs or rollerblades lead to new

Table 1.1   Forms of technical and nontechnical innovation

	incremental product innovation	new concepts for existing products	new products	process innovation	transaction innovation
technical	• new generation of microchips	• new fibres • jet airplanes • DVDs	• fax • video games	• solar energy • ATMs • CAD-CAM • RFID	• chip-based credit cards • e-business
non-technical	• new designs • new fashion • new songs	• flat-pack furniture • SUVs • roller-blades • new franchise formats	• first theme park • fashion consulting	• matrix structure • new pedagogical method	• buzz marketing • leasing • temping agency

material forms. There are also other forms of interaction between the three basic forms of innovation. Increasing productivity (process innovation) may lead to cheaper and, for that reason, more attractive products. New products in the realm of insurance may engender transaction innovations such as product guarantees. Such guarantees in their turn probably lead to more care in the realm of product quality (and related process innovation). In Section 1.7 we will see that innovations in the field of business model innovation concentrate on peculiar combinations of these basic forms of innovation which in themselves lead to a competitive advantage. But let us first look at the relative importance of the different forms of innovations discussed so far.

1.6   THE RELATIVE IMPORTANCE OF THE DIFFERENT FORMS OF INNOVATION

What is the relative importance of each of the basic forms of innovation in the domain of competition? First, I will look at the traditional issue of product versus process innovation. Then I want to zoom in on the relative importance of design innovation. Finally, evidence on the importance of transaction innovations is discussed.

As said in the previous sections, all forms of innovations are important. However, many studies have concluded that firms which concentrate more on product innovation and related market development than on process innovation are more proactive and on average more successful. The reason for this is that product innovation may help the organization to differentiate itself from its competitors. Related to process innovation such firms as a rule invest more than others in organizational renewal and the further education and training of their workforce. On the contrary, emphasis on just competing on productivity as a rule leads to cost competition and a possible 'race to the bottom' (van der Zwan 1987: 76–91; Freeman & Soete 1997: 272; Jacobs 1999a: 178–188).

Further elaborating on an approach proposed by Jens Christensen (1995), we can make a distinction between four kinds of R&D capabilities and then look to which extent they are required in different industries:[20]

- Basic scientific research capabilities are required in industries where new scientific insights play an important role (e.g., pharmaceuticals, nanotechnology).
- Process development competences play a role in all larger-scale industries (manufacturing, as well as distribution) where production efficiency (including cooperation with suppliers) and quality control are of prime importance.
- Product development competences are, of course, important in all industries. Here, an important differentiation can be made regarding the extent to which the technical (functional) or cultural (aesthetic) aspects of innovation prevail.
- Finally, transaction innovation competences play a role in all industries, too, but in possibly totally different forms.

When we look at the products of different industries, we understand the importance of these different competences:[21]

- On one side of the spectrum, we find materials, components and pharmaceuticals for which scientific research and process development competences are the most important. This is also the case in the large-scale food industry, as product design there is mainly related to the (not negligible) design of the packages.
- In industries which produce high-tech components (such as semiconductors, as well as compressors, filters, thermostats, valves and gears) which have to be integrated into specialized equipment, beside similar scientific research and process development competences, also technical and functional product development capabilities are required.
- On the other side of the spectrum, there are traditional industries in the realm of fashion, furniture, entertainment and hospitality, where technical, functional and aesthetic product development capabilities are all important. The more their products are produced on a large scale, the more process development capabilities will be necessary. Think for example about the manufacturing and logistic speed of Zara's fast fashion system.
- The most comprehensive integration of all kinds of innovative competences, from scientific research to aesthetic design, is required in industries

manufacturing modern durables from domestic appliances to cars and nowadays also machines (e.g., in the realm of medical technology).

• In the field of software development, technical and functional product development capabilities are of the highest importance. However, from my own research I have learned that even in software development the aesthetic element gradually has become more important as well, even for more industrial applications (Gemser et al. 2004).

When we zoom in on the industrial design side of product innovation, we find similar positive results, even when studies providing hard financial data on the relationship between design and company performance are more limited in number. However, all studies that are available point in the direction that investing in design has a positive effect on company performance, especially when competitors don't do it (see, e.g., Black & Baker 1987; Walsh et al. 1992; Gemser 1997; Gemser and Leenders 2001; Groupe Bernard Juilhet 1995; CEC 2009: 14–15; Candi et al. 2010). In 2005, Marco Ricchetti undertook an international overview of all studies in which the relationship between investment in design and company performance was investigated. From this emerged a clear positive correlation between investment in design activities and competitiveness, not only at the level of enterprises, but also at that of countries. I quote a few of his examples:

> In 1998 a major UK design company, which counts many large global corporations among its clients, compiled an index based on the Stock Exchange value of its clients—which were therefore businesses that use design in a significant way; it emerged that over the last 5 years, this Design Index performed much better than the Standard & Poor 500, so much better that subsequently a real investment fund was launched, with a portfolio based on those businesses. In 1999, the Design Council in the UK adopted this method of measuring, making the basis of comparison wider and more complex. The new data fully confirms that the Design Index is superior to the stock exchange benchmark indices . . . from 1994 to 2003. (Ricchetti 2005: 11–12)

Functional and experiential aspects of product design

In 2009 researchers from the universities of Rotterdam and Delft researched 163 firms in the Netherlands in a variety of industries (manufacturing and services) on the effectiveness of their design activities. They distinguished between six kinds of industrial design:

- design for technology;
- design for functionality;
- design for usability (ergonomic design);

- sensorial design, aiming at stimulating the senses;
- design aiming at evoking emotions;
- design supporting self-expression.

The first three categories were subsumed under the category of functional design and the latter three under that of experiential design, which corresponds with the technical and cultural aspects of innovation, respectively. Both aspects appeared to contribute about equally to the improvement of financial performance. New product development processes with a high emphasis on functional design on average led to a 10% better financial performance than those with medium emphasis; for experiential design, such a higher emphasis led to a 9% better financial result. High attention to both aspects even led to a 20% better result.

It also appeared that a relative emphasis on functional design led to a negative effect on experiential design quality. Therefore, especially in industries where experiential quality of design is of primary importance, such as the entertainment, hospitality and cultural sectors, innovators have to take care that these experiential aspects get enough attention. Attention for experiential design, to the contrary, is always positive and, maybe surprisingly, mostly when customers are not too much involved. Customers are possibly a bit too conservative, so that listening to them too much may prevent designers from realizing the full potential of their creativity (Candi et al. 2010; Gemser et al. 2011).

Transaction innovation as a comprehensive category has never been researched in innovation studies. In economic historiography there has, of course, been a lot of interest in all kinds of institutional innovation which has stimulated economic development. There has also been quite some comparative research in the field of 'national systems of innovation,' focusing on the influence of institutions on the innovativeness of different national economies (Lundvall 1992; Nelson 1993; Edquist 1997).

Transaction innovations at the micro level are mostly researched as investments in market or marketing innovation. Market research and customer feedback have been frequently recognized as important sources of product innovation[22] (Freeman & Soete 1997: 197–204). Moreover, branding and reputation management are nowadays seen as important vehicles of value creation and value relations (see next section). This is even the case in the arts, where branding (of artists, galleries, auction houses, fairs and collectors) sometimes appears to be more important than artistic innovation itself (Thompson 2008).

Investing in marketing is, however, not the same as investing in marketing innovation. If we concentrate on the latter, we have to know to what extent such transaction innovation leads to competitive success. Think for instance about a fashion brand introducing e-sales beside traditional retail or starting to advertise through SMS messages. Another example could be introducing a new business or retail format—but in many cases, this will also enhance developing new product ranges so that it is difficult to separate the effects of both forms of innovation. H&M's new COS format, for instance, was set up with its own separate headquarters and design team. When, however, a firm is separating an existing product line into a different retail format, this can be seen as a pure transaction innovation. Examples are Nespresso, which has developed its own shops and coffee bars, or H&M's separate lingerie stores, which it has set up in different locations. In the Netherlands, department store V&D was especially successful with its in-store restaurant La Place; as a consequence, they have been opening separate La Place restaurants in shopping malls and along highways. As with all innovation, we know from experience that such moves can be successful but that failures also happen. In the field of marketing, there is a lot of trial and error innovation nowadays as well. It is not clear yet how successful these experiments are, but they seem to be necessary, as increasingly traditional forms of marketing prove to be ineffective (Jacobs & Mossinkoff 2007). As far as there is evidence from innovation cases in the realm of transactions (e.g., e-business), in general the pattern looks similar to that of the field of product innovation: first movers as a rule are not the most successful. Most successful are the early followers who learn rapidly from first movers' experiences and implement these lessons in their practices.[23]

1.7   BUSINESS MODEL INNOVATION

Many innovations combine the basic forms of innovation just discussed. Design innovations (nontechnical product innovation) may enhance more than just the appearance of a product, as a more functional design of its parts can make the manufacture of the product easier and more efficient (process innovation). In fashion, the use of new materials (technical innovation) makes it possible to develop totally new styles. Where we discussed den Hertog's 6-D model of service innovation (Section 1.2) we also saw the relationship with process innovation. In most of these cases, it is nevertheless obvious what the most important dimension of innovation is a new style, a new process, a new service and a new form of marketing.

In some cases, however, the peculiarity of the innovation is not to be found in one of the dimensions but in their combination. The simplest form is the combination of product and transaction innovations into new 'value propositions.' With the concept value proposition—a concept I like as it highlights the values part and thus the cultural side of innovation—it is emphasized that in many cases it is not enough to concentrate on product innovation and quality as such. A new product may be very nice and of high quality, but if it is not introduced in the right environment with the right brand, it still may fail. The same new handbag will not be valued equally when presented in a Louis Vuitton store or an Aldi supermarket, even when objectively the product quality is the same. Therefore, general advice to all product innovators is to not just think about product but about the whole value proposition—in other words, the combination of product and transaction innovation.

Process innovation may be part of the deal as well. McDonald's fast food may look primarily like a transaction innovation or an innovation in services (including successful franchising on a global level), yet this was made possible by the extreme standardization of the product (product innovation) and the use of specialized tools and a strict coordination and quality control regime throughout its whole supply chain (internal and external process innovation). Moreover, an important innovation in McDonald's approach was its special attention to children as customers (transaction innovation) and the development of special products and experiences for them (product innovation plus imagineering).

In the world of fashion, firms such as Inditex (the mother company of Zara, Massimo Dutti, Bershka, etc.) have developed the concept of fast fashion. Zara today launches about twelve new collections per year, which are produced and distributed very rapidly (three to six weeks from design to retail), partly on the basis of the newest ways of monitoring customer demand (rapid processing and interpretation of sales data). Therefore, product and process innovation are strongly linked. In such cases, one could say that each of these innovations in itself is not so special. Zara's clothes are of reasonable quality and McDonald's burgers may be of a somewhat better quality than the average, but the real strength of both approaches lies in the *combination* of aspects.

Therefore, the real innovation in such cases is more in the field of comprehensive *business models*—new, original ways of composing a value chain and earning money—than in each of their aspects. These business models link innovations in various fields and as a whole are more difficult to copy than each of their elements. For firms, devising—inventing!—innovative business models may be the most interesting innovation there is. As Joan Magretta (2002: 48–49) states, 'Behind every successful organization is a business model that in its time was revolutionary. . . . [N]ew business models are all variations on the universal value chain that underlies all businesses. Broadly speaking this chain has two parts. Part one includes all activities associated with making something: design, the purchase of raw materials, the manufacturing or service delivery process. Part two includes all the activities associated with selling something: finding and reaching customers, transacting a sale, distributing the product or delivering the service.'

Thus we see that, as Magretta describes it, the first part of a business model is covered by product and process innovation, the second one by transaction innovation. Den Hertog's 6-D model of service innovation (Section 1.2) also emphasizes the interaction between the different aspects.

Especially radical innovations require deep thinking about ways of earning money with them, as in many cases the market will have to be created. Therefore, adding business development professionals, who are more trained in the field of transaction innovation, to innovation teams may help to clarify and perhaps test possible business models based on the new concept early in the process (Leifer et al. 2000: 93–108; Osterwalder & Pigneur 2009: 226–231). Sometimes radical innovations coming from unexpected corners (like the emergence of the Internet) force whole industries (music, publishing, media) to reconsider existing business models and develop new, viable ones. However, the examples of McDonald's and Zara show that business model innovation also takes place in traditional industries.

Special attention should also be paid to situations where the combination of serving two or more different customer groups is essential to the viability of the business model. A traditional example is newspapers, which have two distinct customer groups: readers and advertisers. Without enough readers, the advertisers are not interested, but without advertisers, most newspapers are not able to survive. Even in the case of free newspapers, serving the readers well is crucial. Google can be viewed as a modern and even more complex example of such a 'multi-sided' business model (Osterwalder & Pigneur 2009: 80–81, 92–93).

Thinking in a comprehensive way about innovation is probably the main advantage of an approach in terms of business models. As will be discussed in the box on technology push versus market pull, in innovation literature there have been endless and repetitive chicken-and-egg discussions about what comes first: a new concept or an unsolved problem. Creative inventors and artists always rightly emphasize that consumers and other users are not able to articulate demand in fields which do not yet exist. Marketing people then answer equally convincingly that these inventors always overestimate the attractiveness of their inventions. Moreover, many inventions have been the result of addressing difficult problems: curing diseases, increasing productivity or tackling traffic jams or even climate change. Thinking in terms of business model innovation (e.g., Osterwalder & Pigneur 2009) helps to look not only for the attractive elements of innovations but also for the possibly missing elements to turn these into real (business) successes.

Technology or science push versus demand or market pull, and more interactive models of innovation

In the field of innovation, heated discussions have been waged about the origin of innovations. The traditional linear model finds the origin of innovations in new scientific insights, which may later on be included in new products or processes. However, many scientific inventions have emerged from dealing with a concrete problem. Moreover, new product ideas may emanate from studying consumers and their daily problems. Developing these products may entail new scientific research—if necessary. In general, the two models represented in Figure 1.3 have been called technology or science push versus demand or market pull. As can be seen from the Airbus A380 example discussed previously, nowadays more interactive views prevail, such as that in Figure 1.4 (inspired by Nederlands Forum 1994: 23). Inventions and innovations may emerge anywhere in the processes of dealing with customer problems or carrying out scientific research. I will come back to this in Section 6.7 on open innovation and cocreation with customers.

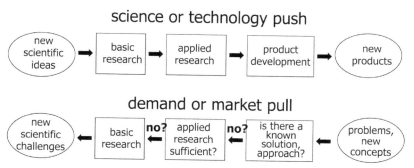

Figure 1.3 Science and technology push versus demand and market pull model of innovation

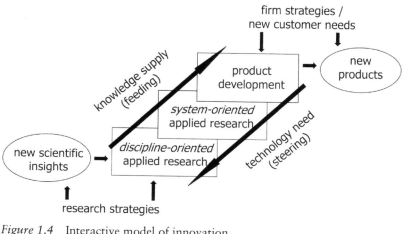

Figure 1.4 Interactive model of innovation

1.8   SYSTEM INNOVATIONS AND CHANGES IN TECHNO-ECONOMIC REGIMES

Comprehensive innovation may also take place at the societal level. Here, two basic forms have to be distinguished. Most large-scale developments start small, for instance, in niches where it is possible to experiment. Think of the introduction of trains, cars or electricity. But, finally, the diffusion of such innovations may lead to social change on a huge scale. This is the reason we call them 'new techno-economic regimes.'[24]

In contrast, *system innovations* reconfigure important elements of a broader system which have to be changed at once through a kind of Big Bang: think of the introduction of the euro, changing the health insurance or the pensions system in a country or changing the side of the road on which cars drive (as happened in Sweden from left to right in 1967, and from right to left in Samoa in 2009). Here it is not really possible to experiment in niches—for instance, trying out how it works when only lorries drive on the other side of the road. In the Netherlands the municipality of Amsterdam wanted to follow a niche strategy to introduce a system of electronic road pricing, as exists, for example, in parts of the centre of London. This was, however, prohibited by the national government, which wanted to introduce a standardized system later on and was afraid that the Amsterdam experiment would limit its technical and organizational options. Therefore, in the realm of system innovations, as a rule, an alignment of all incumbent actors in the system is required, many of whom do not have an interest in change. That is the reason why, for example, changing the health insurance system in many countries has been so difficult. As a consequence, pursuing—or preventing—system innovation leads to cunning strategizing by most actors implied. In most cases, strong pressure and leadership, especially of the government, will be necessary.

Between change towards a new techno-economic regime, where bottom-up experimentation and diffusion is possible, and system innovation, where this isn't the case, there are intermediate cases of innovation in highly interconnected industries. In such cases, bottom-up experimentation is possible in principle, but as many actors have to align their decisions, it remains difficult. As a consequence, innovation in such a situation requires smart strategizing as well (Chakravorti 2003).

Sometimes, however, relatively many new actors are involved which all have an interest in a new basic technology, so that an alternative network comes into being which is able to eclipse the incumbent one. As a consequence, actors of that incumbent coalition then have no alternative but to join the newcomers. Chakravorti (2003: 15–16) describes, for instance, the emergence of digital photography and imaging at the moment it was still unfolding:

> Consider the multitude of motivated players steering toward a common purpose: Kodak not only is interested in defending its core business threatened by the ongoing transformation, but is also looking for

new avenues for growth. Hewlett-Packard's printing capabilities make the firm deeply interested in wrestling Kodak's historically predominant position. Software companies, PC makers, and even cell-phone makers can foresee digital imaging as one of the high-potential consumer applications that could help reposition PCs and cell phones as devices to capture and manage images. Camera manufacturers, such as Sony and Olympus, hope to ensure that their business does not get taken over by the likes of Kodak or Hewlett-Packard. Other players, such as the online photo service Shutterfly, are a part of the digital photography network. Each is motivated by its own interests but is taking actions that one way or another help to enable an *implicit* co-ordination that nudges the network toward a mutually reinforcing, digital future.

In a similar way Freeman and Perez (1988: 46–47) talk about 'far reaching changes in technology, affecting different branches of the economy, as well as giving rise to entirely new sectors' as a consequence of the uncoordinated actions of different actors in the first half of the twentieth century: 'They are based on combinations of radical and incremental innovations, together with *organizational* and *managerial* innovations, affecting more than one or a few firms. . . . An obvious example is the cluster of synthetic materials innovations, petro-chemical innovations, machinery innovations in injection moulding and extrusion, and innumerable application innovations introduced in the 1920s, 1930s, 1940s and 1950s.'

When such 'clustered innovations' have an important societal impact, we call these a change in sociotechnical regime (or paradigm, as these authors do):

> Some changes in technology systems are so far-reaching in their effects that they have a major influence on the behaviour of the entire economy. A change of this kind carries with it many clusters of radical and incremental innovations, and may eventually embody a number of new technology systems. A vital characteristic of this . . . type of technical change is that it has *pervasive* effects throughout the economy, i.e. it not only leads to the emergence of a new range of products, services, systems and industries in its own right; it also affects directly or indirectly almost every other branch of the economy, i.e. it is a 'meta-paradigm.' (Freeman & Perez 1988: 47)

Other examples of such regime changes in the past have been electrification, or the arrival of the car system, leading to the suburbanization of large cities. Clear examples of this have also been the successive waves of new information and communication technologies (ICT) we have witnessed since the 1980s. They have facilitated, for instance, new work and management practices at all levels of society and a new phase in the internationalization of the economy. In economic literature, such regime changes have

Table 1.2   Two basic forms of large-scale innovation

new techno-economic regime	system innovation
• New actors form new network.	• Existing actors have to be aligned.
• Atomistic (market selection), mainly on the basis of a new pervasive technology with superior performance and convincing products.	• Coordination necessary (hierarchical selection), in many cases by government, for which a lot of strategizing is required. Introduction at once through a kind of 'Big Bang.'
• Trial and error and co-evolution.	• Some experimentation possible.
• Bottom-up; societal support based on sales.	• Top-down; political support necessary, based on cunning strategizing.
• Sometimes technological standardization crucial for diffusion.	• In many cases the role of governmental regulation is crucial.

Some of the concepts used in this table, such as market and hierarchical selection and co-evolution, will be discussed in later chapters.

often been related to long waves of economic growth ('Kondratieff cycles') in the economy. As the term 'techno-economic regime' suggests, as a rule, new technology is at the root of a new period of economic growth, allowing for an increase in productivity on a huge scale—for example, the steam engine, electricity, the combustion engine and the related car system, computers and microprocessors. The huge social and economic spillovers of these technological breakthroughs have also provided the traditional justification for governments to subsidize private technology development.[25] This does not alter the fact that only a small portion of new technologies lead to such spillovers.

Nowadays, developments in the direction of a more sustainable economy could lead to a kind of regime change. However, this appears to be difficult without forms of coordinated system innovation. The example about road pricing in the Netherlands mentioned previously and the difficult, prolonged international negotiations in the realm of climate change, illustrate this. In Table 1.2, the differences between system innovations and new techno-economic regimes are summarized.[26]

In Figure 1.5, the more comprehensive forms of innovation are added to the three basic forms of innovation discussed in the first part of this chapter.

1.9   AN INTERACTIVE SYSTEM

In this chapter the realm of innovation has been broadened far beyond what is traditionally presented in innovation literature. Product innovation is not only about new tangible products but also about new services (including new experiences and transformations), new product-service combinations and new

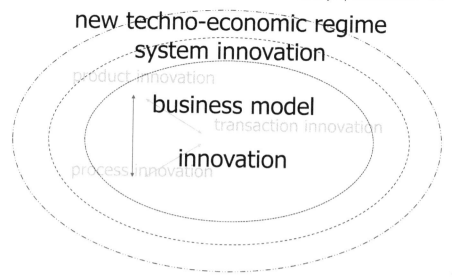

Figure 1.5   Different forms of comprehensive innovation

intangible information products (content). Process innovation is not only about automation but also about new organizational forms (including the realm of innovation itself) and new forms of cooperation within value chains and other networks. Moreover, transaction innovation has to be recognized as an important third basic form of innovation: all kinds of innovations in the realm of institutions, publicity and marketing and sales facilitating economic transactions. Products are continuously qualified and requalified through discussions at all levels of society by possible customers and their environment. As a consequence, suppliers have to position and possibly reposition their offerings.

At the micro level, new value propositions and business models combine these three basic forms of innovation. This is also the case with system innovations and new techno-economic regimes at the meso level of industries and the macro level of society. I have emphasized that it is important to make a sharp distinction between these latter two forms. New techno-economic regimes may develop bottom-up as a consequence of the emergence of new actors who sponsor them. System innovations, to the contrary, require a start via a coordinated Big Bang. As a consequence, they are more difficult to organize as cooperation of most incumbent actors, who usually do not have an interest in this change, is required. As a rule, therefore, strong pressure and strategizing by government will be necessary.

These different forms of innovation all interact with each other and they are dependent on each other. Without continuous product innovation, process innovation would come to a halt. Without transaction innovations, product innovations do not get the necessary attention. Some firms have founded their strength on specific business models—that is, innovative combinations of these three basic forms. On the basis of all these innovations, new techno-economic regimes may spontaneously emerge, but from time to time system innovation has to be organized in order to unlock more comprehensive innovative solutions.

With this chapter the presentation of the variety of innovation is far from complete. In the following chapter, I deal with the distinction between technical and nontechnical aspects of innovation, which was already shortly introduced in this chapter. In the third chapter, we then look at different degrees of radicalness of innovations.

2 Technical and Cultural Aspects of Innovation

2.1 DEFINITIONS

As we all know, many words have more than one meaning, which often leads to confusion and misunderstandings. This is not necessarily bad, as sometimes misunderstandings lead to innovations. Especially in unclear situations—at the fuzzy front end of innovation—we are involved in conversations in which we search for meaning and the clarification of each other's ideas, feelings and concepts. Sometimes different actors involved divide tasks based on an unclear understanding, and this leads to unexpected results (Fonseca 2002; Lester & Piore 2004). However, regularly the cultural difference is too large, as we say; some people don't click with each other. The conversation does not really take off, and finally each goes one's own way.

In a scientific book, however, the author has to clarify his or her position as clearly as possible. Especially because I take a somewhat peculiar position in the innovation field, I have to do this as precisely as possible. In the previous chapter, I already defined innovation, but I haven't yet dug deeper in the distinction between the technical and nontechnical aspects of it. As this distinction is crucial to the main argument of my book, it is important to define it as clearly as possible. Moreover, not everything which is nontechnical is by definition cultural. This has to be clarified as well.

In a lot of the innovation literature, innovation has been equated with technical or technological innovation or change, at least implicitly. In one of the bestsellers on innovation in the 1980s, the index mentioned for the entry 'innovation' was 'see technical change' (Dosi et al. 1988: 640). However, of course, not all innovations are technical or technological. New fashions or designs may have technical aspects, but in the core, they are cultural. The same applies to new pedagogical methods in schools or new ways of dealing with criminals. We might also consider new forms of organization, new art styles or a new procedure for electing members of parliament. Moreover, technological innovations frequently lead to nontechnical innovations in other industries. As stated by the famous evolutionary economists Nelson and Winter, 'Often an innovation is produced by a firm for sale to customers who will use it. Thus there are two acts of innovation . . . that are involved. In the case of the advent of jet passenger aircraft, DeHaviland, the company that produced the first commercial jet, was an innovator. But so was the airline that bought the plane' (Nelson & Winter 1982: 263). To a large extent, the first kind of innovation was technological, implying the development of new technical knowledge. At the level of the airline, the introduction of the new airplane was a combination of technical process innovation with nontechnical product innovation—the establishment of a new service.

These distinctions depend, of course, on the definition of technology. Some definitions are so broad that they encompass all forms of knowledge and capability. McDonough and Kahn (1996: 241) for example, do not define technology itself but make a distinction between 'hard' and 'soft' technologies in the field of product development: ' "Hard" technologies consist of electronic mail, teleconferencing, fax, videoconferencing, and other electronic means in the field of communication. "Soft" technologies on the other hand, reflect managerial behaviors that are necessary to deal with the social and behavioral aspects of global new product development.' Everett Rogers, author of probably the most diffused book on the diffusion of innovations, sees 'innovation' and 'technology' as synonyms. However, these technologies can have a hardware and a software component (Rogers 2003: 13): 'We often think of technology in terms of hardware. Indeed, sometimes the hardware side of a technology is dominant. But in other cases, a technology may be almost entirely composed of information; examples are a political philosophy such as Marxism, a religious idea such as Christianity, a news event, and a policy such as a municipal no-smoking ordinance.'

In one of the best books in the field of evolutionary economics, Eric Beinhocker distinguishes physical from social technologies. The latter are defined as 'ways of organizing people to do things': 'Examples include settled agriculture, the rule of law, money, joint-stock companies, and venture capital'[1] (Beinhocker 2006: 15).

Everybody is, of course, allowed to use concepts in a peculiar way, as long as this meaning is clearly defined and isn't too remote from common understanding. In this sense, nonmechanical or nonphysical associations with techniques and technologies are possible. But how far would they go? I do not think many people talk about Christianity as a technology or even a social technology. Then probably the following question would be raised: A technology for doing what?

In my opinion, such broad definitions of technology lead to a lot of confusion, as they diverge too far from the everyday use of this concept. In practice, they have also led to the neglect of what I see as the nontechnical aspects of innovation. Therefore, I propose to identify what these authors call 'soft technologies' or the 'software or information side of technologies' with cultural innovations or the cultural side of innovations. Let me clarify this a little more.

As is the case with innovation, most textbooks do not define technology.[2] However, when we look for 'technology' in dictionaries we always find a key idea related to 'applying science to practical purposes in the material world.' The Greek source of this combination of two words is, on the one hand, *technè,* which stands for art, craft or practical skill, and, on the other, *logos,* meaning word, discourse or doctrine (Misa 1992: 4). For 'technology,' the *Concise[3] Oxford English Dictionary* (Stevenson & Waite 2011) gives three explanations: ■ 'the application of scientific knowledge for practical purposes. ■ machinery and equipment based on such knowledge. ■ the branch of knowledge concerned with applied sciences.' Without further explication, the adjective 'technological' is simply derived from this.

For 'technique' the same dictionary has ■ 'a way of carrying out a particular task, especially the execution of an artistic work or a scientific procedure. ■ a procedure that is effective in achieving an aim.' In its turn, 'technical' has no less than three explanations: ■ '1 relating to a particular subject, art or craft, or its techniques. ■ requiring special knowledge to be understood. 2 involving or concerned with applied and industrial sciences. ■ relating to the operation of machines: *a technical fault.* 3 according to a strict application or interpretation of the law or rules.'

Therefore, following the *OED* it is nowadays correct to use 'technology' and 'technological' for 'the branch of knowledge concerned with applied sciences, as well as its application for practical purposes and related machinery and equipment. The reader of this book will, however, observe that I still find it useful to make a distinction between the knowledge and scientific side, which I call technology or technological, and the application side, which I call technique or technical. As recalled previously, the suffix *-logy* comes from the Greek *logos.* Therefore, strictly speaking a *technological* invention is an invention in the (intangible) field of sciences and thus in itself nontechnical, even when of course many of these inventions emerge from attempts to deal with practical, technical problems. In many cases a technological innovation—which is scientific—then leads to a series of technical innovations in practice.

Following the common definitions in most dictionaries, I restrict the adjective 'technical' to the realm of practical applications in the material world. This, I hope, helps to clarify what I understand by the opposite: nontechnical innovation and the nontechnical aspects of innovation.

- 'Nontechnical innovation' relates to innovation in the realm of style, content, the development of new concepts, services, experiences or methods or the introduction of new forms of organization. This requires knowledge and competences in fields such as art and style history, semiotics (understanding signs and symbols), psychology and sociology (understanding customers or employees and dealing with them; organizational behaviour), political science, economics and the practical sciences based on these such as design, marketing and strategic management. But, of course, nontechnical innovations may have technical consequences, for example the use of new materials and other artefacts. Conversely, new technical opportunities may lead to nontechnical innovations as we saw in Chapter 1.

- 'Nontechnical aspects of innovation in general' relate to the environment, the organizational or institutional setting within which innovation takes place, from the level of organizations (see the literature on organizational culture or learning, total quality management and new forms of organizing innovation) to that of networks, industrial or regional clusters or even national systems of innovation (Porter 1990; Lundvall 1992; Nelson 1993; Edquist 1997). Moreover, most innovations are the object of continuous discussions in society about their relative value (Callon et al. 2002).

- 'Nontechnical aspects of technical innovation' relate to the fact that even innovations which are mainly technical (e.g., new applications of biotechnology or nanotechnology) may profit from an awareness that nontechnical aspects are important in their possible adoption. To put it negatively, not taking aspects such as the organizational and business side of innovation[4] or societal concerns about a new technology into serious consideration may precipitate its rejection. To increase possible success (selection) of technical innovations, potential lead users may be involved in forms of co-development (von Hippel 1988, 2005) or other forms of demand articulation, or public discussion may be organized.[5]

When we try to turn the term 'nontechnical' in these three categories into positive qualifications, we can subsume them under two concepts: cultural and institutional. However, this depends—again—on the definitions we use.

Let me start with institutions. According to Nobel Prize winner Douglass North (1990: 3), '[i]nstitutions are the rules of the game in society, or, more formally, are the humanly devised constraints that shape human interaction.' Later, he clarified: 'They consist of both informal constraints (sanctions, taboos, customs, traditions, and codes of conduct), and formal rules (constitutions, laws, property rights)' (North 1991: 97).

Following Eelke de Jong (2009: 32), I will further equate culture with North's informal constraints and institutions with his formal rules. In his book on *Culture and Economics,* de Jong also gives a nice overview of definitions of culture (2009: 6–9, 34). From this overview, I want to highlight Ronald Inglehart's: 'By culture, we refer to the *subjective* aspect of a society's institutions: the beliefs, values, knowledge, and skills that have been *internalized* by the people of a given society, complementing their external systems of coercion and exchange.' It is important to emphasize this highly internalized character of culture. Even when sometimes we discuss our norms and values and try to clarify them more explicitly, to a large extent, we are not aware of them. Our actions and reactions based on these are, therefore, mostly spontaneous and instinct-like.[6]

Following these definitions of culture and institutions, the adjective 'institutional' refers to the nontechnical aspects of innovations which are more formalized—the legal and organizational settings in which innovation takes place. For the remaining in each of the three categories, 'nontechnical' stands for cultural: the soft or software side, the content or information elements of innovations, the related norms and values and the subjective evaluations based on these. As clarified previously, when we talk about technology as the *logos* of *technè*, we also talk about content, information and science, all parts of culture. Despite this, we mostly concentrate on functional, measurable and more objective elements of innovations when we talk about technology. When we talk about the cultural elements, we concentrate on the intangible elements related to subjective norms and values.[7]

What then is the meaning of 'material culture'—a phrase one encounters regularly in the realm of technical or art history? With this concept, the fact is expressed that many ideas are materialized in artefacts such as paintings, statues, cars, buildings or apparel. Some historians are highly interested in the material embodiments of these ideas—the kinds of canvas or paint used in a painting, for example—but when they talk about culture, as a rule, they will concentrate on the intangible side of these artefacts.

In practice, it will not always be easy to disentangle the material, technical side and the cultural side of innovations, but conceptually it is not only possible but also important to do so. Culture is about shared norms and values, not only at the level of a whole society but also at that of smaller groups, and these are the basis of our valuation and selection of innovations. According to this value system, some innovations will be quite attractive, whilst others will encounter opposition. Being aware of this and taking these values into account will improve the chances for success of innovations. In the economic realm, these values are mostly called 'preferences.' Innovation always entails changing an existing preference to a new one, at least marginally, as otherwise there would be no change in buying behaviour. That is the reason why a one-line summary of this book could be 'there is no economic added value without adding (or changing) cultural values.' The second part of the title of this book is an even shorter version of this one-liner.

This book further concentrates on nontechnical innovations and nontechnical aspects of innovation which are cultural. The more formalized institutional aspects are also interesting but have already received much more interest, for example, in the literature on national (and other) systems of innovation (Lundvall 1992; Nelson 1993; Edquist 1997). Besides, in this institutionally oriented literature, innovations are mostly regarded as technical. Innovations in the field of services, fashion or industrial design have only rarely been dealt with. For this reason, I try to restore the balance by concentrating on the cultural side of innovation in this book. However, of course, the relationship between the technical, institutional and cultural aspects of innovation will not be neglected.[8] In Chapter 5, we will see, for example, that technical aspects of innovation and even plain technical innovations are culturally valued as well. In addition, in Chapter 8 the organizational settings in which innovation routines are embedded will be discussed.

2.2   WHY HAS CULTURE BEEN NEGLECTED SO LONG IN INNOVATION LITERATURE?

Has culture indeed been neglected in innovation literature, and, if so, why? As I showed in the box on technology push versus demand pull in Section 1.7, there have been regular debates on which was first: the inventor's idea or a market need. Continuously, all main books on innovation have been arguing that a one-sided technology-push approach is in danger of helping innovation to fail. Freeman and Soete, for instance, remind us of the Scientific Activity Predictor from Patterns with Heuristic Origins (SAP-PHO) project in the 1970s in which in different industries' pairs of similar attempted innovations were compared with each other to better understand patterns of success and failure. These comparisons 'showed that most failures were associated with either neglect of market requirements or relatively poor understanding of the customer's needs' (Freeman & Soete 1997: 204–218, 381).

In French innovation literature especially, another aspect of culture related to innovation has been emphasized. Especially in the realm of the arts, Pierre Bourdieu (1993) has shown how valuation of innovation is the object of strategic fights between upcoming and incumbent schools of artists and related experts. As a consequence, cultural valuation of works of art has never been stable, even when certain works enjoy a more lasting appreciation than others do. Authors such as Bruno Latour (1987) and Michel Callon (Callon et al. 2002; Akrich et al. 2002a, 2002b) have extended these observations to the broader field of innovations and related research and development on the basis of many case studies. This dynamic perspective on the cultural side of innovation has been an important source of inspiration for this book.

In another strand of innovation literature, authors such as Eric von Hippel and Bengt-Åke Lundvall have emphasized the benefits of involving lead users from an early stage of development of new products. More recently, von Hippel has even written about such lead users who actually initiate innovation, for example, in the realms of software and extreme sports[9] (von Hippel 2005). This short overview shows that most innovation specialists agree that it is quite important to take the cultural side of innovation seriously in order to improve the chances for innovative success.

However, all of this only makes it more striking that most popular handbooks on innovation (e.g., Freeman & Soete 1997; Tidd et al. 2005) don't deal with consumer trends or lifestyles and do not even mention concepts such as stylistic innovation, fashion, industrial design or experiences.[10] One could argue that these innovation thinkers delegate the consumer side to marketing literature. It is certainly true that in this literature more attention is given to how consumers view new products and services, and sometimes even feedback of this information to R&D departments is discussed.[11] However, apart from the fact that a large part of the marketing literature still has a strong push orientation—starting with a product that has to be rammed down the consumers' throat—such a division of labour only reinforces one-sided approaches to innovation.

So why is it that most literature on innovation continues to neglect the cultural side of innovation? I see two main reasons for this. First, for a long time, economic history, and especially the history of industrial revolutions, has been written from the perspective of technological development. Most authors were so impressed by continuous technological innovations that they forgot to ask about the environment in which these emerged—the technology-push model discussed in Section 1.7. Only in the last decades has more attention been given to cultural (Mokyr 2002; Hård & Jamison 2005) and institutional factors (North 1990) in that history, the development of demand (de Vries 2008) or at least the co-evolution between such factors and technological developments (Bijker et al. 1987; Misa 2004).

A second reason why the cultural side of innovation has been neglected is probably the fact that many economists interested in innovation are also active in the field of innovation policy. A traditional legitimization of such policies—especially when we talk about subsidy schemes—is that investment in technology- or science-push innovation in many cases has spillover effects to the broader environment. New scientific or technological breakthroughs may lead to all kinds of new developments in other industries. Therefore, when a firm invests in developing a new technology which is difficult to protect from being copied by others, many people—amongst them, competitors—may profit from this development. Early followers in the industry may learn from the innovating pioneer without investing as much in technological research and development as the pioneer. As a consequence, possible innovators could refrain from investment in innovation, which from society's perspective would be a harmful development. For this reason, government subsidies are considered legitimate as a reward for innovators who make socially useful investments. The higher the risk involved and the further a new development still is from commercialization, the more such government intervention is viewed as legitimate. In terms of Figure 1.2 (Section 1.7), it doesn't matter whether basic research started from new scientific ideas or from a market need; basic research is seen as precompetitive. Even when the need came from the market, it can take some time before it leads to useful applications. This reasoning is graphically represented in Figure 2.1: the more basic the research, the more it is seen as a public interest and therefore eligible for subsidizing. Moreover, in some cases there may also be more direct social benefits from publicly supported basic and applied

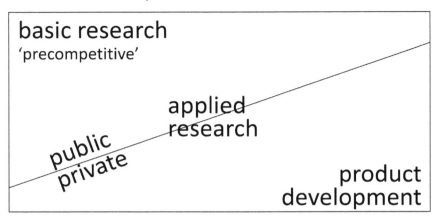

Figure 2.1   Public and private roles in research and development

The time arrow in this figure shouldn't be understood as an endorsement of the traditional technology- or science-push model. Basic research can be stimulated by new demands or problems to be solved, but it then takes some time and may afterwards lead to new, socially useful applications.

research, apart from increased competitiveness of firms, when, for example, health or environmental problems are addressed. In certain fields, where no rapid return on investment is expected, as a rule there is private underinvestment in innovation. Think, for example, of malaria research. Then there is an especially clear case for public support of such research (Freeman & Soete 1997: 377–378).

The nearer industrial R&D comes to the market, the more it is connected to solving concrete market needs, the more the firms will be convinced that they will be able to capture the value they create themselves. Moreover, less social spillovers are to be expected. As a consequence, there is a lesser need for government subsidies. Freeman and Soete go even as far as saying that a lot of R&D in consumer industries has dubious foundations: 'Consumer industries have very little [R&D] and much of these limited R&D and other scientific inputs are used for product differentiation in oligopolistic markets, and in the closely related activity of planned obsolescence. The growth and welfare implications of this kind of industrial R&D are dubious' (Freeman & Soete 1997: 382). As a consequence, in such cases there would be no legitimization for public support of private R&D. In spite of this, most public subsidy schemes do not differentiate between different kinds of R&D. As long as such investments fall within the boundaries of the following general definition of R&D according to the OECD's *Frascati Manual* (OECD 2002: 30), they are considered eligible for being subsidized:

Research and development (R&D) comprise creative work undertaken on a systematic basis in order to increase the stock of knowledge, including knowledge of man, culture and society, and the use of this stock of knowledge to devise new applications. (. . .) R&D is a term covering three activities: basic research, applied research, and experimental development. (. . .) Basic research is experimental or theoretical work undertaken primarily to acquire new knowledge of the underlying foundation of phenomena and observable facts, without any particular application or use in view. Applied research is also original investigation undertaken in order to acquire new knowledge. It is, however, directed primarily towards a specific practical aim or objective. Experimental development is systematic work, drawing on existing knowledge gained from research and/or practical experience, that is directed to producing new materials, products or devices, to installing new processes, systems and services, or to improving substantially those already produced or installed.

For a long time there has been discussion to what extent design is part of R&D. Basically, a lot of what in this book is called 'marginal product innovation' (see Chapter 3) and 'transaction innovation' are not recognized as innovation.[12] The later OECD *Oslo Manual* clarifies this: 'Design is an integral part of the development and implementation of product innovations. However, design changes that do not involve a significant change in a product's functional characteristics or intended uses are not product innovations. . . . Routine upgrades or regular seasonal changes are also not product innovations' (OECD 2005: 48–49). As I will demonstrate in the next chapter (Section 3.1), I do not agree that upgrades or seasonal changes are not innovations. Such innovations may be marginal regarding their degree of radicalness, but in quantitative terms, they are quite important. Of all innovations, 99.9% (including style changes and upgrades) are probably marginal.

At the same time, I totally agree that such marginal innovations, as well as transaction innovations, should not be eligible for government subsidies. Following Freeman and Soete's comments quoted previously about the fact that the welfare effects of many industrial developments activities are questionable, I would even plead for a more restricted definition of R&D related to subsidies. Therefore, a clear distinction should be made between the issue of which kind of innovation is in principle eligible for public subsidies—less than all R&D that falls within the boundaries of the *Frascati* definition— and the definition of innovation in itself. The *Frascati* and *Oslo* definitions of R&D have led not only to pointless nitpicking discussions about where precisely the boundary lies between real and apparently unreal innovation (see CEC 2009: 11–13) but also to an overemphasis on R&D statistics as a measure of investment in innovation. As a consequence, a huge number of innovations which take place on a daily basis and which contribute to the culture of continuous innovation in which we live is neglected. In the next box, and also the next chapter, this is further clarified.

Hidden innovation and the decreasing relevance of R&D statistics

In many studies and statements about innovation, investment in R&D is used as the key indicator for innovativeness. However, the increasing importance of stylistic, service and transaction innovations has led to the decreasing relevance of this indicator, as much of investment in innovation is not covered by it. For example, in service firms, other departments—such as business development—often play an important role in innovation (Jacobs & Waalkens 2001: 29, 42, 54), developing products such as new shop formats, new mortgage forms,[13] forms of health insurance which stimulate more healthy forms of living or other examples already given.

In other cases, R&D is the core business of service organizations, provided on a commercial basis to other firms—by, for example, design agencies, architectural or engineering firms, organization or marketing consultancies, private research institutes and laboratories. However, many of such innovative or innovation-supporting services are not recognized in the 'official' R&D statistics (den Hertog 2000; Jacobs & Waalkens 2001: 49–59).

From this perspective, official objectives, such as that put forward by the European Union in its Lisbon Declaration (2000), to increase the level of R&D investment to 3% of gross domestic product in 2010, are old-fashioned, certainly not innovative and often even counterproductive. In advanced countries such as the United Kingdom and the Netherlands, official R&D investments have been lagging behind, without negative consequences for innovative success. For this reason, the National Endowment for Science, Technology and the Arts (NESTA) in the United Kingdom coined the concept of 'hidden innovation' (Harris & Halkett 2007). As advanced countries, as a rule, have a large service industry, high R&D figures could even become an indicator of backwardness.[14] Therefore, I was not surprised when Hendrik Snijders (2008) even found a negative correlation between R&D investment and economic growth.

Of course, advanced economic countries may also have a large presence of high-tech industries with high R&D investments. A conclusion therefore could be that as the average R&D investments between industries and the industrial structures between countries are quite different, differences between average R&D investments of countries at the same time do not tell much. The objective therefore shouldn't be to increase that average but to increase innovation success as efficiently as possible, which means with as little investment as possible (Hamel & Prahalad 1994: 152; Snijders 1997: 226, 246–247; Jacobs 1999a: 283–284). Following Porter (1990), I see, for instance, success of different countries on world export markets—which, contrary to R&D investment, is an output indicator—as a more relevant indicator of innovative performance.

Again, just as with the neglect of culture in innovation, the question can be posed as to why R&D statistics and the linear innovation model on which it is based remain so popular in innovation literature. Firms have known for a long time that the quality of investment in innovation is more important than its quantity. Depending on their industry, for many of them, stylistic, service and transaction innovations are more important than technological ones. So why are innovation researchers lagging behind? A simple, materialistic hypothesis could be that universities profit most from the traditional linear model, as they are the typical site for independent basic research. When in the framework of cost-cutting or innovation policy universities are asked to economize or to align their research more with that of industry, their usual reaction is that this will hamper innovation in the end. Of course, this could be the case, and I also defend free space for independent free scientific research, but with such statements, they adopt too easily an old-fashioned model of innovation. A hypothesis which is a bit less materialistic is that many authors do not feel happy with the fact that most discussions about innovation are based on efficiency or economic reasoning. In advanced economies especially, culture, science, innovation and creativity should be about more than just money and efficiency. Again, I sympathize with them. However, the picture they paint about the cultural and scientific world is also a bit too idealistic, free of conservatism or material interests. Moreover, this old-fashioned linear-push model of innovation hampers pursuing interesting opportunities for productive co-evolution with smart customers.

3   Degrees of Radicalness of Innovations

3.1   INCREMENTAL INNOVATION AND THE FASHION SYSTEM

In the variety of innovation presented in Chapter 1, different degrees of radicalness of innovation can be distinguished. In the literature, a distinction is traditionally made between incremental and radical innovation. Incremental innovation entails step-by-step improvements or style changes in existing products or services based on, for example, customer feedback. Incremental innovation may also be a form of 'marginal differentiation' (Lipovetsky 1994: 131) vis-à-vis products of competitors or products from the previous season. In the field of information products, there is even a continuous need for new content: new daily newspapers, magazines, books, songs and movies. If nothing new were provided, people would get bored.

Some people question whether such incremental innovation is real innovation, but wouldn't it be strange to exclude this form of innovation which, quantitatively, is the most important? Incremental, even marginal, innovation supports the economic system on a daily basis. Without this continuous flow of new styles, designs and content, most economic life would constitute nothing more than replacement purchasing and remain at a much lower level.

According to Gilles Lipovetsky, this continuous flow of style, design and content innovations and small improvements can be seen as an extension of the fashion logic to all kinds of industries:

> '[T]he overall process that forces companies to innovate, to keep on introducing new articles that are sometimes truly new in conception, but that sometimes (most often) simply incorporate minor refinements in detail. . . . [A] firm that does not regularly create new models loses its market penetration and weakens its image of quality in a society where consumers spontaneously hold that the new is by nature superior to the old.' (Lipovetsky 1994: 131)
>
> '[O]ur economic system has been propelled into a spiral in which innovation is sovereign whether on a large scale or a small one, and in which obsolescence is accelerating.' (Lipovetsky 1994: 135)

'We have reached the era of *consummate fashion,* the extension of the fashion process to broader and broader spheres of collective life. . . . Everyone is more or less immersed in fashion, more or less everywhere and the triple operation that specifically defines fashion is increasingly implemented: the operation of *ephemerality, seduction* and *marginal differentiation.*' (Lipovetsky 1994: 131)

'Marginal differentiation' is a concept quite close to incremental innovation, but without the latter concept's connotation of improvement. A new product is not necessarily better; it does not necessarily lead to a higher degree of well-being, except possibly the well-being found in the newness itself and a larger degree of choice.[1] 'Ephemerality' emphasizes the temporal character of many of these innovations, leading to at least increased economic obsolescence. Many people argue that this leads to a lower level of welfare as a consequence of the problem of increased waste. 'Seduction' draws attention to the fact that there is an increased need for marketing investments (and related transaction innovations) to make product innovations succeed. In many cases, these marketing endeavours cost more than the expenditures necessary to originally develop the innovation. However, as I shall show in the Chapters 6 and 7, in such cases marketing is clearly a part of the value-creating innovation process.

Some innovators do not like this association of innovation with fashion, as they focus on the longer term. Hulsman (2005), for instance, reveals how many architects still nurture the illusion of designing buildings lasting for eternity but, at the same time, increasingly follow short-term fashions. This is only gradually being recognized by the architects themselves. Lipovetsky illustrates the degree to which fashion and marginal differentiation have become the rule as far as product innovation is concerned. This has increased the interest not only in style and design innovation as such (more recently also in the realm of innovation policies) but also in another aspect of fashion: fads and hypes, and related marketing issues. I will come back to this in Chapter 6. In any case, the emergence of the fashion system has led to a culture in which novelty rather than tradition has become the norm (Lipovetsky 1994: 23, 47–48, 84, 127, 229). The more this system has developed, the shorter the product life cycles have become. In the field of management concepts themselves, we can also observe this phenomenon (Carson et al. 2000). In this respect, Abrahamson talks about a proinnovation bias which may even harm organizations (Abrahamson 1991).

In Lipovetsky's view, however, the fashion logic does not necessarily entail uniformity at a certain moment—such as Paris's fashion 'Diktat' as it existed before. On the contrary, through their choice of clothes and other products, from cars to mobile phones, people establish, develop and present their identities as individuals and as members of certain subgroups within society. All of this leads to a fragmentation of lifestyles and the increasing unpredictability of consumer behaviour. As a consequence, investment in marketing and branding has also increased, becoming part of continuous innovation itself (transaction innovation). More frequently than before, products need to be aligned with certain subcultures and lifestyles—a very important element to make product innovations successful (I will return to this in the Chapters 6 and 7). Thus far, this aspect of innovation has received little attention in innovation literature as it traditionally belongs to the realm of marketing. The consequence of this has been that many authors have overlooked some of the aspects which are of the utmost importance for the success of innovations.

In addition to incremental product innovations, there are also incremental process and transaction innovations which involve firms improving their production and transaction processes and their supply chains—for example, banks upgrading their e-banking facilities. Consider also total quality management, Japanese kaizen (continuous improvement) systems, knowledge management systems and firm ambitions in the direction of learning organizations. Ideally, all of these are leading to higher productivity, better service delivery and more customer satisfaction and not just to the multiplication of management fads. At the same time, management fads illustrate Lipovetsky's point that the fashion system has been extending to all spheres of the economy and society. Of course, when successful, some of these new ambitions—such as that of the learning organization—may lead to more than just incremental innovation. However, in many cases the difficulties related to continuous improvement and learning are underestimated, so that many attempts in this realm fail (Bessant et al. 2001).

3.2   RADICAL INNOVATION: DISCONTINUITY

If marginal innovation is on one side of the spectrum of innovation, then radical innovation is on the other one. In innovation literature this is one of the most popular themes for which various other terms exist, such as 'revolutionary,' 'discontinuous,' 'paradigmatic,' 'out of the box,' 'disruptive,'[2] 'breakthrough,' 'really new,' 'game-changing,' or 'pioneering' (Veryzer 1998; Green et al. 1995). Despite this, most authors emphasize that the distinction between incremental and radical innovation is better seen as gradual or continuous rather than as a strictly binary opposition. In a book which is totally devoted to radical innovation, Leifer et al. (2000: 5) state that

> A radical innovation project is one with the potential to produce one or more of the following:
>
> - an entirely new set of performance features;
> - improvements in known performance features of five times or greater; or
> - a significant (30 percent or greater) reduction in cost.

Thus a radical innovation is a product, process or service with either un-precedented performance features or familiar features that offer potential for significant improvements or cost. In our view, radical innovations create such a dramatic change in products, processes, or services that they transform existing markets or industries, or create new ones.

This quote seems to move in two directions. On the one hand, there is talk about an 'entirely new' set of features and dramatic change which 'transform' markets and industries, but no clue is given as to what this means. On the other hand, huge increases in performance or reductions in cost are mentioned related to 'known performance features.' The former is clearly more radical than the latter.

Based on a study of 213 R&D projects in twenty-one large industrial firms, Green and others (1995) arrived at a four-dimensional scale of radicalness of *technological* innovation. The four dimensions are:

- *Technological uncertainty*: the extent to which an innovation incorporates technology that is embryonic and rapidly developing in the general scientific community
- *Technical inexperience*: the extent to which an innovation incorporates a technology that is new to the firm but may be well understood by others
- *Business inexperience*: the extent to which an innovation represents a departure from the firm's existing management or business practices
- *Technology cost*: the extent to which an innovation requires a sizable financial risk

Of these four dimensions, the first seems to be the most important, especially as Green and others looked at the firm level. However, the other dimensions illustrate the degree to which radical technical innovations require related innovations and changes in organizations as I argued in Section 1.3. When we look, however, at the level of industry, all four dimensions become more important. Again and again, it is emphasized by many authors that more radical innovations lead to changes in skills, knowledge, designs, plants and equipment (e.g., Utterback 1994: 200).

In the literature, at least one external dimension has been added to these four dimensions: *commercial discontinuity,* or the fact that the market is not yet familiar with a new product class and its possible value for customers or users. It is even possible to introduce radically new products which do not require new technology (Veryzer 1998: 307). New nontechnical concepts (see Table 1.1 in Section 1.5) especially seem to fit into this category. However, we can also think about new paradigms in the realm of science or the arts (Wijnberg 1995: 226–230). For this reason, in my opinion, commercial discontinuity can be understood better as *cultural discontinuity*—that is, incompatibility with existing concepts, norms, values and routines. I will develop this idea from Chapter 5 onwards. In the meantime, it is surprising that none of the publications just quoted states the issue in this way—again an illustration of the neglect of the cultural aspects of innovation.

In their book on *Radical Innovation,* Leifer et al. only mention 'culture' when stating that '[o]ne of the executive's greatest contributions to innovation is to shape the *organizational* culture in ways that make radical innovation a more natural, accepted, and valued activity' (Leifer et al. 2000: 164, 181–182; my emphasis). Remaining questions about customer resistance to adopting the new *technology* and the changes the customers will possibly have to make in order to use the innovation are only addressed very briefly (Leifer et al. 2000: 100–101, 105). This one-sidedness again illustrates the degree to which the broader cultural aspects of innovation are mostly neglected. Even when it is broadly recognized that most failures in the realm of innovation are due to this neglect of the consumers' perspective, at best the firm's internal cultural problems related to innovation are dealt with!

Alternatively, for Markides and Geroski (2005: 4), the first defining characteristic of radical innovations is that 'they introduce major new *value propositions* that disrupt existing consumer habits and behaviours'—I have emphasized 'value propositions' because this concept clearly emphasizes the cultural character of innovations. The second defining character of radical innovations is that the competences and complementary assets on which the different competitors have built their success are undermined.[3]

New consumer habits and behaviour which radical innovations induce often cannot be predicted even by the innovators themselves. In addition, mental models related to one kind of use may prevent seeing alternative practices and innovations based on these. In this way, cultural discontinuity also affects innovators.

Mental models hampering the development of telephony, radio and mobile telephony

Graham Bell invented the telephone in 1876 based on Michael Faraday's scientific and technological insights, which had already been known for more than forty years without many people seeing a social need for such a device. At that time, telegraphy, which originally also had had to negotiate quite a few obstacles, had become so popular and integrated in social life that many people could not imagine a need for telephony. Even after it was introduced, it didn't take off rapidly. Originally, an important application was even one-way communication (Hård & Jamison 2005: 209–214).

Similarly, when Guglielmo Marconi invented radiotelegraphy twenty years later, the possible relevance and use of the invention was not rapidly understood, as Petroski recalls (2006: 103–104):

> 'Since the 'wireless,' as the name suggested, was designed to replace the telegraph, it was perceived at first to be a failure in that it did not just carry signals point to point but broadcast them so that anyone with the

proper receiving instrument could listen in on what were intended to be private communications. It took a while before this failing was seen as an advantage, but in a different context. Ships at sea could broadcast calls for help. . . . It was not until after World War I that the advantage of broadcasting programs to what came to be called radios was fully realized and exploited.'

Later, the mental association between wireless and radio hampered the development of mobile telecommunication, which was in an altogether different realm. Ericsson, one of the few companies active in both fields, was one of the most vociferous about the difficulties of merging these two industrial cultures (Lester & Piore 2004: 16–17).

Culture not only entails norms, values and habits, but also, of course, language and concepts. From Immanuel Kant we have learned that our perception is steered by concepts and categories. Such concepts and categories are of course cultural constructions related to larger or smaller communities. The more familiar they become, the more natural they seem to be. Conversely, '[t]he more at home you are in a certain community of practice, the more you forget the strange and contingent nature of its categories seen from the outside. Illegitimacy, then, is seeing those objects as would a stranger—either as a naïf or by comparison with another frame of reference in which they exist' (Bowker & Star 1999: 294–295).

In a way, it is difficult to value and sometimes even to see something for which we do not have appropriate categories and interpretation schemes. An example of this is the German quip about contemporary art: 'Ist das Kunst oder können wir das wegwerfen' (Is this art or can we throw it away?). Radical innovation leads to new concepts or categories which by definition are far from our common understanding. One way to decrease the *cognitive distance* of a radical innovation from existing reality is the adaptation of well-known concepts to explain such a radical innovation. 'The first automobile, for example was called a "horseless" carriage' (Ries & Trout 1986: 32); a recumbent bike is a kind of bicycle, even when its design is quite different from what we see as the dominant design of bicycles.

Cultural speciation: The coming into being of new product categories

Linking innovation to existing concepts and categories resembles the emergence of new species from existing ones in biology. *Homo sapiens,* for instance, is a relatively young species (about 130,000 years old) within the genus *Homo,* which came into existence some 2.4 million years ago.

In a similar way, we can sometimes trace the remarkable lineages of different concepts: a large grocery becomes a supermarket, whereas later on the small grocery store is called a minimarket! After the bikini (the originally explosive bathing suit named after the atoll where the fourth and fifth nuclear tests were performed at around the time the bathing suit came into vogue) came the monokini. From impressionism we moved to expressionism and even abstract expressionism—quite different from the original expressionism. After men's suits, we got women's suits and later on even catsuits. Thus linking new species to existing ones is an interesting tactic to decrease the inherent cognitive distance which radical innovations entail.

The fact that a number of competitors copy a relatively successful product may even help in the establishment of a new category. In this way, a strange kind of brown lemonade at a certain moment got widely recognized as cola. In this way, having competitors—early followers—in a new area may be an advantage, as they help to spread the message.

On the basis of this kind of experiences, Richard Lester and Michael Piore argue that especially in the first stages of radical innovation, research is primarily focused not on solving technical problems, which requires analytical thinking, but on interpretative search—interpretation and sensemaking— which tries to completely understand new realities for which new concepts and categories have to be developed. In many cases, this requires a great deal of debate and incisive conversation, a dimension of innovation which often has been neglected:

> The interpretive process has much in common with the ways that people within a linguistic community come to understand and communicate with one another and with others in different linguistic communities. In this interpretive way of looking at business, the role of the manager has less to do with solving problems or negotiating between contending interests than with initiating and guiding conversations. . . . To maintain their innovative capabilities, firms must continually seek out and participate in exploratory, interpretive conversations with a variety of interlocutors, and this will require a rebalancing of management strategies in the direction of interpretation. (Lester & Piore 2004: 8–9)

Such new realities may be not only in the realm of the application of new technologies but also in that of new social developments, or in the adaptation of new styles or technologies to an uncertain, not yet clearly defined field, in other words a nonexistent market. The still-evolving use of the Internet is a good example of such largely unexpected new combinations between new technical opportunities and new forms of social behaviour. In such cases, many trials are performed, errors are made and attempts to understand, learn and develop new initiatives occur, leading to more trials. The more radical the innovation, the higher the possible technological, commercial, linguistic and interpretative uncertainties are. As a consequence, the development process of these innovations is messier and less structured than is the case with incremental innovations. The process may take a long time, partly because people from various professional backgrounds and related language communities often take part in this process (Lester & Piore 2004: 69–73, 101–103).

Lester and Piore therefore conclude that innovation needs both approaches: interpretative work in order to better understand radically new issues and opportunities, and analysis and problem solving when what one is looking for has been clarified. In a way, these are two totally different forms of creative work which have to complement each other. In innovation literature, it has been emphasized regularly that both activities may call for different kinds of people. Interpretative search requires people who are interested in many fields and as a result can switch more easily between different perspectives. For this reason it is remarkable to hear Lester and Piore, professors at the Massachusetts Institute of Technology, argue in favour of a more humanistic, holistic education, involving the study of subjects such as literary critique, history, language and the arts at an undergraduate and secondary level, as such fields prepare students for dealing with ambiguity. In addition, within the realm of science itself, they claim there should be more conversations and cooperation *between* disciplines than is now the case. By contrast, analytical search, which solves problems, is more favourable to the linear thinking and monodisciplinary approaches most people know best (Lester & Piore 2004: 165–167, 187).

Another conclusion we can draw from this discussion is that with radical innovation we have to prepare for experimentation, co-evolution and learning in the longer term, as the most promising opportunities are revealed only gradually.

Myths related to pioneers

In management literature, a common myth is the one about first mover advantage. This myth is based on the fact that many successful firms which are seen as pioneers in their industry were actually only early followers. The reason for this is that the real pioneers didn't survive and are now forgotten. For example, Tellis and Golder (1996: 67), who did a pioneering study on this theme, give the following quotes from *Financial World* about a leading firm in the restaurant business:

- 'World's biggest chain of highway restaurants'
- 'Pioneer in restaurant franchising'
- 'Most fabulous success story in restaurant chains'

I suppose most readers would guess that these quotes are about McDonald's. They deal, however, with the Howard Johnson's restaurants which in the 1960s and 1970s were the largest chain in this industry in the United States and Canada, with about 1,500 restaurants and motor lodges. After this, they came into decline. After a series of takeovers and partial sales, according to Wikipedia in 2011 only three of these restaurants are still in existence.

Tellis and Golder give more examples. Disposable diapers have been sold in the United States since 1935, but most people think that Procter & Gamble, which only entered this market in 1961 with its Pampers, was the pioneer. The first personal computers were sold in 1975 by MITS. Apple, which by many is seen as the pioneer, was only established one year later and introduced its first computer in 1977.

Tellis and Golder studied the long-term history of fifty product groups introduced in the twentieth century and found that only in 11% of these categories the pioneers were the market leaders, whereas 47% of the pioneers didn't exist anymore. In most cases, early followers were the market leader, and they had a minimal failure rate. They weren't even that early as, on average, they came on the market thirteen years later than the pioneer. These early followers had much more expertise in mass production and marketing and prepared their market entry very carefully.

3.3   A FUZZY APPROACH OF INNOVATION

From many years of studying innovation and trying to stimulate it, I have learned that it is important to really appreciate incremental innovation. Sometimes I ask people who want to innovate not to think outside the box but to remain within the box, just thinking about improving products and production and transaction processes. Many people are quite relieved with this approach, as they find thinking outside the box quite intimidating, and in most cases, it only leads to a lot of funny ideas which are all thrown away. From experience with inside-the-box exercises, I know that these quite often lead to ideas for radical improvement which are not that easy to implement, so even then, there is still a lot of work to be done.

In the meantime, it remains true that not all innovations are equally radical. From the previous observations, it emerges that the more comprehensive innovations discussed in Section 1.8 (system innovations and changes in techno-economic regimes) are in most cases also more radical.[4] Incremental innovations may be the most important quantitatively, but their social impact is smaller. Some stylistic innovations may be more radical and lead to more social turbulence (e.g., new art forms, or in fashion, miniskirts and monokinis). However, there are also radical innovations with little social spillover. The string theory in physics, for example, is a radically new paradigm, but with no apparent major impact on society yet. In addition, the commercial exploitation of wind and solar energy may be a radical innovation but its social impact is not necessarily very large, as these energy systems can be integrated relatively easily into existing infrastructures. In countries where up to now such energy infrastructures have been largely insufficient, this impact could, however, be more important—for example, because these energy sources facilitate more decentralized power generation.

In discussions about innovation, the question is regularly asked relates to whether this—usually a relatively minor innovation—is really an innovation. Following the definition I have proposed, nearly everything new with even a marginal added value is considered an innovation. In literature, qualifications can be found, such as 'new to the firm' or 'new to the world,' but these do not solve the issue. A new kind of coloured paperclip may be new to the world, but it is a marginal innovation. In many cases it is, however, difficult to draw a line between marginal and what then should be called real innovations. How radical would we, for instance, call the adding of a camera function to a mobile telephone? For this reason, I propose to follow a fuzzy approach instead of a binary logic.

A fuzzy approach

In binary logic, we have to make a black or white decision: something is new or not new (i.e., already existing). Therefore, when a new coloured paperclip did not exist before, it is new. I can understand that many people do not find this a satisfying conclusion, but neither is the option of suggesting that it already existed—as it didn't.

In order to avoid such an unsatisfying dilemma, I propose to follow fuzzy logic and adopt a scale. When people ask me whether I am young or old, I find it difficult to answer. I am older than fifty but I still feel young. Binary logic, such as that followed by people arguing about real innovations, forces me to say whether I am young or old. When we put young (1 young or 0 old) at 0 years and old (1 old or 0 young) at 100 years, then when I will be sixty, fuzzy logic allows me to say that I am 0.4 young or 0.6 old. This scale could of course be constructed in a different way (e.g., adding indicators such as energy levels or traditional versus nontraditional lifestyles), but the principle of a scale between the opposites remains a better option than adopting a black or white approach.

Nothing—even the most radical innovation—is totally new, because 100% innovation would not be understood by its environment. Therefore, following a fuzzy approach with the help of Figure 3.1, the most radical and comprehensive innovations—for example, electrification when it first happened—might be rated as 0.8 new, whereas a small change in the style or colour of a dress might be no more than 0.01 new. A new car model would probably fall into the lower categories of around 0.05 new, whereas a new car category (e.g., SUVs at the time of their first introduction) would be around 0.1, and a new car concept requiring a totally new engine (e.g., hydrogen fuelled) and a related new infrastructure would be about 0.5 new. The first introduction of electricity can be considered even more radical. Think of the fact that many more activities could be organized at night; also the

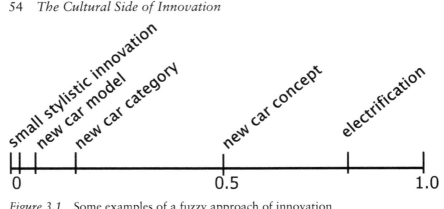

Figure 3.1   Some examples of a fuzzy approach of innovation

design of most machines could be concentrated on their precise function, as the generation of energy could take place on a distant location and power lines enabled energy transmission over long distances. Also nowadays when a distant village in the developing world for the first time gets electricity—for instance, with the use of solar energy—literally a whole new world is opened for its inhabitants with all cultural shocks this brings about.

The opposite approach: Holding to an essential definition of innovation

A few years ago, Harold Evans, a famous historian and journalist, together with two colleagues wrote *They Made America,* a book in which some fifty American innovators are celebrated. The book did not follow a narrow technological approach as, for example, Levi Strauss, Walt Disney and Estée Lauder were present among these fifty greatest innovators. A less known woman such as Martha Harper was also included. This woman invented franchising, when from 1891 she developed a chain of hairdressers and beauty salons following a special philosophy (the Harper method) and related products.

In his introduction, Evans emphasizes the traditional distinction between invention and innovation with which I started Section 1.1 of this book. More than other writers, he even underlines the importance of practical innovations. I couldn't agree more until he comments quite severely on Graham Bell (which he doesn't include in the fifty): 'He was not an innovator.' Evans's reason not to call Bell an innovator was the fact that 'the Bell Company phone was calculated more to develop the American voice and lungs than to encourage conversation. . . . The problem of indistinct and muffled sound was solved by Thomas Edison (with Charles Batchelor)' (Evans et al. 2004: 12). Evans basically says that Bell as an inventor was not good enough, or that he tried to make an innovation of it too rapidly. The reason for this was, however, that just as many other commercial innovators, Bell wanted to be the first to file a patent application. After some years, with the help of this patent he became successful enough with his Bell Company to buy Edison's patent for the carbon microphone from his competitor Western Union. In my opinion, Evans's essentialist definition of innovations and innovators hampers him from learning the real lessons of what good innovators do: start with imperfect innovations and then learn on the basis of experience.

Nachoem Wijnberg, whose definition of innovation was discussed in Section 1.1, relates the radicalness of an innovation to its impact on processes of selection in innovation—and in this way to culture (Wijnberg 2004: 1474): 'The importance [i.e., the degree of radicalness] of an innovation is the extent to which the innovation is connected with changes in the relative valuations of products satisfying the same set of preferences, of the set of preferences, of the composition of the set of selectors or of the characteristics of the selection system itself.'

Wijnberg distinguishes four possible degrees of radicalness:

- Incremental innovations lead existing selectors to reconsider the relative value of products satisfying the same set of preferences. When I see a new type of mobile phone, do I want to replace the one I have?
- A more radical innovation causes the selectors to reassess their preferences. At a certain moment many young people started to spend more money on mobile telecommunication than on clothes.
- Even more radical is the case where the set of selectors is changed. This also happened with mobile phones. Their main customer base moved relatively rapidly from business people to younger people.
- Most radical or important in Wijnberg's view are innovations which lead to a change in the selection system itself. Previously, telecommunications were seen as a public utility, but as a consequence of new technological opportunities and social developments, this industry has become highly competitive and deregulated.

Changes in techno-economic regimes seem to be even more radical innovations than the most radical stage envisaged by Wijnberg. We could say that such changes change not only selection processes or systems but nearly the whole world, the whole environment. After electrification or after the establishment of the Fordistic car system, the world had been fundamentally changed.

3.4 THE DIVERSITY OF INNOVATION FROM A LIFETIME PERSPECTIVE

We can now look at the diversity of innovation from a kind of lifetime perspective. Radical innovations do not happen regularly. They may be the result of new scientific insights or experimentation by inventors. A nice

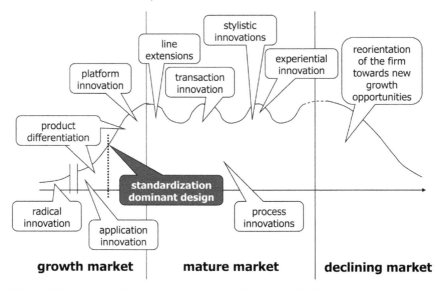

Figure 3.2   Forms of innovation emanating from a radical innovation

example of the latter is provided by the bicycle mechanics Orville and Wilbur Wright who laid the foundation for a new age of flying, warfare, business organization and tourism. This example also illustrates the extent to which radical innovations in one industry may lead to a wave of all kinds of innovations in a variety of sectors. Figure 3.2 illustrates this to some extent. With this figure, I do not look at all innovations stemming from one radical innovation, but I concentrate on one product *category*—for example, airplanes themselves.[5]

As one can see in this figure, there is not one peak as is the case in most diagrams about product life cycles. This is related to the fact that I do not look at single products (e.g., one airplane or car model) but at product *categories*—airplanes, cars, health insurance or computer games. Product categories may also experience decline at some point, but due to renewal, they can also be revived. Some categories will come to an end at a certain time, but others will not, possibly because they fulfil a basic need, such as clothing or housing.

Let us now look at the different stages represented in Figure 3.2. A new development starts with a new concept, paradigm, technology or business model. Again, we should consider not only new technologies[6] such as steam engines, biotechnology or microprocessors, but also bicycles, disposable diapers, hip-hop, McDonald's or low-cost airlines. As we know, radical innovations are not necessarily successful—to say the least. To emphasize this point, Geoffrey Moore draws a vertical line after radical innovation in all his publications. In his opinion, at this point, a chasm has to be crossed[7] in order to move from the small group of possible early supporters of an innovation (technology enthusiasts or visionaries) to broader audiences of more pragmatic customers (Moore 1995: 18–21) who are looking for useful applications. This is a very important phase in which many promising radical innovations fail as a consequence of an overconcentration on technology. For the same reason, many pioneering firms fail in the commercialization phase of radical innovation, whereas fast followers with more experience in and focus on mass production and marketing succeed. As clarified in the box on myths related to pioneers (Section 3.2), Procter & Gamble did not introduce disposable diapers, but they made them successful. Neither Apple nor IBM were the pioneers of microcomputers, but because of their subsequent success in the field, many people think they were (Tellis & Golder 1996).

Thinking in terms of solutions or having a flexible mind?

Many observers state that, in order to succeed, it is important to think in terms of customer solutions. It certainly is useful to concentrate on specific customer groups with a pressing unsatisfied need. Viagra seems to be a good example of this—even when it was developed with another need in mind. However, this does not deny the fact that solving the most pressing needs—such as curing AIDS or malaria—requires a lot of energy, whereas many radical innovations come about in a more accidental way, without much consideration of solutions. Like Post-it, Viagra was originally a failed product—it was intended to cure high blood pressure. However, Post-It and Viagra are good examples of cases in which the firms developing these innovations were successful in commercializing them. Therefore, a flexible mind which is able to shift rapidly from an accident to an application in another field is probably more useful than any dogmatic approach.

Moore warns, however, of targeting mass markets too rapidly when trying to cross the chasm. He emphasizes that concentrating on applications is easier in niche markets. Therefore, the first pragmatic customers to allow an innovation to cross the chasm will probably be found in relatively small niches where there is a clear need. Spreadsheets were initially adopted by financial professionals only. In such niches, it is easier to know one's customers and to learn from their feedback. Once the specialists in these niches are convinced of the added value of the innovation, word may spread rapidly (Moore 1995: 28–29). As a result, these useful applications may be further differentiated in the direction of other niche markets and in this way evolve into a more generic product. But Moore, as well as Tellis and Golder (1996), emphasizes that profiting from mass markets as a rule requires the elaboration of a totally different business model than earning from niche specialists. As a consequence, quite often firms with experience in addressing mass markets perform this step.

Why have Velotype and Veyboard not been more successful?

For more than thirty years, different actors have tried to introduce Velotype, an innovative keyboard with the help of which syllables are typed rather than letters, as shown in Figure 3.3. In this way, it is possible to write twice as rapidly as usual. In principle the necessary Velotype keyboards can replace existing QWERTY or AZERTY keyboards quite easily. In the beginning, Velotype had some success and at least in the Netherlands some larger organizations started to use it. However, probably due to the rapid rise of the personal computer, diffusion stalled. Since 2001 a new model, better adapted to PCs came on the market, now branded as the Veyboard. Even when the product has been continuously improved, it has remained a niche product. Especially in the Netherlands and Sweden, it is used by professionals who have to write very rapidly, such as writing interpreters for deaf people.

Figure 3.3   Velotype's Veyboard

Through the conquest of various groups of pragmatic users, the transition to a mass market becomes possible. In literature on technologies, *standardization* is emphasized as a precondition for this transition. Competing standards mean that there is probably too much insecurity and that many potential customers keep waiting.[8] As a result, standards today are mainly associated with a set of undisputed technical specifications.[9] However, standards also have a possible cultural meaning in the sense of a *dominant design*.

Dominant designs

If we look at many radical innovations, we can observe that it takes some time before a dominant design is established. In an illuminating case study, Pinch and Bijker (1987), for example, describe how the selection of the final bicycle design at the end of the nineteenth century was the result of a complex interaction between totally different social groups. Women and older cyclists saw the possible advantages of this new transport vehicle but especially valued safety and comfort. In contrast, younger cyclists appreciated sports aspects, such as challenge and speed. As a result, various bicycle designs were presented to different groups with all kinds of real and rhetorical answers to the concerns of each. The basic design, which finally won and which still represents our basic idea of a bicycle, apparently fitted the criteria of most of these constituent desires best. It is probably not a coincidence that this model at that time was marketed as the 'safety bicycle.' The establishment of this dominant design was quite important for the ultimate diffusion of the bicycle.[10]

In a similar way, it is said that the Ford Model T was important in setting the standard for cars: 'Almost all cars designed and produced after the Model T are recognizable descendents of the Model T, while most of those that appeared before the Model T seem to be interesting and eccentric one-offs. . . . A dominant design is basically a standard. It defines what a product is and what its core features are. It is, if you like, a platform, from which come a wide range of product variants that are distinguishable from each other without seeming to be fundamentally different' (Markides & Geroski 2005: 52).

Once a dominant design is established, the broader public has a genuine awareness of the product category. The radical innovation may not necessarily be accepted but at least it is recognized. As a consequence, the phase of radical innovation is over and societal discussion about the new product probably becomes a bit more stable. Product differentiation now receives a new meaning. Before standardization, applications in diverse niche markets were sought in the hope of launching the product. Now differentiation from a known, established standard takes place, possibly adapting the product to different audiences.

One diffusion curve or a series of different ones?

In much innovation literature, the diffusion of an innovation is represented as an S-shaped curve. An innovation—say mobile telephones—makes a slow start but when successful reaches a rapid growth stage. When most possible adopters actually have adopted the innovation, the curve necessarily levels off. As Geoffrey Moore clarifies, however, each successive group of adopters may have different preferences to which the innovation has to be adapted. That's why Akrich and others (2002b: 208) state, 'To adopt an innovation is to adapt it: such is the formula which provides the best account of diffusion. And this adaptation generally results in a collective elaboration, the fruit of an growing interessement.' It is through using innovations that people learn what they can possibly do with them, which leads to adaptations and new incremental innovations (Bhidé 2006: 16–21). Nowadays mobile telephones with all their specialized features are seen as a radical innovation. In a way one could call them 'personal telephones' containing private data in different forms, but as far as I know, no one actually invented the concept of personal telephones. All additional features were added gradually. Who could have thought before-hand that SMS, Twitter or visual messages would become important elements of this? Thus gradually the mobile telephone became a radical innovation. As Bela Gold showed many years ago, for this reason a diffusion curve of an innovation is not really that of one stable innovation through time but the adaptation of this innovation to ever-new groups of potential users. This is represented in Figure 3.4 (inspired by Gold 1983: 107).

Akrich, Callon and Latour (2002b: 213) summarize this quite nicely: 'The innovation transforms itself at every loop, redefining its properties and its public.' Well, of course the innovation does not do this itself.

With the possible advent of the mass market, process innovation be-comes important. The more the product becomes differentiated, the more it becomes crucial to look behind the facade of the products to the possible efficiencies in the realm of production (including the back offices of service organizations) on the basis of *platforms*. Car models from different car brands (Volkswagen, Audi, Skoda) of the VAG group nowadays are built based on the same platform, which leads to economies of scale.

Looking at Figure 3.4, we have now arrived at the mature market. At this stage, production processes continue to be organized more efficiently (process innovation). At the level of product innovation, there are possible *line extensions* (small variations of the product targeting diverse customer groups),[11] marginal *stylistic innovations* (in the field of fashion and design) and also *experiential innovations* based on the feelings, emotions or even transformations customers experience when they consume the product. The more the variety of products on offer increases, the more intense the

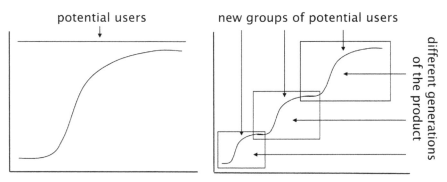

Figure 3.4   Traditional model of diffusion versus diffusion as adaptation, as a series of innovation-diffusion curves

competition for the attention of consumers becomes and hence the relevance of *transaction innovations*.[12]

As stated previously, in many industries this mature stage in the lifetime of product categories may continue forever, as there will always be a need for products in such realms as housing, clothing or education.[13] This does not deny the fact that some organizations are no longer capable of competing in these industries—for example, because they do not have the necessary scale—and may be forced to look for opportunities in other fields.

Of course, some product categories at a certain moment actually come to their end—for example, the Pony Express, telexes, typewriters, tape recorders and fax machines. At that moment, the enterprises supplying such products or services must reorient into new activities or die. This is the third phase represented in Figure 3.3.

Looking back on our discussion in this section based on Figure 3.3, we can observe that cultural issues play an important role in any trajectory from radical innovation onwards. Some radical innovations are more technology based whereas others are more conceptual (paradigmatic). The establishment of a new product category may sometimes require the acceptance of a technical standard, but in all cases, it requires a common cultural representation in the form of a dominant design. Once the category is established, a huge escalation of product differentiations and line extensions takes place based on all kinds of dimensions and values: stylistic, emotional, or experiential. The result of this can be observed every day. Although many innovations succeed, many more fail.

Are we able to better understand the reasons for failure and success? An important and often neglected issue has been highlighted: culture. However, highlighting this still leaves it quite general and vague. Can we come to a more precise understanding? This I do in the second part of this book. But first, we have to make a short detour and revisit Charles Darwin to provide a final building block.

4 Darwinian Selection at Different Levels

4.1 INNOVATION AND THE GENERALIZED DARWINIAN RESEARCH PROGRAMME

This chapter provides a fourth, more theoretical building block with the help of which in the second part of this book the cultural side of innovation will be analysed more in depth. Some readers may prefer to skip it right now and come back to it later, when its usefulness becomes clearer on the basis of the application of its basic concepts in the later chapters.

In the previous chapters, Darwinian terminology was used a few times. For example, the Darwinian concept of 'selection systems' is central in Wijnberg's treatment of radical innovation, which was discussed in Section 3.3. It is probably not a coincidence that especially economists who have been dealing with innovation were the first to adopt evolutionary approaches. Each step in the evolution of humankind can indeed be seen as an innovation. As a consequence, many economic historians describe the development of the economy through different stages—for example, the transition of an agricultural economy to an industrial one and later on to a service economy or even a creative or experience economy. However, peculiar to a more Darwinian way of looking at evolution is always to question why a certain development took place. Many people may see progress as inevitable, but the fact is that for long stretches of time there was not much progress. Throughout history, many inventions did not develop into successful innovations. Therefore, we always have to ask why a certain innovation was adopted—selected—or not.

Indeed, one of the most promising scientific developments in recent decades has been the emergence of generalized Darwinism as a paradigm, with the help of which different disciplines are able to exchange findings and integrate them into a more comprehensive framework.[1] However, Darwinian concepts are sometimes used in economics in a rather sloppy way. Geoffrey Moore for example, a few years ago published an interesting book on innovation called *Dealing with Darwin* (2005), which inspired my treatment of life cycles of product categories in Section 3.4. However, neither Darwin nor the concept of 'selection environment' appear in Moore's entire book, so apparently 'Darwin' in its title is nothing more than a metaphor for competing on markets which have become ever more demanding. Many economists indeed equate Darwinian selection with competing on the market with price as the main selection criterion, whereas in most cases selection is much more complex—as we will see in the following chapters. For this reason, I clarify what in general is meant by a Darwinian approach of innovation.

As this book deals with the cultural side of innovation and Darwinism originated in biology, I also have to say something about the relationship between biology and the social sciences, which will become most clear when we talk about gene-culture co-evolution.'

4.2 GENE-CULTURE CO-EVOLUTION

Let me start from the biological basics, which should be obvious but nevertheless are not always well understood by social scientists. Our *Homo sapiens* species evolved out of other species and for this reason for the most part functions on the basis of biological instincts and mechanisms. However, like other more evolved animals, we have developed more brainpower and related information-processing capabilities and behavioural flexibility. As a consequence of its long development out of other species, ours is equipped with a relatively large brain size which at a certain moment led to the development of culture. More than any other (surviving) species, we are aware of what we do and seem to be able to change the direction of our behaviour.[2] The development of languages and later of whole scientific systems increased the speed of our development and led to the supremacy of our species over all others—with the exception of some bacteria and virus-infected organisms from time to time.

Like all primates, our species is a social one, which means that cooperation was essential in our survival. Compared to other apes we are even supersocial. As a rule, we take others' feelings into account, and because of this, we are able to cooperate.[3] Sarah Hrdy, for example, hypothesizes about what would happen if other apes were crammed together in an airplane for a long flight: 'What if I were travelling with a planeload of chimpanzees? Any one of us would be lucky to disembark with all ten fingers and toes still attached, with the baby still breathing and unmaimed. Bloody earlobes and other appendages would litter the aisles. Compressing so many highly impulsive strangers into a tight space would be a recipe for mayhem' (Hrdy 2009: 3).[4]

There is probably a direct relationship between our supersocial character, the size of our brains and the development of human culture and language. Human survival and evolution has been dependent on the creation of ever-larger groups and societies. According to evolutionary psychologist Robin Dunbar, the development of *Homo sapiens*' brain is directly related to people's integration in ever larger groups.

> There is a correlation between social group size and the volume of the neocortex in primates which suggests that is has been the need to manage the complex social world in which primates live that has driven the evolution of ever larger brains. . . . Group size in humans is about 150: this is the number of people that you know personally and have some kind of meaningful relationship with—as opposed to the people you know by sight or those with whom you have a strictly business relationship. Chimpanzees live in communities that have an average size of about 50–55, and their neocortex is proportionally smaller. (Dunbar 2004: 72)

Human societies, however, have grown much larger than 150. Language and, more generally, culture (e.g., through religion) helped to monitor social relationships of larger groups with nonvisual methods of social control. Language is a practical tool not only to pass on knowledge to other people but also to gossip and to talk about other members' behaviour, in this way helping to control them and repress free-riding and other unwanted actions. Compare this with chimpanzee groups, where social control can only be performed visually (Barrett et al. 2002: 244–260, 325–344; Dunbar et al. 2007: 118–135).

What really sets our species apart is, therefore, the development of human culture. This does not mean, however, that our nature and culture can be dealt with in a totally separate way. As Peter Richerson and Robert Boyd, two biologists who have written more than any of their colleagues about culture and biology, state, '*Culture is part of biology.* . . . Culture affects the success and survival of individuals and groups; as a result, some cultural variants spread and others diminish, leading to evolutionary processes that are every bit as real and important as those that shape genetic variation. These culturally evolved environments then affect which genes are favored by natural selection. Over the evolutionary long haul, culture has shaped our innate psychology as much as the other way around' (Richerson & Boyd 2005: 4; their emphasis). For this reason, the development of our species has been dependent on the co-evolution of genes with culture. As one can imagine, these statements lead to a very interesting research programme to which different sciences contribute.

Many researchers have taken up this challenge: among many others in biology are, beside Boyd and Richerson, for example, Edward Wilson (1998), Niles Eldredge, and Stephen Jay Gould (Eldredge 1985, 1997; Eldredge & Gould 1972); in psychology, Robin Dunbar and colleagues (Barrett et al. 2002; Dunbar et al. 2007) and David Buss (2009); in economics and management science, Richard Nelson and Sidney Winter (1982), Michael Hannan and John Freeman (1989), Geoffrey Hodgson and Thorbjørn Knudsen (Hodgson 1993; Hodgson & Knudsen 2010), and Eric Beinhocker (2006); in sociology,[5] Gerhard Lenski (2005); and in the humanities, Joseph Carroll (2004), Denis Dutton (2009), Brian Boyd (2009) and David

Rothenberg (2011). With this book, I contribute my part to this emerging generalized Darwinian research programme, even when it is not always easy to oversee all discussions and other contributions in this field.[6]

4.3 THE BASIC DARWINIAN FRAMEWORK

From a Darwinian perspective, successful innovation can be considered in terms of the survival of any new product, process or transaction which apparently fits into its selection environment—an environment which is not necessarily much larger than a niche within a larger ecosystem. To be clear, survival of the fittest does not necessarily mean that only one can survive—most often this is not the case—nor that the survivor is the strongest, the healthiest, the best or whatever superlative is used. Apparently, the surviving innovation fits to some extent, not necessarily perfectly, in its relevant selection environment. Fitting is more about 'satisficing' than about perfection; a later innovation may fit better and for this reason replace the previous one. But this replacement is not necessarily better in quality—as quality is mostly measured with a kind of absolute yardstick—whereas fitness is related to the criteria of its specific selection system, which, moreover, may change.

As a rule, for a long time evolution has been a blind process in most cases which has led to more complex species through time, but not necessarily more perfect ones. In addition, our species may disappear at some moment, without being replaced by a better one.

Darwinian evolution—through natural selection—proceeds by means of a kind of three-stage rocket: (1) variation, (2) selection, and (3) retention (inheritance), multiplication, and possibly speciation. Therefore, in the Darwinian framework we can see an innovation as a kind of genetic recombination or mutation (variation) which is accepted (selected) or not by its environment (its selection system) and then possibly survives for a longer time (retention, multiplication[7] and maybe speciation). For Darwin, evolution meant descent with modification. In biology, most variation relies on a mere recombination of the genes of the parents (comparable with incremental or marginal innovation). Mutations (random mistakes in copying) happen continuously but only rarely lead to the emergence of a new species. As a consequence of mainly external shocks (e.g., the impact of meteorites or volcanic eruptions), however, sometimes more rapid evolution takes place.[8] More radical innovations—originating from new concepts or new technological insights—in turn are comparable with such sudden radical biological evolutions. As we saw in the previous chapter, such innovations may lead to new *categories* (comparable with speciation or phylogenetic development, the coming into being of a new species through natural selection).

In biology, natural selection is a blind and wasteful process.[9] A lot of variety is created continuously, but most biological innovations are not viable and therefore not selected. Most of the time evolution proceeds quite slowly. Our planet has been in existence for about 4.5 billion years, but multicellular organisms came into existence only 610 million years ago. However, in the next 10 million years afterwards, the Cambrian explosion, biological diversity developed quite rapidly. About 500 million years ago, plants and fungi colonized the land, soon followed by smaller animals. Another 300 million years later, the first mammals appeared. Some 7 million years ago, the first hominids appeared. *Homo sapiens* entered the scene about 130,000 years ago. Only one hundred thousand years later do we have the first evidence of a more settled lifestyle, including trading between groups. Increasingly, through the development of culture, learning became an additional form of human development which led to its increasing acceleration. Therefore, human evolution to a large degree has acquired a more cultural nature as knowledge and competencies can now be rationally transmitted between different people quite rapidly.[10] In this way, selection has become less blind, even when many of our preferences and our behaviours remain hidden from our consciousness. Most of our preferences have a biological basis, but culture in the form of values and routines also plays a role. In this book, this extended Darwinian framework is used to understand and possibly improve the selection of innovations.

From creativity to productive creativity

When we look at the Darwinian three-stage rocket, we can observe that in most discussions about creativity, the first stage of variation—the development of as many ideas as possible—is emphasized. This is important, as without variation the evolutionary process is not fed and comes to a standstill. Think of difficult problems (e.g., curing cancer) for which new solutions are continuously devised and tested. In many cases, of course, the issue is not that complicated and is more about inventing a new mousetrap or designing a new style.

As many books have already been written about creativity in the sense of generating variation, I, on the contrary, want to concentrate on the second stage of evolution—selection—in terms of what I call 'productive creativity' (Jacobs 2006b: 23). How should we proceed in order to increase the chance for selection of the innovation on which we have been working? What can we know about the selection system or systems where our proposals will end up? How can we influence selection? As we have seen in the previous chapter, incremental innovations, as a rule, will have more chance to be selected than radical ones. However, the most promising ideas in the longer term may be those based on radically new concepts. How can we possibly improve the chances for selection of these more radical innovations, too? For all of this, in the rest of this book, I will present a series of frameworks and approaches.

4.4 UNITS OF SELECTION: ORGANIZATIONS AND THEIR INNOVATIVE PRODUCTS

When we apply the Darwinian framework to the economy, an important question arises in relation to the units of variation and selection: what is selected? Many answers have been provided: individuals (leaders), products, technologies, teams, routines, strategies, firms, clusters of firms, successful regions and countries, institutions and even cultures of whole continents (Hodgson 1993: 46–48; Aldrich 1999: 35–40; Nooteboom 2000: 83–85; Knudsen 2002: 458, 462–463; Acemoglu & Robinson 2012). All these answers are correct to some extent, as evolution takes place on various levels which co-determine each other. Quite remarkably, in evolutionary economic literature, which has a special interest in innovation, innovative products have not often been studied as units of selection. Of course, creativity, entrepreneurship and the act of innovation have frequently been seen as the source of variation (Hodgson 1993: 44–45; 1997: 406–407; Nooteboom 2000: 80; Knudsen 2002: 457), but the products emanating from these have not to the same extent. Hodgson and Knudsen for instance say, 'Goods in a store do not necessarily struggle to survive or pass on knowledge to others through replication or imitation' (2010: 93). In a literal sense this is, of course, true. However, as these authors confirm (2010: 95–97), firms to a large extent compete through product innovation, and thus through this competition between goods in stores. Part of this is that they imitate and replicate as many successful products of their competitors as possible. In this way, knowledge of products is replicated.[11] Eldredge and Wijnberg are a few exceptions in the realm of evolutionary economics who have looked at products as units of selection.

In an excursion into evolution in the marketplace, Eldredge takes this one important step further, suggesting that different designs of the same product also compete with each other *within firms*. He illustrates this by looking at the evolution of the 'Desideratum' cornet in the last decades of the nineteenth century as a consequence of selection processes within the Besson company, where it was invented, and in cross-firm competition with companies which made imitations of it. He concludes, 'If firms compete only in part through the products themselves; if each produces a spectrum of designs that in a sense compete with themselves; if firms have births, histories and deaths, similar to, but generally independent of, the births, histories and deaths of their products, clearly the world of economics, just like the biological world, is hierarchically structured' (Eldredge 1997: 395–396).

Of course, both selection processes—that of innovative products and that of firms—are linked, as Eldredge also observes that sometimes the better quality products of smaller firms do not survive competition from inferior products produced by larger firms (Eldredge 1997: 396–397). This leads to the question as to why some firms have grown bigger than others in the first place. Apparently, they have been good in competing with their products and services—at least for some time.[12] Therefore, much of the business literature has been dealing with the question as to what kind of features set successful, excellent organizations apart from less successful ones. As a rule, these features have been summarized under headings such as a 'creative' or 'innovative' culture, but the question remains as to what then are the important elements of such a culture. Moreover, organizations cannot just be innovative. They also have to provide continuity—in different degrees according to their competitive environment. We don't want, for instance, railway companies or schools to change their schedule and programme every day. Organizations, therefore, always have to deal with the tension between continuity and renewal. Part of such an innovative culture are routines by which organizations—in a similar way as other living organisms—are able to respond adequately and flexibly to all kinds of threats and opportunities. In Chapter 8, I will come back to the theme of successful innovation routines.

Group selection: Competing with culture

For a long time, group selection was unpopular in biology, although this concept was already proposed by Charles Darwin himself. As a consequence of more cooperative or altruistic forms of behaviour, certain species—or groups within species—would increase their chances for survival.[13] In contrast, many biologists were convinced that free-riding individuals would have a higher survival rate than altruistic ones and therefore in the end would dominate their populations. However, for their part populations with only individualistic behaviour could have a lower chance for survival.[14] Therefore, nowadays multilevel selection theory, which evaluates the balance between individual and group selection on a case-by-case base, is more accepted (Hodgson & Knudsen 2010: 153–158). In addition, in human societies there are different degrees to which cultures favour individualism versus cooperation, but all of them exhibit strong social values. Pure egoistic behaviour is mostly disapproved, even when since the rise of capitalism the positive aspects of egoistic behaviour are more appreciated. Throughout history, the urgency of cooperation and conformism for humans was probably larger than it is today. In general, however, humans nowadays cooperate more and fight less for their survival than was the case before. In this respect, our ecosystem and related selection criteria have changed as well.

The fact remains, however, that groups and whole societies still have different success rates related to their environment and the ways they deal with it—that is, their culture (including their technologies). For this reason, groups have always been forced to imitate elements of other, more successful cultures.[15] This was most true for weapon systems, but as a rule, these were related to their social and economic organization and innovativeness. As Hodgson and Knudsen (2010: 217) summarize, 'Organizations promoting the production of necessities, their pillage from elsewhere, and their protection from outside plunderers will have some survival value for the community. The evolutionary fitness of each social formation will relate to some degree to the efficiency and viability of its organizations concerned with production, acquisition, and military capability.' Nowadays, business enterprises may be at the forefront of human competition, but differential success rates between enterprises are also related to their integration in more comprehensive national systems of innovation (Porter 1990; Lundvall 1992; Nelson 1993; Edquist 1997). At the other side of the spectrum, the competitiveness of organizations depends on the integration of smart individuals, but successful organizations have additional properties and capacities not possessed by these individuals (Hodgson & Knudsen 2010: 141). Part of their successful routines are, indeed, the hiring and further development of such smart individuals. All in all, multilevel selection remains relevant.

As any culture, organizational culture is tacit to a large extent and internalized in the form of routines. In evolutionary theory, habits are nowadays attributed to individuals and routines to organizations. Both are developed through repetition of behaviour or thought. They are influenced by prior activity and are the basis of both reflective and nonreflective behaviour (Hodgson & Knudsen 2010: 137–142). 'Habits' and 'routines' are clearly words which express continuity, repetition and thoughtlessness, but at the same time they are not as inflexible as instincts. People may change these habits and routines on the basis of reflection and the evaluation of their own experiences and those of others. Routines may be replicated from one organization to another by spin-offs, by mobility of employees and managers, by mergers and takeovers of units or whole organizations, by imitation and learning or by diffusion through articles, books or consultants. Despite this, such replication is never precise. Moreover, what works in one environment is not necessarily successful in another one.

In management literature, routines are mostly seen as a necessary evil: necessary for organizations to function on a daily basis, but in the end possibly hampering adaptation and innovation and therefore threatening the organization's survival. Acquiring smooth-running routines is a critical factor in the survival of an organization. The survival rate among young companies therefore remains low. The organizations that succeed in surviving into adulthood have acquired not only the necessary routines but also a kind of peculiar character—in line with their strategic profile and to a large extent based on investments that are difficult to undo (e.g., buildings, technology and specialist knowledge). They have conquered an accepted place in their environment and have become reliable partners for other stakeholders, such as financiers, suppliers and customers. To acquire key routines, characteristics, investments and external links is essential to organizations, but all of these also restrict their adaptability. They possibly lead to structural inertia. Moreover, organizations reflect the environment in which they have developed—think of the dual nationality of companies such as Unilever and Shell, with all the double structures that this involved for almost a century. Thus change is difficult, especially when it involves the most characteristic features of an organization. In fact, many organizations do not survive their attempts to adapt, even if the changes are essential, for change itself endangers an organization's coherence (Hannan & Freeman 1977; 1989; Lammers et al. 1997: 421–434; Aldrich 1999: 168; Baum & Amburgey 2002: 304–309).

Organization ecologists such as Hannan and Freeman (1977; 1989), therefore, see the working of the Darwinist evolutionary mechanism foremost through the creation of new organizations and the dying out of old ones. This process gives rise not only to new organizations but also to new *types* (species) of organization (e.g., supermarkets, accountancy firms, Internet shops and business schools).Over time, variation occurs within each type. We can regard the generation of variation as a learning process—strategic or otherwise—but the organization ecology school regards the process, from a more Darwinian perspective, as the development of new ecological niches, which will eventually be populated by new organizations that are fit for the environment in question. In fact, this is how organization ecologists express their lack of optimism about the ability of organizations to adapt and change. Most organizations adapt too slowly, with all the risks this entails for their long-term survival.

However, when an organization succeeds in making a successful transition, it is more likely to repeat such a process in the future. The change process itself may become a sort of routine. In most cases, not everything has to change. Core features exhibit greater inertia than peripheral features. Some inertia can prevent organizations to respond too rapidly or frequently to uncertain developments in their environment (Aldrich 1999: 169–170; Baum & Amburgey 2002: 309–311). In addition, Nelson and Winter recognize that organizational routines may be changed. Following Joseph Schumpeter, they state, 'Innovations in organizational routines similarly consist, in large part, of new combinations or existing routines.' They also mention Schumpeter's observation in his 1950 book, *Capitalism, Socialism and Democracy,* that 'sometime during the twentieth century the modern corporation "routinized innovation"' (Nelson & Winter 1982: 130, 133), but they do not elaborate on that idea. With the examples of industries such as pharmaceuticals and fashion in mind, my colleague Hendrik Snijders and I coined the concept of 'innovation routines' to which I will come back more extensively in Chapter 8. Some firms and, indeed, whole industries innovate in a routine manner.

Evolutionary theory focuses on the fit between an organization (or its products) and its specific ecosystem. Ultimately, it is this ecosystem—the selection system—that determines whether the organization will survive. This survival rests on the organization's key routines at different levels: an organization itself is a selection environment for selecting the best innovative ideas and proposals; for this, it has to be able, to some extent, to foresee selection of its future products in its relevant markets and to realize its plans internally and externally. Moreover, each organization has a kind of—at least implicit—strategic concept or profile which functions as a kind of overall filter for the selection of different proposals. Therefore, here the evolutionary mechanism works at different levels as well:

- The level of proposals (product ideas and ideas for new strategic directions) within the organization
- The level of products that have to survive in the market
- The level of strategies that have to prove their value in the outside world
- The level of departments that want to survive—or even grow—within their organization
- The level of organizations that have to survive in their industry (or industries)

On the basis of this, Hendrik Snijders and I (Jacobs & Snijders 2008) came to the visualization of the important subroutines of an organization's innovation routine, shown in Figure 4.1.

Most important is the organization's learning subroutine. This helps the organization to continuously monitor its basic strategic direction and product range. To a very large extent, the success of innovation depends on trial and error and listening to feedback from customers—in other words, co-evolution and continuous learning. The existing strategic profile, as a rule, is the filter with the help of which new proposals for innovation projects are continuously selected. Finally, the organization has to be able to implement these proposals and present them to their relevant selection system. In the second part of this book, we will see how to navigate these different kinds of selection systems. When successful, innovations may possibly lead to not just their own success but to that of all kinds of descendants.

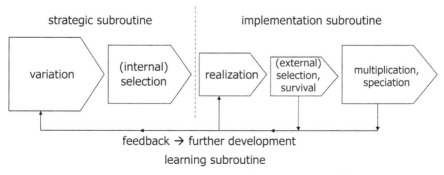

Figure 4.1 Darwinian innovation routines at the organizational level

4.5   EVOLUTION AND LEARNING

Selection in socioeconomic systems differs from selection in biology the most in the fact that learning is possible in the first. In contrast to simple biological variation and selection, which are random and do not allow for hereditary transfer of learned skills, cultural information can 'jump' from one lineage to another (Eldredge 1997: 395). Of course, group processes and the emergence of cultures originally have been the results of the more simple, blind evolutionary processes, which are at the core of the Darwinian approach. Like other social animals, humans were only able to survive by cooperating. Thus, social and cultural development evolved from natural selection itself.[16] However, in socioeconomic systems, at a certain moment more rapid developments became possible through the evolution of the human brain, of language and culture, and as a consequence, imitation, learning and the purposeful transfer of acquired knowledge and competences to newer generations (Hodgson 1993: 47).

Despite this, in human cultural systems there is still a lot of trial and error—random variation and selection, which we do not understand. Because we are not always aware of our preferences, it is often not easy to understand why certain innovations are successful and others aren't. In the next chapter on fitness in an economic environment, I will try to dig deeper into this.

Preferences may also not be personal but systemic. Seemingly inefficient or useless innovations may fit and therefore be successful for different reasons in their history. When the QWERTY keyboard was adopted, its design had its use as it helped to prevent the cluttering of typewriter keys. Now it is an example of lock-in: as so many people use this standard across the world, it is difficult to change it (David 1986)—as we saw in Section 3.4 with the example of Velotype's Veyboard. This example illustrates that fitness, adaptation and learning are always related to a specific environment. When we study the selection of innovations, it is therefore necessary to relate these to their relevant selection systems, each with its specific rules, culture and selectors.[17] As we will see in Chapter 6, sometimes selection is more rationally and hierarchically organized in a top-down way, and sometimes it is more tacit, bottom-up and anonymous.

4.6   CO-EVOLUTION AND STRATEGIC THINKING

An environment is never static. Volcanic eruptions take place, big meteors may collide with the earth, people burn more and more fossil fuels, and as a consequence of such events, the climate is continuously changing. All living species constantly change the environment, and sometimes the environment strikes back. For some time different species in a certain ecosystem may maintain a kind of equilibrium through self-organization and negative feedback, but such equilibria are regularly disturbed by relative overpopulations of one kind, possibly destroying others.

Positive and negative feedback: Self-organization

Positive feedback reinforces certain developments—even negative ones! The rich become richer and the poor become poorer, for example. Negative feedback, on the other hand, halts a development and may therefore result in equilibrium. A thermostat is a good example of the latter. When the temperature in a room is too high, the heating switches off. This process keeps the temperature more or less constant. If the poor become too poor, there is a risk of revolution, particularly if they see the rich becoming richer. When the situation is becoming too dangerous, the rich are usually prepared to make a sacrifice. Negative feedback helps us to understand that there is more order than we sometimes expect. Disorder quickly generates opposing forces that counteract it. A spontaneous reaction of this type is called self-organization.

Many species not only adapt to their environment but also change it; they really *construct* niches: 'To varying degrees, organisms choose their own habitats, mates, and resources and construct important components of their own, and their offspring's local environments, such as nests, holes, burrows, pupal cases, paths, webs, dams, and chemical environments. . . . Niche construction starts to take on a new significance when it is acknowledged that, by changing their world, organisms modify many of the selection pressures to which they and their descendents are exposed' (Laland & Odling-Smee 2000: 123).

Therefore, evolution to a large extent is co-evolution, in which the selection environment itself is changed. This is certainly true for human societies where many kinds of purposeful, strategic behaviour can be observed. As a consequence, innovators partly build on opportunities provided by social and cultural change, on the one hand, and try to stimulate certain developments in their selection environment which fit their purpose, on the other hand. As Hodgson and Knudsen state, 'It is important to emphasize that the selection environment is not necessarily fixed and that it is endogenous to the selection process. Powerful (groups of) entities can sometimes change the selection rules' (2010: 97–98).

However, powerful groups are not the only ones able to change the rules. I am always struck by the competences of all kinds of entrepreneurial people to turn elements in their environment to their advantage. Innovators may take all kinds of features of, and developments within, their environment as a starting point for new initiatives. Innovators do not act alone but co-evolve with all kinds of other developments in their environment. They take part in the continuous dialogues about their offerings. I already dealt with this issue when talking about diffusion as not one but a series of different curves in Section 3.4. Co-evolution and co-development will therefore regularly come back in this book.

Learning and artificial variation and selection

Interactive learning on the basis of experimentation is especially similar to artificial variation and selection or selected breeding in biology. Comparable with horticulturalists or pigeon breeders who combine different individuals with certain traits in order to grow new variants, innovators may learn from market information in order to improve their products. However, the products of artificial variation also have to be tested in their environment. Artificial selection may be somewhat less blind than normal natural selection, but it is still dependent on its basic mechanism (Hodgson & Knudsen 2010: 50–51).

In recent decades, Darwinian evolutionary theory has proved to be a promising paradigm in a variety of scientific disciplines. On the basis of this, bridging the gap between more individually and more culturally focused disciplines appears to be possible, providing a way out of the existing Balkanization in the social sciences (Boyd & Richerson 2000: 159–160). Moreover, in the realm of strategic management, evolutionary theory helps to mitigate managerial hubris and pretentiousness. All of us may try to influence our environment, but ultimately it is the environment that selects. Even the president of the United States is not the master of the universe. In this way, evolutionary thinking stimulates outside-in thinking without necessarily succumbing to fatalistic pessimism. Because we are not the masters of the universe, we have to be as clever as possible and learn to think strategically.[18] The previous chapter has already taught us that the more radical our innovations are, the more daunting this task will be.

We now have all the building blocks assembled to start building. In the second part of this book, the Darwinian framework presented in this chapter is used to understand selection in the realm of innovation at different levels. From understanding fitness in an economic environment, we will move to the mapping of complex selection systems and, on the basis of these, to navigate strategically in co-evolving environments.

Part II
Making Innovation Succeed

5 What Constitutes Fitness in an Economic Environment?

5.1 FITNESS IN INCREASINGLY DIFFERENTIATED ECOSYSTEMS

From a Darwinian perspective, selection is about survival of the fittest, where fitness means fitting into a certain environment, a certain ecosystem.[1] So when we apply this framework to innovation in order to enhance productive creativity, we have to address the question of what 'fitness' means in a socioeconomic environment. The first thing we have to understand is that environments are not undifferentiated plains. Moreover, in all ecological systems, including human ones, we observe a development in the direction of more differentiation (Jacobs 2000: 16–17). All kinds of species find or construct niches into which they fit best. As a result, increasingly there is room for more species, which only compete to some degree for the same resources. As a consequence, fitness never involves the one-size-fits-all criterion.

In spite of this, scientists always search for a simple general criterion. In biology, such a general criterion for success has been defined in terms of the relative increase in the descendants of a lineage. From this follows Dawkins's formulation that selfish genes try to multiply themselves as much as possible. In a similar vein, Stan Metcalfe (2008) has proposed to identify the fitness of economic units with their propensity to accumulate, which he associates with economic efficiency. Metcalfe rightly connects economic efficiency with the ability to innovate, as economic competition is never static. In economics, however, efficiency has been mostly associated with the lowest cost and price. Think, for example, of Oliver Williamson's statement that 'economy is the best strategy': economic units have to adapt rapidly to lower prices and rigorously eliminate all waste (Williamson 1991b: 76, 87). Of course, in most markets price (and therefore also cost) constitutes an important element of fitness, but certainly not the only one. Not every customer is just looking for the lowest price, as this does not necessarily provide the best value for money. Customers may look at other values in the value proposition of a firm. Moreover, as a consequence of Williamson's advice, there is a danger of an undifferentiated race to the bottom.

Michael Porter corrected this traditional economist's view a long time ago, when stating that, besides cost leadership, '[a] second generic strategy is one of differentiating the product or service offering of the firm, creating something that is perceived *industrywide* as being unique. Approaches to differentiating can take many forms: design or brand image. . . , technology. . . , features. . . , customer service. . . , dealer network. . . , or other dimensions. . . . It should be stressed that the differentiation strategy does not allow the firm to ignore costs, but rather they are not the primary strategic target' (Porter 1980: 37).

So, cost may be an important criterion for valuing process innovations—certainly, even when not all firm reorganizations can be reduced to this—but not necessarily for product or transaction innovations. Porter's differentiation strategy leaves more room for strategies aimed at a variety of niches. In every niche, customers value products differently. In this respect, economic literature talks about customer preferences, which for a long time have been seen as fixed and given, or at least exogenous to the economy. These preferences are, however, continuously endogenously reconfigured based on innovative economic activities (Bowles 1998) and social developments.

5.2   ADDED VALUES

From the supply side, added value in economics is the value which is added in each step of a production process. At the firm level, it is the difference between total revenue and the cost of all inputs: raw materials, intermediate products and the cost of finance, outsourced services and labour. As a rule, a firm will invest in these inputs when it expects that it will be able to at least recoup these investments. This requires that from the demand side enough customers recognize the value of the firm's output literally in the sense of selecting—that is, buying—its products.[2] When talking about innovation, we say that the firm has to be able to capture the value of its innovations. Fitness of an innovation in economic terms therefore boils down to a matching of the characteristics of this innovation (supply, a value proposition) with the values of the relevant selectors (demand). This is represented in Figure 5.1.

As we will see in Chapter 6, these selectors are not necessarily end consumers—they may also be intermediate clients, government bureaucrats, juries or editorial boards—but in all cases we talk about values, translated into preferences, in more or less institutionalized environments. In Chapter 6, these selection environments will be mapped more precisely. In this chapter I concentrate on the valuation from the demand side.

As said, values are at the basis of preferences (demand) on the one hand, apparently recognizable in certain offerings (supply) on the other hand. From the demand side, added value of an innovation means relative advantage compared to existing offerings.[3] That value is the best economic translation of fitness from an evolutionary point of view also appears from

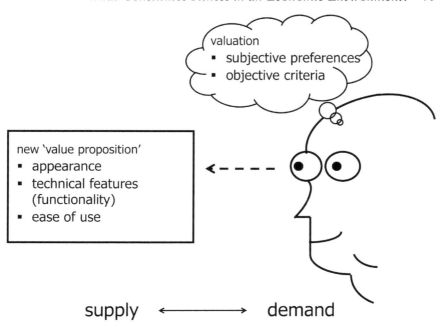

Figure 5.1 Values as a mediator between supply and demand

Wijnberg's definition of innovation quoted in Section 1.1: 'Something new which is presented in such a way that the value will be determined by the selectors.' My shorthand version reduced this to 'something new which is realized, hopefully with an added value.' Apparently, a set of values proposed in an offering is connected with a set of values (preferences) held by the relevant selectors. In most cases, economic selectors are ultimately consumers, but the latter are not the only relevant selectors. Organizations producing and supplying products and services also need to see an added value in this activity. This means that the valuation by different types of (also intermediate) customers has to be high enough to make the activity rewarding[4]—if not profitable—for each of the suppliers in a value system.[5]

Valuation is largely subjective, determined differently by various actors or selectors: '[T]his means that the value of an innovation can only be determined within the context of a set of preferences of selectors' (Wijnberg 2004: 1472). Does this mean that all valuation is strictly personal or individual, as has been assumed *in principle* by most economists since the marginalist revolution at the end of the nineteenth century?[6] Sociologists and institutionalist economists definitely do not agree. Preferences may be subjective, but they are never completely individual. By the beginning of the twentieth century, institutionalists such as Veblen and Commons had already argued that value is socially constructed (Mirowski 1990; Throsby 2001: 21–23). All of us are part of different groups in which we influence each other (e.g., in our buying behaviour) based on our norms, values and expectations. In the realm of fashion, more than one hundred years ago the German sociologist Georg Simmel already observed that the essence of individual dress, for example, lies in individual differentiation within the confinements of group norms and tastes (Simmel 1904).[7]

Each selection system functions within a culture, with its norms and *values,* which can be general or more specific. Moreover, these norms and values are never static but are the subject of numerous discussions which take place at all levels of society. As a consequence, there is a multitude of selection systems, none of which function according to the same fitness criteria. Some of these norms and values may look quite peculiar or even inefficient from another value perspective but can still be decisive in their own environment. Just taking a look in a book on costume history illustrates this quite easily. However, as we will see in the next section, some values may be more attractive than others, so that one may enhance the chances for success of an innovation by adding them.

I already said it before: the one-line summary of this book is that there is no economic added value without cultural added value. In this respect, creativity guru Edward de Bono talks about 'valufacture,' the deliberate process of creating values. As key value drivers, he sees convenience (simplicity of operation), quality of life (health, lifestyle, family, working habits), self-importance (exclusivity) and distraction (de Bono 1992: 131, 134–139). These values, however, are not created by the designers. Designers only make a more or less real link between their product and existing values. For instance, as a rule, Volvo cars are associated with the value of safety. That's why I prefer to talk about adding values. Such adding of values solves what Rob Walker calls the 'pretty good problem: nowadays the functional quality of most products is "pretty good."' So what makes these products to stand out? 'Even companies like Apple and Nike, while celebrated for the tangible attributes [i.e. the functional quality] of their products, work hard to associate themselves with abstract notions of nonconformity or achievement' (Walker 2008: 6–9).

Culture does not simply play a role on the demand side of the economy. In all industries there is a kind of socially constructed industry recipe, a mental model or paradigm of what is valuable, of what the critical success factors are[8] (Porac et al. 1989; Debackere et al. 1994; Jacobs 2010: 134–146). As stated in Section 3.4, innovations at a certain moment lead to a dominant design for what we understand as a certain product category. Later on, of course, radical or paradigmatic innovations may try to change this mental model again.

As a rule there, is a lot of variety within these mental models and recipes. A multitude of car models fit our mental model of a car, leaving room for a huge variety of strategies and preferences. Actors (suppliers and customers) make different choices between competing value propositions, allowing for a multitude of strategies. Consider consumer values in the realm of television: some consumers mainly use their television for entertainment or sports programmes, others for information or culture. Some television channels try to cover all these interests, whereas others target only a few. Some channels will establish a more critical or experimental identity and others a more conservative one. Similar forms of differentiation are found in all industries from yacht building to cheese production. They are the consequence of co-evolutionary strategic profiling and niche finding. Therefore, as a rule, the economic environment consists of a multitude of niches, each with its own fitness criteria. Behind the general concept of economic value, there is a variety of cultural *values* in continuous development. As a result, at the core of economic fitness we can observe the importance of the non-technical aspects of culture, norms and values in their many manifestations. These include different ideologies, the cultures of professions and other peer groups, paradigms, fashions and stylistic movements, all of which lead to more general basic criteria such as price and status, on the one hand, and very particular and sophisticated criteria in the realm of quality, defined in a multitude of subcultures (from wine lovers to kite surfers), on the other.

Finding out what customers really value

In innovation literature, it is always emphasized that market research is not very useful, as consumers do not know their future needs and preferences regarding products they are unaware of. As the saying goes, 'If Henry Ford had asked consumers about their preferences, they probably would have asked for a faster horse.' This may be true for more radical innovations; in addition, the future success of new designs is difficult to predict. Nevertheless, much information can be obtained in the realm of product and service improvements—as emerges from a lot of customer frustrations and complaints. Zyman therefore contends that firms spend too much energy trying to innovate and too little trying to renovate—his term for incremental innovation—taking into account that winning new customers costs six times more than retaining existing ones (Zyman 2004: 5, 17). Therefore, much more can be done with customer complaints and other forms of feedback. In addition, firms may proactively research what customers really value.[9]

Designers at the famous American design firm IDEO, for instance, take a lot of time to observe as closely as possible in real life how users handle current products and services: what they like and hate about them, what confuses them, where possibly latent needs are not addressed. They also take a special interest in rule breakers, people who have their own uses for certain products (Kelley 2001: 6–7, 25–52).

Quite useful is also Bradley Gale's (1994) Market-Perceived Quality Profile tool. Customers in a targeted market (including competitors' customers) are asked to list the factors other than price that they find important in their purchasing decisions related to certain product categories—for example, cars. They are then asked to weigh these factors by distributing one hundred points among them. Finally, well-informed customers have to rate the most important competitors on each of these quality attributes. Multiplying these scores with the weight of each of the attributes gives an overall assessment of the market-perceived quality score of the various competitors (Gale 1994: 24–54, 200–221). These scores can be charted on a customer value map on which one can see which products provide more value for money than others and also where producers have been investing too much on attributes customers don't want to pay money for.

From this comparison, factors on which firms should really improve their performance may emerge, whereas in relation to other factors it may appear that they are already doing too much.

Such approaches provide an invaluable basis for discussions about strategies and investments in the realm of innovation, as they help to improve the value connection between firms and their customers. However, this kind of customer knowledge is only the starting point. The challenge of innovation is always to *surprise* customers with unexpected value propositions. As Zyman (2004: 160) maintains, '80 percent of people who switch brands were actually satisfied with the brand they switched from. The only way to build loyal customers is to deliver experiences that create value *beyond* satisfaction.'

5.3   BASIC INSTINCTS

In modern and postmodern societies especially, values are the subject of continuous discussion and redefinition. Clothes are not only susceptible to fashions, but ideologies as well, as for example emerges from increasingly volatile election results. Ever more after each election incumbents are replaced by their opponents. So is all value ephemeral and socially constructed? Yes and no. Nowadays in literature, the yes answer receives most of the attention, and in this book on the cultural side of innovation, I also contribute to this. But let us not forget the no part: the biological predispositions of consumers and the purely technical performance of products play a role, too. In this section, I deal with the first biological issue and in the next with the latter technological one.

In Section 4.3, I discussed units of selection within a Darwinian framework. In the realm of innovation, organizations and their products were seen as the most important units of selection. We could, however, go a level deeper and look at the attractiveness of ideas. In this respect, Richard Dawkins proposed the concept of memes in analogy with genes. A meme is then a simple idea, the smallest particle of a culture which can be transmitted. Comparable with genes memes would also compete with each other in the struggle for survival. The question then is why one meme—let's say the latest gossip about Lady Gaga—is more easily diffused than the other one—for instance, Darwinism within the social sciences. The examples already illustrate that it is not easy to define a meme. Darwinism is probably too large to be an elementary cultural particle, but how could one split it in smaller particles? Moreover, even a small piece of gossip will probably never be as faithfully replicated as a gene. So it is not surprising that the concept of memes has raised a lot of controversy.[10]

Richerson and Boyd therefore prefer to talk about cultural variants: beliefs, ideas, values, skills or attitudes that are transmitted between people through different kinds of communication and learning. All such cultural transmission is biased, which means that people preferentially adopt some cultural variants rather than others.

Therefore, cultural variants compete with each other, from relatively simple units such as a Nokia cell phone versus an iPhone, to more complex belief systems such as Catholicism versus Southern Baptism, Buddhism or atheism. Moreover, sometimes one doesn't have to choose and can have both the Nokia and the iPhone.[11] In general, the question can be posed as to which cultural variants are most likely to be adopted. A person's family background and education certainly play an important role in this. Richerson and Boyd hypothesize, however, that in traditional societies people learn more from their broader environment than from their parents alone. In addition, Hrdy (2009) contends that more than in other species, humans are educated and socialized by a broader group of people. Moreover, when the environment is changing and more varied, there will be more nonconformist learning than when it is not. Especially when new ideas are practical and easily testable, they will more easily be adopted. The drawback of this is that maladaptive forms of superstition are more easily developed than more elaborate forms of scientific research (Richerson & Boyd 2005: 60–93, 156–169).

Within the Darwinian framework, one usually goes one step further. There is an evolved adaptive basis for many of our preferences. We acquire preferences through genetic inheritance combined with social learning. We need oxygen, water, sleep, warmth, nutrition and affection, but most of these needs are secondarily reinforced through cultural socialization processes. Consider the example of diverse tastes in food occurring in different cultures (Witt 1991: 564–569; Bowles 1998: 79–84). From the biological *basis* of many of our preferences it follows, however, that Darwinism can never be totally relativistic. Socially constructed cultural valuation of innovation to a large extent is related to basic instincts our species has acquired through a long evolutionary process of adaptation through natural selection. Sometimes psychologists refrain from using the term 'instinct' because instincts would only refer to innate behavioural patterns which are modified very little by environmental contingencies or culture, of which there are only a few (Richerson & Boyd 2005: 277). Instead they refer, for example, to evolved (psychological) mechanisms[12] (Buss 2009), basic emotions or action tendencies (Frijda 1986). However, not everybody agrees about the terminological restriction related to instincts. It is important to observe that a lot of our behaviour is the result of unconscious brain processes and that in this realm instincts are more basic than habits and both are more basic than beliefs and reasoning (Hodgson & Knudsen 2010: 79, 134). Instincts are innate behavioural tendencies in response to a certain stimulus in the environment and as such part of human *nature*. Of course, people (and many other animals) regulate to some extent their impulses and emotions. As a consequence, in many cases actual behaviour is a combination of innate and learned components, but even with humans this is only to a small degree a rational process (Frijda 1986: 401–418). There is also a consensus that whereas there are many instincts, we do not know how many precisely. Buss (2009: 94–96), for example, enumerates ten different kinds of fear with their corresponding adaptive problem (e.g., fear of snakes or spiders which could bite us with poisonous substances, fear of heights, separation anxiety or stranger anxiety).

In his *Evolutionary Psychology* textbook, Buss (2009) classifies 'evolved psychological mechanisms' according to four basic human problems or challenges:[13]

- First of all, of course, there are problems of survival (food, health, shelter, combating predators and other environmental dangers); in this category, we find the different kinds of fear just mentioned.
- Second, we find challenges of sex and mating (sexual selection, which includes finding an attractive partner, which for both sexes doesn't mean the same, with the mirror issue of being attractive to the opposite sex).
- Third, we find the challenges of parenting, kinship and protecting one's offspring.
- Finally, we find problems of group living (cooperation and reciprocity, being part of and being accepted and respected by our relevant group or groups, aggression and warfare, status and social dominance).[14] A part of this last group of social instincts is the most peculiar, as it sets humans most apart from other animals, even other primates and other supersocial species.[15] Richerson and Boyd (2005: 196–197) here make a differentiation between ancient social instincts that we share with our primate ancestors and 'tribal instincts . . . that allow us to cooperate with a larger, symbolically marked set of people, or tribe. As a consequence, humans are able to make common cause with a sizeable, culturally defined set of distantly related individuals, a form of social organization that is absent in other primates.'

Love for puppies and the design of cars

'In a seeming contradiction to all that is Darwinian, many birds and mammals are surprisingly susceptible to the charms not only of babies that are no kin to them but even babies belonging to different species altogether' (Hrdy 2009: 209). Many birds and mammals are born quite different from adults in a way that elicits adoration and care. 'Konrad Lorenz identified a suite of traits contributing to the perception of infants as adorable, what he called *kindenschema* (infant schema). These include a relatively large head; large, low-lying eyes; and pudgy cheeks. Together with short, thick extremities and clumsy, gambolling movement, such infantile features render baby animals luscious and irresistibly appealing. . . . Given such propensities, it is perhaps not surprising that so many members of our species become attached to puppies and other pets with babylike attributes' (Hrdy 2009: 221). Our species likes not only babies and puppies but also products or brands which look like them. Think of the Volkswagen Beetle (the 'Love Bug'), the Mini Cooper or the Nissan Micra. Think of logos such as the ones of Innocent Smoothies or Hello Kitty. Thus it is not surprising that Lidwell and others (2003: 28–29) recognize 'Baby-Face Bias' as one of the universal principles which enhance the attractiveness of product or brand designs—of course, related to the kind of message one wants to convey.

In Darwinian literature, other instincts are regularly mentioned, which easily could be subsumed under Buss's headings but which merit separate consideration:

- *Conformism, docility and imitating others' behaviour.* An important social instinct, as it reinforces groups, partly through socialization as is not possible to learn everything by understanding. This instinct is clearly related to Buss's fourth category. It helps to reinforce specific characteristics of certain groups (also their maladaptations) and in this way supports group selection (Simon 1990; Richerson & Boyd 2005: 114–126, 162–169, 205–206; Hodgson & Knudsen 2010: 159–161).
- *Flexibility, curiosity and learning.* An evolved characteristic of higher animals such as humans is their behavioural flexibility. People are also able to modify what they learn and in this way are able to innovate (Hodgson & Knudsen 2010: 160, 186–187). Moreover, humans, and especially children, appear to be universally curious and looking for new and varied experiences and sensations. These actions tendencies can, of course, be related to survival instincts as people have to continuously train their learning capability and their ability to react flexibly to new circumstances. Risk-taking by young males is also associated with sexual selection, as it shows to potential mates how healthy they are and capable of defending their family (Frijda 1986: 345–350: Lenski 2005: 46; Richerson & Boyd 2005: 126–127). However, people also avoid too much stress. This reminds us of the Yerkes-Dodson law (first published in 1908) according to which performance increases with physiological or mental arousal, but only up to a point. When levels of arousal become too high, performance decreases. See the next box, on 'Fitness with an Edge' (Frijda 1986: 112–118).

- *Language and love for art.* In recent years, books have been published on the language instinct (Pinker 1994) and also the art instinct (Dutton 2009; Rothenberg 2011). There is more consensus about the former than about the latter, even when quite a few researchers have been dealing with Darwinian explanations of arts and aesthetic emotions. From time to time a religious instinct is also postulated.

The Darwinian hypothesis is then that ideas, concepts, products or innovations which appeal to more basic instincts have a higher probability of success than others. Gad Saad, who follows Buss's basic classification, enumerates, for example, advertising slogans which appeal to these (Saad 2007: 156–157). A few of these:

- Survival: 'Designed to save lives' (Bridgestone tires), 'Here's health' (Pepsi)
- Reproduction (sexual selection): 'Health is vital. Start with healthy looking skin' (Vichy skincare)
- Offspring care: 'Choosy mothers choose Jif' (Jif peanut butter), 'Look Ma, no cavities' (Crest toothpaste)
- Reciprocity: 'We love to see you smile' (McDonald's), 'I love what you do to me—Toyota,' 'Like a good neighbor, State Farm is there' (State Farm Insurance)

In the previous section, I talked about adding values, and in this respect, I briefly discussed the contributions of Edward de Bono and Morris Holbrook. It is probably not too difficult to relate their different value drivers or value dimensions to basic Darwinian evolved psychological mechanisms. Anyway, the Darwinian hypothesis would be that the closer you stay with basic instincts when adding values to your value proposition, the more you increase the chance for success. I suspect that this has been the source of Rupert Murdoch's success with his tabloids in different countries. Of course, more intellectual audiences do not like the more simple elaboration of these themes, but this can also be related to basic instincts. On the one hand, such intellectuals want to be challenged on a higher level of their intellectual capacities—otherwise they do not really learn. On the other hand, apparently being able to cope with such a higher-level challenge makes oneself feel better than the rest—also a very basic instinct.[16]

Fitness with an edge

Fitness can be a misleading concept. One of the remarkable features of the human mind is that what is perfectly fitting seems not to arouse our attention. There has to be some edge. As Frijda states (1986: 113), 'It is generally assumed that the relationship between emotion and performance follows the so-called Yerkes-Dodson law. According to this "law," the relation between motivation and performance can be represented by an inverted U-curve (see Figure 5.2). Increase in emotional intensity (or in motivation) from some zero point upward is supposed to produce increase in quality of performance, up to an optimal point. Further increase in intensity then leads to performance deterioration and, finally, to disorganization.' As Frijda recognizes, the Yerkes-Dodson law is often referred to, but evidence supporting it has been scarce. In most cases where the supposed law is mentioned, the independent variable (emotion) is translated as 'arousal' or 'strength of motivation.' The attractiveness of this law appears to be in its recognisability in the sense that something which slightly differs from what we know raises our attention more rapidly. In fashion, experts say, for instance, that a new style should have an edge, rendering it looking somewhat odd in the beginning. When a new style is far from what is generally expected and accepted, however, it will be probably be rejected more rapidly, as we saw in Chapter 3 on radicalness of innovations. For different people in different environments optimal arousal levels vary to a large extent. It seems, for example, quite difficult to arouse children who are used to complex video games. The Yerkes-Dodson law also helps us to understand why people in small villages react more stressfully to the arrival of immigrants than inhabitants of large cities who are used to a high level of diversity.

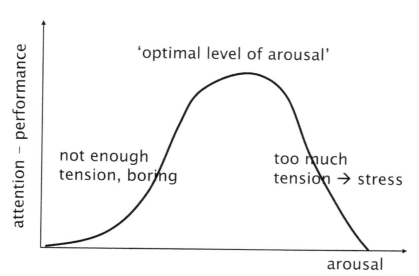

Figure 5.2 Arousal and attention according to the Yerkes-Dodson law

5.4   TECHNICAL AND NONTECHNICAL VALUATION

A second reason why valuation of innovations is never totally a social or cultural construction is to be found in the technical or functional elements of this valuation.

In selection of products, technical criteria play an important role. This is quite obvious for more purely technical products, such as steel or microprocessors. In general, an innovation has to work, to fulfil its promise. Of course, besides technical criteria, nontechnical preferences, in the form of conventions, tastes and fashions, will play a role. Why is a certain material selected for a certain application? Why choose steel for a building and not aluminium, marble or wood? Based on which technical criteria do we evaluate the performance of a car engine: acceleration, maximum speed or fuel efficiency? Changing criteria with which we evaluate technical performance are a nice example of co-evolution. Because of ecological awareness, people nowadays, for instance, tend to look more at fuel efficiency and the emission of carbon dioxide than they did before. However, most customers do not select a car only based on technical features. The more technical performance of different products has become similar, the more they have to be differentiated with their nontechnical aspects. I will come back to this in Section 5.6 on industrial design. However, technical and functional aspects will always play a role, at least in a minimal way, as I just said. The innovation has to work; it has to fulfil its promise.

Thus, we have come back to the basic distinction between the technical and nontechnical aspects of innovations discussed in Chapter 2. Once we have decided which technical criteria are most important, technical assessment can take place relatively objectively:

> The aspects that are technically necessary are those aspects of a product which selectors can specify in advance and which could, in principle be checked by other actors, or even robots. If such other actors exist, they have a purely technical role and not an economic one; they have no personal sets of preferences. The role of the other actors still leaves selectors with the task of determining or attributing value in an economic sense. The other actors could check the speed of microprocessors, but the selectors would have to specify beforehand (a) that speed makes a microprocessor valuable and (b) which type of measurement of speed are acceptable to them. (Wijnberg 2004: 1477)

The evaluation of the nontechnical aspects, to the contrary, is difficult to objectify. Why does one person prefer a certain car or piece of furniture to another? Even people who agree on their selection criteria in many cases come to different decisions. This is not only a question of changing fashions and tastes but also of the difficulty making explicit one's preferences. Think, for example, about a computer programme with which one could try to model as precisely as possible the preferences of a person on the basis of her detailed explanations about which paintings she likes or not. Do you think this programme would be able to predict this person's preference when it assesses a new series of paintings? A few times I have listened to teachers coaching students in fashion and art schools and I always had the feeling that these teachers could as well have told the opposite. Cultural valuation, even when it is on the basis of agreed criteria, remains subjective and in this sense arbitrary. This renders the cultural side of innovation much more difficult to assess beforehand than the technical side.

In literature on the diffusion of innovation, this basic dichotomy between the technical and nontechnical aspects of an innovation can be recognized as the two most important features, which determine its speed of adoption. In this regard, in his famous book *Diffusion of Innovation,* Everett Rogers (2003: 229–257) discusses five factors. Three of these are relatively straightforward and only briefly mentioned (Rogers 2003: 257–259, 266):

- *complexity,* the degree to which an innovation is perceived as difficult to understand, hampers diffusion;
- *triability,* the degree to which an innovation can be experimented with, enhances diffusion;
- *observability,* the degree to which the results of an innovation are visible, stimulates its diffusion.

To an important degree, these factors are related to the two factors which Rogers views as the most important: the relative advantage of an innovation on the one hand and its compatibility on the other. Let us look at both these factors in more detail.

Relative advantage, or 'the degree to which an innovation is perceived as being better than the idea it supersedes' (Rogers 2003: 229), most resembles the technical aspects of innovation. However, as can be seen from Rogers's definition, relative advantage to a large extent is a *perception.* Even with technical innovations, perceptions may be more important than precise measurements. Moreover, relative advantage also relates to status aspects. In particular, the adoption of highly visible innovations, such as new cars, clothing, hairstyles and advanced technical gadgets, may be status conferring. Rogers gives the example of a certain type of expensive Harvestore silo, which was very popular with American farmers because of this status aspect (Rogers 2003: 231).

Compatibility, Rogers's second decisive feature of an innovation, is mainly understood as compatibility with existing cultural ideas and values, as well as recognized needs, but of course this may have a technical component as well: compatibility with existing technical standards (Rogers 2003: 240–253). Many radical innovations fail by being incompatible with existing demand or values and also by not complying with existing technical and nontechnical systems of testing, implementation, production, commerce or distribution. Such lack of fit has been called the 'Leonardo effect,' referring to Leonardo da Vinci, who conceived many ideas that could not be realized or even tested with the existing technologies of his time (Nooteboom 2000: 11, 182, 194).

Table 5.1   Technical and cultural aspects of Rogers's factors stimulating innovation

factors stimulating diffusion	technical aspect	cultural aspect
relative advantage	**measurable technical advantage**	status effect of acquiring an innovation
compatibility	compatibility with existing technical standards	**compatibility with existing concepts, norms and values**

So, if we look again that Rogers's two main factors explaining diffusion of innovations, relative advantage has mainly a technical connotation, but with a cultural aspect, whereas compatibility is mainly cultural, but with a possible technical aspect. This is summarized in Table 5.1.

Holbrook's framework

Morris Holbrook (1999: 9–24) provides a three-dimensional framework which can possibly help map consumer values—that is, what are the motivations to consume a certain product:

- *Extrinsic versus intrinsic value.* Extrinsic value pertains to a means-end relationship wherein the consumption of certain goods or services mainly has a functional, utilitarian instrumentality related to certain objectives. In contrast, intrinsic value suggests that the consumption experience is appreciated as an end in itself (e.g., listening to music simply for pleasure).
- *Self-oriented versus other-oriented value.* I may like certain clothes because they feel good or warm, or simply because I like them, but also because I want to impress others in a certain way.
- *Active versus reactive value.* Active values require action, such as driving a car or trying to solve a sudoku. With reactive value, it is rather the product or service acting on us, such as getting a haircut or watching TV.

These three dimensions can be combined, leading to a matrix with eight possible cells.

Holbrook treats these dimensions, however, too much like dichotomies instead of providing possibilities of combining the opposites or providing room for positions in between. In Table 5.2, I have listed a few motivations to consume with Holbrook's interpretation, confronted with my own for his last column. In addition, for other categories not integrated in this list, I would give more hybrid valuations. For instance, what about health: we enjoy being healthy (reactive), but we possibly have to undertake certain activities (including consuming) to maintain this condition. In a final column, I have added the distinction between technical and cultural valuation. From this it emerges that five out of the six motivations are basically cultural—albeit most of these also have a biological base (as we saw in Section 5.3).

Table 5.2 Holbrook's dimensions of consumer values and some of my interpretations of these

Motivation		Holbrook			DJ	
Efficiency[1] (of a tool)	extrinsic	active	self-oriented	self-oriented	technical
Status[2]	extrinsic	active	other-oriented	other-oriented	cultural
Play	intrinsic	active	self-oriented	self- and other-oriented	cultural
Aesthtetics	intrinsic	reactive	self-oriented	self-oriented	cultural
Ethics	intrinsic	active	other-oriented	other- and self-oriented	cultural
Spirituality	intrinsic	reactive	other-oriented	other- and self-oriented	cultural

[1] Holbrook also has a category 'excellence,' in which a characteristic of a certain tool is not used (e.g., the speed limits of a Ferrari) and therefore is placed in the reactive category. I do not see the usefulness of this extra cell.

[2] Holbrook also has a category 'esteem,' in which consumption is apparently reactively sought through forms of conspicuous consumption. Holbrook concedes that the distinction between status and esteem is difficult to articulate. I am, indeed, not able to distinguish such esteem from more active status seeking which Holbrook associates with impression management and dressing for success.

5.5 SUBJECTIVE VALUATION VERSUS INTRINSIC, OBJECTIVE VALUE

In economic theory, it has been accepted for a long time that price formation is never objective because in the end it comes down to what the fool is prepared to pay for an item—the value this item apparently has for this fool. Despite this, the farmers who selected the Harvestore silos for status reasons, mentioned in the previous section, probably did not want to pay too much for them. So even when the subjective theory of value has been accepted for a long time, we are still confronted with the opposite issue of intrinsic value. So what is the real price or real value of what we want to buy, so to speak? It is striking that even in the literature on jewellery or haute couture, the price of such luxury items is usually legitimized on the basis of the cost of higher quality materials and the labour costs of very expensive specialists involved in design and production. Apparently even experts—and customers—try to avoid a purely subjective valuation. Apart from the people for whom money really does not matter, most customers attempt to obtain some clue or expert opinion on what the intrinsic value of a product is, independently of their own subjective valuation or the rhetoric of the seller, in order not to pay too much.

This intrinsic or natural value of products has been haunting econo-mists for a long time, even after the marginalist revolution. Ultimately, this intrinsic value is based on the cost of production, including all pos-sible overheads, and a reasonable profit margin. Most economists still view this intrinsic value as the equilibrium price over time, even when there are possible fluctuations related to temporary supply and demand conditions (Throsby 2001: 20–21). The more transparent a market, the easier it will be to know about this real value of products. However, the more informa-tion asymmetry between seller and buyer, the more need for independent expert valuation (e.g., reports of consumer organizations). I will come back to this important role of experts in the next chapter on mapping selection systems. However, let us now look at their role in the valuation of cultural products.

The Valuation of Cultural Products as an Example

Even in the realm of cultural products, the discussion of intrinsic value has never ceased. Think, for example, about Andy Warhol's replicated Brillo boxes. I suppose many people will have experienced this in exhibitions: peo-ple loudly questioning whether this or that item is really art, worthy of being displayed in a museum, and—more importantly in this respect—wondering about their price. At some moment, established experts and informed buy-ers apparently concluded that it was worth the money. Such an example cer-tainly helps us understand that value is a social construction. In this respect, Bourdieu speaks about the production of belief, in which certain cultural products are being 'consecrated' by recognized authorities. 'The question can be asked in its most concrete form . . : who is the true producer of the value of the work—the painter or the dealer, the writer or the publisher, the playwright or the theatre manager?' (Bourdieu 1993: 76).[17]

However, is this valuation *only* a social construction, or is there a deeper, intrinsic value? Many cultural experts are not relativists and therefore try to define intrinsic universal cultural values—even if they generally concede that these universal values change over time. David Throsby has tried to define some of possible more universal criteria for valuing art, even when he recognizes the pitfalls related to this (Throsby 2001: 27–29, 84–85):

- Aesthetic value: beauty, harmony[18] and form
- Spiritual value: apart from its significance for certain groups, that which makes us think about important issues, providing understanding, en-lightenment and insight[19]
- Social value: connection with others and contributing to the compre-hension of society
- Historical value: inheritance and relation with the past
- Symbolic value: conveying meaning
- Authenticity value: being unique and original

Throsby's exercise is interesting because it illuminates the difficulty of defining general valuation criteria for cultural products. It appears to be very difficult to define any of these dimensions in an acultural or ahistorical way. At the same time, many will probably agree that there is much to be said for Throsby's proposal. We may value artefacts from other cultures and periods, even when it is impossible to look at these in an acultural way. Throsby's exercise is also interesting because it provides us with some perspective to understand the cultural value of any product, its compatibility with values and beliefs (Rogers 2003: 243–246). A design may appeal to us because of its aesthetic value (its connection to what in our culture is understood as beautiful or harmonious) or its symbolic value (its connection with our semiotic understanding). When one works within the framework of a certain culture, the integration of these values may happen quite automatically and implicitly. However, the more we cross the boundaries between cultures with our products, the more pressing it will be to think about these aspects beforehand (Jacobs 2004). To give an example from the opposite site, before the German Nazi Party started using the swastika symbol, it was widely used as a symbol of good luck, as one can see from old American postcards. On the Internet one can find a lot of such pictures, even of an old Coca-Cola badge in the form of a swastika. And, of course, people travelling to India will meet this symbol quite often.

In relation to many products, we simply follow our intuition in our valuation and buying behaviour. We buy a certain item because we like it (maybe despite that price!). The status aspects of selection help to clarify that selection is often made based on criteria that selectors do not always like to recognize. To a large extent, mental models, cultural values, paradigms and industry recipes are tacit, socially constructed cultural phenomena which simply emerge from generations of discussions by all kinds of actors. Moreover, some of these constructions may appeal more to us because they are connected with deep-rooted evolved psychological mechanisms related to our survival and that of our offspring, our mate choice and our integration and status within specific groups—as we saw in the Sections 4.2 and 5.3.

However, especially with more radical or paradigmatic innovations which challenge our existing set of preferences (as discussed in Chapter 3), more extensive explanations and related rhetoric will probably be necessary. The introduction of such radical innovations (including totally new art styles) therefore as a rule require the emergence of new experts who are able to defend and explain their value. The more radical the innovation, the further it will be from our existing norms and values and the more difficult its adoption.[20] As Bourdieu has shown, this leads to incessant, innumerable strategic struggles to establish the value of these innovations (Bourdieu 1993). In such cases, we can observe the actual strategic construction or at least negotiation of new meanings. As a consequence of this, cultural valuation is never static.

To conclude, this chapter established a broad framework to clarify how values and thus culture provide the basis for the assessment of fitness in an economic environment. In Chapter 6, this Darwinian framework for understanding innovation is further developed with a clarification of how different economic selection systems work and interact with each other. Before that, however, in the following section I illustrate the technical and nontechnical aspects of fitness in an economic environment on the basis of the case of industrial design.

5.6   THE ADDED VALUES OF INDUSTRIAL DESIGN*

In order to clarify and qualify the framework presented in this chapter, especially Section 5.4, I delve a little deeper into the diverse aspects of the added value of industrial design. From this, the close connection between different technical and nontechnical aspects of added value will clearly emerge.

On one of the first pages of his book on design, the famous British designer Terence Conran asks the question with which this section is concerned: 'How can design add value?' (1996: 18). His immediate answer is that 'if something is well designed it can improve the quality of life of the user,' directly followed by the comment that

> something which is well designed should not necessarily cost more than the equivalent object which has been designed without care, thought or professionalism. To this end the designer must fully understand manufacturing, marketing and selling processes, and ensure that the product he or she designs can be economically and efficiently made, and competitively priced. . . . It is not about pushing up price or creating elite brands through the mystique of the label. . . . The identification of design with elite goods and snob value has helped to bring about its poor profile today, a misrepresentation of its true purpose to producers and consumers alike. . . . The remedy, I believe, is not to hive off design into ever-more esoteric areas, but to integrate it more fully in the entire process of product development, manufacturing and retail. (Conran 1996: 18)

Conran's claims are, of course, rather normative and partisan. More than a few designers actually do try to create an aura of exclusivity and mystique around their designs in order to be able to extract a higher price. Some consumers apparently see an added value in such an aura and are prepared to pay for it. This does not deny the fact that Conran's main point

*Parts of this section have been published in the report of a study I conducted in 2004, together with Gerda Gemser and Ritzo ten Cate, on the added value of design in the Dutch software industry, for Premsela, the Netherlands Institute for Design and Fashion (Gemser et al. 2004 & 2006).

is clear and straightforward: well-designed products can improve the quality of life of the user, and in order to succeed in this ambition, as a rule it is desirable for the designer to be integrated into the entire process of product development, including manufacturing and retail. It is also striking that Conran moves directly from a general statement about the possible added value of industrial design for the consumers to a more extensive exposition about the back-office requirements to realize this.

However, now that Conran has drawn our attention to the supply side, let us follow this logic and start our investigation of the added value of design by looking at it from the producer's perspective. In order to create an economic activity, added value must be perceived not only by the buyer but also the supplier. From the latter's perspective, what might the added value of well-designed products be? From the perspective of the innovating firm, adding value through design may manifest itself in performance measures such as:

- increased profitability or turnover as a consequence of more sales, possibly at a higher price;
- lower production costs as a consequence of well-designed (maybe standardized) components;
- less complaints and reduced support and service costs on the customer side as a consequence of better and more functional products;
- a higher degree of customer satisfaction and more loyal customers;
- design for disassembly and design for recycling, a better ecological performance and related improved image;
- clearer differentiation of the brand and its products from competitors;
- a more attractive image of the firm or brand which generates goodwill and, for instance, allows it to recruit better qualified people.

In Section 1.6, we saw that from the few studies available it appears that at least many of these possible promises are fulfilled. Investment in design innovation leads to better company performance. From Section 2.1 it emerged, however, that an overemphasis on the technical aspects of design may have a negative effect on the cultural side and as a consequence on selection. Therefore, both sides have to be taken care of, especially in sectors such as the entertainment, hospitality and cultural industries, where the experiential side of innovation is of primary importance. Attention paid to experiential design is always positive, especially when consumers are not too much involved—as appears from a Dutch study (Candi et al. 2010: 18–21).

Let us now turn our attention back to the customer side, as firms will not reap the fruits of investing in design unless they also realize the added value on the demand side. In the literature on design, Conran's added value of improving the quality of life is usually reduced to the following three main value dimensions: functionality, usability and aesthetics. The challenge of what I call productive creativity is to make sure that these dimensions are addressed. Let us briefly look at each of these separately and in relation to each other.

'Functionality' refers to the functions or tasks a product has to perform. This is clearly the most technical aspect of a design. So it is no surprise that in existing literature one usually looks to engineers to design the aspects of a product that relate to technical and functional performance. In contrast, the contribution normally ascribed to the designer entails designing the aspects that relate to the user—that is, the aesthetic and ergonomic product features (e.g., Harkins 1994; Muller 1990; Potter et al. 1991; Ulrich & Eppinger 1995). Pruys (1972: 24) puts it another way, stating that the engineer is mainly concerned with the relations which are internal to the product and the designer with the relations between the product and its user.

'Usability' can be defined as a measure of a product's potential to accomplish the goals of the user in an efficient, healthy, easy and pleasant way. Usability thus includes not only efficiency in use (functionality and consistency), but also ergonomic (healthy, easy) elements, and to some extent the aesthetic (pleasant) elements. The latter are related to the so-called aesthetic-usability effect, according to which aesthetic designs are perceived as easier to use than less aesthetic designs. As noted by Lidwell and others (2003: 18), 'Aesthetic designs look easier to use and have a higher probability of being used, whether or not they actually are easier to use.' The relationship between usability and functionality on the one hand, and aesthetics on the other, is especially clear when we look at design consistency: 'The usability of a system is improved when similar parts are expressed in similar ways' (Lidwell et al. 2003: 46). These authors distinguish four kinds of consistency in design:

- Functional consistency: consistency of meaning and action (e.g., traffic lights) and the consistent use of well-known symbols which enhance usability and learning;
- Internal consistency: consistency with other elements in the system which enhances trust in the system and its designers;
- External consistency: consistency with other elements in the environment (e.g., standards also adopted by designers of other products and systems);
- Aesthetic consistency: consistency of style and appearance which enhances recognition, communicates membership and sets emotional expectations.

Usability also has to deal with the paradox of simplicity: adding more features may increase the usability of a product related to some aspects but decrease its overall usability.

Usability seems most difficult to classify according to the technical-nontechnical dichotomy presented in Chapter 2. Usability is partly about function and thus has a technical dimension.[21] Whereas consistency can be checked relatively objectively with the help of a kind of design manual, usability appears to be highly subjective. We just saw that as a consequence of the aesthetic-usability effect we tend to overestimate the practical usability of something we like. Ultimately, this dimension is, however, more technical than nontechnical. It is, for example, possible to measure the productivity obtained quite objectively using different tools and to base selection on the outcome.

Finally, 'aesthetics' concerns the visual and sensory beauty and appeal of a design. This may be determined by, for example, the proportion, contours, colours, shape, sound, material, and texture of the product. This appearance ideally increases the acceptance of the product by the targeted customer group. According to Conran (1996: 14),

> [D]esign is 98 per cent common sense. What makes design so interesting and challenging is the other two per cent: what one might call 'aesthetics.' . . . Many products which achieve 98 per cent are demonstrably good: but those with the extra two per cent have a magic ingredient which places them in another category altogether. That two per cent makes the difference between something which is perfectly acceptable and something which is so special that everyone wants to possess it. When the magic ingredient is present, the quality of life is improved. . . . If something is aesthetically pleasing—if it strikes a chord, creates excitement or a surge of desire—people are often willing to overlook or overcome less-than-perfect performance in other areas.

In a similar vein, Lidwell and others (2003: 18) note that '[a]esthetic designs are more effective at fostering positive attitudes than unaesthetic designs, and make people more tolerant of design problems.' This aesthetic aspect of design brings us most closely to their cultural side, as aesthetic taste is closely related to cultural values.[22]

The physical appearance of a product is important because visual images are remembered and recognized more directly than words and texts (Wheeler 2003: 7; Kazmierczak 2003: 52). However, certain appearances can convey different meanings to different people. Some form and colour combinations have, for example, an exotic connotation, whereas others may give a design a modern or a more classic appearance. This can be summarized under the heading of 'design as sensemaking,' the object of visual semiotics, which tries to decode the sometimes hidden, possibly unintended, codes which connect signs and meanings (van Leeuwen & Jewitt 2001).

Thus, the appearance of products is not just a matter of aesthetics; it is also about the value the chosen aesthetics convey, intended or not. The colour green, for example, has connotations with nature, environmental awareness, permission to cross and Islam. The design of brand logos also has to take such connotations into consideration. Especially when products are exported or adapted to other regions of the world, it may be important to look at one's designs from a semiotic point of view, as more often than not a certain design may have a totally different, even undesirable meaning in another culture. As a consequence, designers increasingly try to deal explicitly with this value connection of design: the fact that some designs appeal to some values more than to others.

Thus, designers may try to imbue their designs with a certain meaning. However, what is most important is the meaning which the customers, the receivers, attach to a design. It has been suggested by Kazmierczak (2003) that a designer is successful when able to make the intended meaning cross to the receiver. However, it may be just as interesting to learn from un-intended meanings, which might provide unforeseen opportunities. As a consequence, Press and Cooper (2003: 32) state that the 'essential task for designers is to understand how people make sense and meaning of the things they design, and how they create new experiences with them.'

Aesthetics is clearly the most subjective, nontechnical dimension of the three dimensions discussed. With the help of knowledge in the field of the visual arts and semiotics, much can be understood or at least rationalized in this realm. However, this knowledge will not help in the slightest in defining what it takes to make the crucial 2% difference Terence Conran is talking about—sometimes also called the 'X-factor.' In a similar vein, fashion critics talk about the signature of certain designers, but nobody can clearly state what a designer should do to develop or find a signature. Thus, again we come to the role of experts and critics. It is said that there is no accounting for taste, but this does not alter the fact that many people want guidance in this respect. To some extent, this may be related to the search for the in-trinsic value of certain products, which was briefly discussed in the previous section. However, an important reason for this also lies in the social aspect of the added value of design. To many, buying design products is an invest-ment in what Pierre Bourdieu (1979) called 'cultural capital,' an investment which has to lead to higher returns in terms of status and reputation. Such an investment necessarily also has to be intellectual, as the buyer must be able to talk intelligently about it in order to realize these returns.

Design Inside-Out and Outside-In

Let us now return to Conran's remarks about the desirable integration of the design function within the entire process of product development, in-cluding manufacturing and retail. In this respect, in most industries we can observe a movement of design, first from the inside out and later on from the outside back in.

The first movement inside out means that in many cases the initial de-sign of a new product, at that time probably a more radical innovation, does not receive much attention. For example, the first microcomputers were not very user-friendly and looked awful. However, as Ulrich and Ep-pinger (1995) argue, whenever the underlying technology of a product has levelled out, this provides room for, or rather necessitates, investments in design for the creation of differentiation—as we saw in Section 3.4 about the diversity of innovation from a lifetime perspective. Gemser and Leenders

(2001) provided empirical evidence for this based on the Dutch instruments industry. From the moment product technology began to level out, the use of professional design expertise to develop pleasing product appearances and increase product user-friendliness became a successful strategy to create differentiation within this industry. We can call this the movement from the inside out. Firstly, the engineers try to fix and debug the inside of the product, related to its functionality. The more developed an industry and its products, the more it is necessary to pay attention to the design of the outside aspects: the interface with the user and aesthetics.

The second movement is then in the direction of integrated design—defended by Conran—which brings design so to speak from the outside back in. In order to improve both usability and functionality, designers try to simplify the product and its components. They have to move their attention from the outside in. In relation to this development sometimes a model is presented with the following stages (von Stamm 2003: 15):

- *Design as styling.* The basic features of the product are designed independently from its wrap. The aesthetics of the product is the last stage of the design process.
- *Design as making better products.* There is some integration in the process between engineering, industrial design and marketing research.
- *Design as interface between the company and its audiences.* Now real communication between the firm and its audiences becomes more important.[23]
- *Design integrating the whole process.* A multifunctional team works on the design process from the start and is seen as central to corporate success.

All of this, however, does not deny the fact that many creative designers are still quite happy with a purely external role, concentrating on the external styling of products. If this is the only competence they really master, it is probably the best they can do. As we saw in Section 1.6, for relatively simple products such as clothes, shoes or traditional furniture, this can, however, be more easily done than for cars or other modern durable consumer goods such as television sets or even shavers, as in the latter cases there will be a more direct link between aesthetic design and design for manufacturing.

In the previous chapter, a general Darwinian framework was presented for studying all kinds of evolution. In this chapter, I addressed the question what constitutes fitness in an economic environment. Part of the answer was found in Darwinian psychology as consumer preferences might be rooted in evolved psychological mechanisms. Now we can take an important step further, increasing the level of complexity a few degrees. In the next chapter, our Darwinian framework for understanding innovation in order to improve productive creativity is further developed with a clarification of how various economic selection systems work and interact.

6   Mapping Selection Systems

In Chapter 4, we saw that economic actors mainly compete with each other with their products and their routines. When we deal with innovation, important questions are how we can increase the chances for success—adoption or, in Darwinian terms, selection—of innovations and what the most successful innovation routines are. In this and the following chapter, I deal with the first question. In Chapter 8, the latter question will be addressed.

6.1   INTERNAL AND EXTERNAL SELECTION

Economic selection deals with the distribution of resources in the framework of scarcity. In this regard, a distinction can be made between internal and external selection: selection internal or external to organizations (Aldrich 1999: 22). Of course, these two forms are related in various ways.

Let us start with internal selection. 'Where there is a competitive process, there is a selection system. The selection system inside the organization determines the outcome of the internal process of distribution' (Wijnberg 2004: 1479). It is obvious that an organization cannot pursue all possible innovative ideas, so first an internal selection has to take place—as we also saw with the help of Figure 4.1 in Section 4.3. This internal selection may already be the subject of a strategic fight, as not all proposals can be selected.[1] Of course, one can argue that the criteria for internal selection to a large extent will be the same as the criteria which determine success in the outside world. As such, we might follow Knudsen when he states that 'the selection pressure is exerted by market forces and mediated by managers' (Knudsen 2002: 461) or '[t]he firm's criteria for performance are established by the expectation of the market' (2002: 466). However, Knudsen also concedes that '[t]he possibility remains however that the manager may apply idiosyncratic or biased criteria' (2002: 466). Indeed, there may be all kinds of social or political processes within organizations or definitions of what is appropriate in a certain situation as a consequence of norms and values within certain professions or industries (e.g., the 'industry recipes' referred to in Sections 5.2 and 5.5). 'Fitness necessarily refers to the proliferation of practices and strategies associated with professional identities developed within particular teams and firms' (Knudsen 2002: 467). In Chapter 8, I come back to this in the framework of more or less successful innovation routines.

Regarding external selection of innovation, Wijnberg (2004: 1471–1472) distinguishes between three possible selection systems, each with a different type of selector:

> The first type is the traditional type, market selection, where consumers are the selectors and producers[2] the selected. The second type is peer selection, where the opinion of other producers, the peers, determine the outcome of the competitive process. The third type is expert selection, where competitive success or failure is determined by the opinions of a category of people who are neither consumers nor producers but to whom particular knowledge or expertise is ascribed.
>
> In every industry a particular selection system can be identified in each context where there is a competitive process. The academic world provides an example of peer selection;[3] ethical drugs provide an example of expert selection. The opinions of physicians, who do not produce and usually do not consume the drugs they prescribe, determine the competitive success of producers of pharmaceuticals. An actual selection system can also be a particular mix of these ideal types.

As emerges from this chapter, I found Wijnberg's approach quite stimulating and I certainly have been inspired by it. In the end, however, I did not agree with his classification. Therefore, what follows is my different approach.

6.2 HIERARCHICAL SELECTION: INTERNAL AND EXTERNAL

In general, as can also be seen from Figure 4.1, the internal selection of an innovative proposal, the internal assessment of its value, is a preliminary stage before its implementation and possible external valuation. As I just said, the assessment of the possible external success of an innovation in many cases is only one of the internal selection criteria. Managers may have their hobbyhorses, certain prejudices for or against certain ideas, or they may have conflicts with people who advocate certain ideas. Thus internal selection is possibly a first sphere in which strategizing to get one's ideas realized has to take place.

Looking more closely at various innovation cases, we can observe that a first form of preliminary hierarchical selection of innovative proposals often also takes place outside the firm. Many products are only developed with the help of public subsidies, or at least are subject to forms of public regulation and approval: airplanes, building projects, infrastructural works, cultural projects (including subsidized movies), weapons systems, educational programmes and biotechnological experiments. Medicines have to be officially approved before they can enter the market. Some products (e.g., public roads or space rockets) are totally dependent on hierarchical selection. Historically there have been societies (ranging from traditional ones to communist experiments) in which a large part of economic selection took place through hierarchies.

Democratizing hierarchical selection of innovation: Constructive technology assessment

Hierarchical selection of innovations in most cases is not the subject of democratic procedures. Sometimes people who are normally outside these selection processes have tried to influence such selection by forms of social action, for instance, by trying to prevent public investment in nuclear energy or experiments with nanotechnology or genetic plant modification. Related to this, proposals have been made to institutionalize technology assessment (TA). The aim of TA is to assess the possible dangers and ethical issues related to new technologies as much as possible beforehand. Different authors in the TA field have defended that TA should not be reactive or defensive, but proactive, constructive or even participative, defining the conditions for experiments with certain possibly harmful new technologies (Smits & Leyten 1991; Schot & Rip 1997). As a consequence of these endeavours, in different European countries, institutes for TA have been established, mostly related to their parliaments.[4] This does not alter the fact that only seldom do public discussions about new technologies—which sometimes rage vehemently on the Internet—really affect selection. An exception was the temporary ban of genetically modified food in the European Union as a consequence of societal concern (Benkler 2006: 333–335).

Internal selection is mostly hierarchical and therefore can be seen as one of the basic forms of hierarchical selection, the other one being external hierarchical selection. Moreover, Wijnberg's peer selection seems to be a special case of this latter form: the editors of a scientific journal or the members of an award jury may be peers of the selected author, but when selecting they act as hierarchical superiors (as a rule within the framework of a set of preestablished selection criteria).

How about Wijnberg's expert selection—is this also a form of hierarchical selection? As an expert, the physician can be seen as the superior of the patient; he or she selects the medication which the patient has to buy but does not pay for it. In a similar way, a teacher may select the course books for his or her students. Medicines and course books are, however, brought on the market, and their success is not guaranteed by hierarchical selection. Therefore, this looks like a combination of hierarchical and market selection, which I call hybrid selection.

Wijnberg also gives other examples of expert selection which are even less clear cut. 'In the case of an haute couture dress the selectors will also include primarily experts, such as the editors of women's magazines. The difference these selectors are able to perceive will determine the value the dress has for the customers and consumers, who will do their best to perceive the same differences to enjoy some of this aspect of the value of a dress' (Wijnberg 2004: 1477). This may be even more interesting, although we might still argue about the detail of this example.[5] The experts here co-determine the value, but again they are not the buyers. However, in contrast to the cases of medicine and textbooks, they do not even *determine* actual purchasing. These experts possibly draw the attention of customers to certain innovations. In this sense, they may sometimes be important *preselectors*—without them, we would perhaps never take notice of an innovation. They may give expert advice on the possible value of innovations in this realm. However, quite importantly, they do not buy them, nor do they have a decisive influence on ultimate market selection. As a consequence, consumers may or may not be convinced.

There is also a third possibility: consumers are convinced of the value of certain innovations without buying them. People may appreciate in principle the value of an innovation but not actually spend money on it. They may even be frustrated that they are not able to buy the product. However, economic selection is always about the allocation of scarce resources. From an economic perspective, only actual buying plays a role. So we are confronted with a subjective valuation, which possibly remains just that: positive valuation without economic selection. In other words, paying attention[6] to an innovation and possibly appreciating its value is a necessary but not a sufficient condition for selection in economic terms. This does not mean that these nonbuyers are unimportant—quite to the contrary. Buyers will always be a subgroup of potential buyers, the larger group of people who know about your product and have become interested in it. Initiatives can possibly be undertaken to turn more of these nonbuyers into buyers. In the end, without sufficient buyers, however, there is no viable business model.

In the cultural realm, this kind of purely subjective positive valuation is quite normal. Many cultural objects such as monuments or famous works of art are valued, although apparently few consumers would be able or prepared to pay for them,[7] whereas less culturally valued[8] tear-jerkers find more than enough buyers. As economic decision-making is about the allocation of scarce resources, it is obvious that cultural and economic valuation are not always reconciled, at least not in the market[9] (Throsby 2001: 33–34, 159–160). As a consequence of this cultural market failure, public authorities at different levels play a role in funding the arts, convinced as they ideally are that there is an added value of this at the societal level.[10] However, at this level many possible options must also be assessed as there are never enough resources to pay for all. As stated previously, this is a typical form of external hierarchical selection.[11]

As a consequence of spending cuts in the public realm, thrifty policymakers have resorted increasingly to subsidy and tax schemes (forms of what I would call hybrid selection), through which they stimulate private actors to invest in, donate to or sponsor valued cultural objects and initiatives (investing in monuments, film projects or scientific institutes, sponsoring museums and exhibitions, or donating to sociocultural, scientific, ideological or environmental organizations). Then selection is not hierarchical—the authority only supports in principle a cultural product *category*—but neither does it take place purely in the market. Apparently, an important selection criterion for policymakers in such cases is that private actors also take part in the cultural and economic valuation.

Cultural and economic valuation in cultural and creative industries

Many artists and designers primarily have a cultural motivation. They want to create something special which is recognized by relevant peers and experts. For a long time selection in the art environment (including applied arts such as design, architecture and fashion) was mostly culturally based, which could lead to a kind of art trap. Many artists remained within a purely subsidy-dominated hierarchical selection system and did not learn to work in a more economic environment. It is, of course, nice when governments provide a stimulating environment in which new talent can develop. However, when artists do not learn to break out to private selection environments, they remain too dependent on the whims of a relatively small and sometimes fickle hierarchical selection system. As this book explains, in the private realm cultural valuation is key also and partly dependent on what experts and opinion leaders tell. However, more than in the world of high culture, economic considerations play a role as most people have only limited resources. Therefore, artists and designers should also map their selection environment in order to be able to develop a revenue model on the basis of which they can survive and realize their cultural ambitions.

For this reason, we can say that for artists and creative enterprises especially, a double success criterion applies. On the one hand, they have to develop a cultural reputation on the basis of expert reviews, attention in specialized journals, awards, invitations to show their work in exhibitions and work sold to museums or well-known art buyers. On the other hand, they have to develop a viable revenue model (Jacobs 2012). In Figure 6.1, a few possible developments of such enterprises are mapped (based on Jacobs 2013). Number 1 is, for example, an architectural firm which gradually builds on its cultural reputation and grows as an enterprise. Number 2 is a clear victim of the art trap: rapid cultural recognition without developing a working revenue model. Number 3 is, for example, an artist who escapes from the art trap, but, maybe because of the suspicion of having become too commercial, gradually is seen as less interesting culturally. Number 4 could be a designer who gets a certain reputation and then grows as a firm, providing consistent quality.

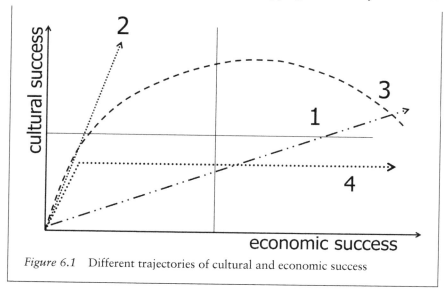

Figure 6.1 Different trajectories of cultural and economic success

6.3 EXPERT AND PEER INFLUENCE

Returning to the experts, when experts value something but no money is spent, either by private consumers or public authorities, from an economic point of view there is no willingness to pay and therefore no real valuation and selection.[12] Therefore, in situations where experts provide a valuation without having the power to make customers buy, we can only speak of expert influence, not expert selection.

We can also discuss peer influence in a similar way. We are continuously influenced by different peers in our (buying) behaviour: colleagues, friends (and also rivals within our peer group) and family members, some of whose valuations we especially value—opinion leaders. All products are the object of an unceasing dialogue at different levels of society. As a consequence, they are continuously qualified and requalified. Value is added or subtracted. Implicitly or explicitly, different offerings are classified and an order of preference is established with no more than an ephemeral validity (Callon et al. 2002).

As intrinsically social beings, the opinions of our environment are quite important to all of us. More than one hundred years ago, the German sociologist Georg Simmel already observed that the essence of fashion lies precisely in the combination of social belonging with individual differentiation. Basically, we comply with the rules of our environment and within the limits of these we play with the margins to affirm our individuality (Simmel 1904). From this perspective the fashion logic boils down to what Lipovetsky calls 'marginal differentiation' (Section 3.1), a logic which has spread to the whole economic realm.

Section 5.2 discussed some methods for learning more about what customers value in relation to certain product categories. We can certainly learn more about such needs, but at the same time, it remains difficult to predict customer behaviour in general, as many customers do not know precisely what they want or need. Customers have many needs and preferences which they acknowledge, but also many they are not aware of. Why? First, because these choices are only partially rational. Second, because they are open to the continuous stream of new offerings. Third, because they are influenced by continuous discussions in their environment, the future development of which they do not know. So all of us are continuously learning, individually and socially, about ourselves and our preferences also, by doing, trying, looking, talking, listening, and finding clues in all directions. In this way, we develop our values, tastes and preferences. By listening to the comments of other people, we might learn to what extent we have to change our tastes and values. Taste is about individual expression *and* social adaptation (Simmel 1904; Janssen & Jager 2001). As a consequence marketing and market research become a bit easier when organizations know more about the environment and related values of their customers and take part in ongoing dialogues (Mossinkoff 2012).

Both peer and expert influence are important, but in the end, it is each individual customer who makes the buying decision. When the influence of experts or peers is necessary to make customers buy, these experts or peers are clearly *taking part in the creation of economic value,* just as they can destroy value by influencing the customer's valuation in the opposite direction. Therefore, it is important to understand that actors, who do not touch a product, actually may add value to it—or deduct value from it. Cultural valuation is a continuous discourse, in which some people have more influence than others. To give a possibly extreme example, in the visual arts value is added to all works of an artist when a famous art collector buys one of his or her works. Therefore, it may be in the artist's interest to sell an artwork quite cheaply to a branded collector such as Charles Saatchi: 'When Saatchi buys the work of a new artist through a dealer, the commission may be waived. This means Saatchi pays half or less of the gallery asking price. The value added by Saatchi's ownership is such that neither artist nor dealer complains, or feels exploited' (Thompson 2008: 98).

In this chapter, I try to map selection systems in order to be able to influence them. Who are decision makers who have a relative influence on cultural and thus economic valuation? When we talk about hierarchical selection, it is easier to identify those decision makers than when we talk about market selection or hybrid selection. Marketers have, of course, understood this kind of game for a longer time, so that in the case of hybrid selection they address their endeavours more at, for example, physicians or teachers than plain consumers when medicines or course books are concerned.

6.4 HIERARCHICAL, MARKET AND HYBRID SELECTION

On the basis of the considerations in the previous sections, I propose to make a basic distinction between two ideal, typical forms of economic selection— mirroring Williamson's (1975) traditional distinction between markets and hierarchies[13]—which are often combined in one or other hybrid form.

- *Hierarchical selection.* Selection by selectors who have received the authority for this. Policymakers and managers at higher levels in organizations are typical examples of people with such authority. Other examples include juries and editorial boards. It has to be emphasized that in hierarchical selection the selectors as a rule are not acting as private persons but as actors within a preset structure (a hierarchy) with preset criteria (the norms and values of this selection system, usually embedded within the mental model of a certain sector). Therefore, it is important to understand the structure and culture of this system. Of course, in hierarchical selection there will usually be some room for the personal preferences of the selectors, but within the boundaries of the formal and informal rules and criteria of the system. The editorial board of a scientific journal has to work within the framework of its publishing house, combined with the rules of the scientific community in general and of a certain discipline and maybe even a paradigm in particular. Moreover, all hierarchical systems are governed by informal political rules and games with which people with innovative proposals have to deal.
- *Market selection.* Selection by customers in a marketplace. As many markets are large, this kind of relatively blind selection most resembles natural selection. It is, however, important to understand that these customers do not select in a vacuum. Of course, they also have certain personal preferences, but apart from their basic instincts (as defined in Section 5.3), they are usually influenced by their broader culture and their direct environment: family, colleagues and other members of peer groups, and by experts they especially value (reviewers, DJs, critics, etc.). From communication theory, we know that opinion leaders have an influence, but we also know that people select the opinion leaders they like. Opinion leaders, for their part, take into account the opinions of their followers. Therefore, there is mutual selection and co-evolution. Again, all these people are part of a culture and possibly one or more subcultures (ethnic, professional, age group, peer group) with specific values and role models.
- *Hybrid selection.* There are many hybrid combinations of these two basic forms. One is Wijnberg's first form of expert selection in which someone with special authority selects what the customer buys: firms or schools may decide on uniforms, teachers on schoolbooks and physicians on medications.[14] As said, in such cases the marketing departments

of supplying firms (publishers, pharmaceutical companies) as a rule will direct their endeavours towards these decision makers.

From a strategic point of view, it is important to recognize that hierarchical and market selection function according to totally diverse mechanisms. Where markets are directed by an invisible hand, the hand of hierarchical selection, to the contrary, is quite visible.

As stated in Section 6.1, when hierarchical selection is the preliminary stage before market selection, we may expect that the ultimate market perspective directs this hierarchical selection, but this is not necessarily the case. The success factors related to internal selection (e.g., secret or more open agendas, favouritism between departments, short- and longer-term political games within organizations) may be completely different from those on the market. People initiating innovative proposals should take this into account.

When we look at hierarchical selection outside the organization, the success criteria may be even more different compared with those on the market—for obvious reasons. Many public regulations are specifically devised to remedy market failure, so we may expect a divergent logic. Governments may intervene to align private actors who, as a consequence of the rules of the game, are not able to select the outcome with the highest added value from a societal point of view—as we have seen with the example of system innovation in the realm of health insurance in Section 1.8. Public hierarchical selection may also promote values which are undervalued by the market. In order to be subsidized, in many cases, theatre or music productions, for example, have to be experimental (i.e., not commercial), or research and development has to be fundamental and precompetitive. In concrete terms, this may sometimes mean that high art has to be difficult to digest or that R&D may not lead to practical results.

As a consequence, innovative entrepreneurs as a rule will have to shift continuously between different selection systems. When they are part of a larger organization, first they must get their proposals selected within the hierarchy. When successful, they sometimes have to acquire outside funding in the form of subsidies. Maybe they have to persuade essential external partners (hierarchical selection within other organizations). Going to the market, in some cases they have to convince preselectors (buyers of supermarkets, directors of theatres, etc.) and preferably also important experts and opinion leaders. All of this requires a lot of strategic and tactical flexibility. As a consequence, mapping one's selection environment may be a fruitful exercise in order to address each of the different steps sequentially as prepared as possible.

6.5   AN ILLUSTRATION: COSELECTION IN FASHION

As an illustration of the many ramifications of hybrid coselection, let us look more closely at selection in the realm of fashion. In the following section, I will map diverse forms of market and hierarchical selection, including expert and peer influence in the fashion value system. First, it is important to develop a better understanding of fashion selection. There is probably no other industry with a higher a degree of continuous innovation and related discussions as fashion. Nowhere else is it so easy to actually *see* cultural values changing. Fashion selection has traditionally been described on the basis of three social mechanisms labelled as 'trickle-down,' 'trickle-up' (or 'bubble-up') and 'trickle-across' (Jenkyn Jones 2002: 33–35; Solomon & Rabolt 2004: 20–21):

- *Trickle-down.* Subordinate groups look at and emulate the status symbols of the groups and role models above them (e.g., movie and music stars or high-level executives in firms[15]); as a consequence, the latter groups in their turn have to adopt ever new innovations in order to be able to differentiate themselves from the former. This is one of the traditional forces driving fashion innovation.
- *Trickle-up or bubble-up.* Grass-roots innovations from subcultural groups or lower classes are sometimes adopted by higher classes, mostly mediated by fashion designers who are inspired by these innovations and make more stylized versions of them. These include, for example, blue jeans, overalls, hippie styles, styles from music subcultures such as punk, grunge and hip-hop.
- *Trickle-across.* Much adoption also takes place horizontally within peer groups, whether these are based on class, profession, age or other subculture, as many consumers are more influenced by opinion leaders who are similar to them. Based on Simmel's (1904) remarks, fashion is about individual presentation within the limits of the rules of your group. Or as emerges from network theory: '[W]e still tend to be influenced disproportionally by the opinions or actions of our immediate friends, contacts, sources, or coworkers' (Watts 2003: 228).

Fashion is an industry in which we can observe a clustered network structure—I shall return to this concept in Section 6.7. Basically, this means that we are mainly influenced by our direct environment, but within broader frameworks. Fashions are at the same time local and global. People are influenced by global fashions, but this influence is filtered by their direct environment. As a consequence, global fashions sometimes only reach diverse clusters—different kinds of in-groups or peer groups—in a diluted way. Trickle-down may remain weak, unless the role model wearing a certain item is very popular in a certain subculture. Some clothing styles remain within restricted peer groups (trickle-across), but some are picked up from these, for example, in designs inspired by these subcultures and possibly translated to a larger environment (trickle-up).

Most of the mechanisms just discussed find a place in Figure 6.2 (inspired by Solomon & Rabolt 2004: 82). The main thrust of the diagram appears to be trickle-down, which in fashion theory traditionally has received most

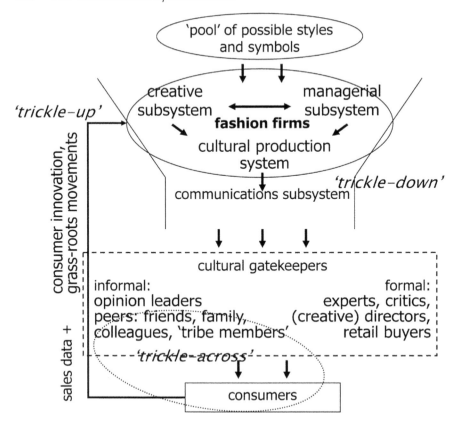

Figure 6.2   Innovation, production and selection in fashion

attention. New designs emerge from the creative subsystem and are cose-lected by the managerial subsystem in order to be able to be produced and presented to the world (the communications subsystem). In the end, con-sumers select the items they like, so they can be considered to be the ultimate selectors. However, in between are all kinds of intermediate gatekeepers who influence final selection: buyers from the retail industry, experts, critics and journalists on the one hand, and opinion leaders and other peers with a possible influence within the peer groups on the other hand. Designers, moreover, always belong to certain environments. The internal selection sys-tems of firms also play an important role in selecting the designers—and to some extent in disciplining them. In addition, these designers are part of in-formal networks: some of them see themselves more as artists, others maybe as average designers working in a commercial environment.

In Figure 6.2, the second mechanism, trickle-up, is only represented with one arrow. Compared with the original figure by Solomon and Rabolt (2004:

82), I have added 'sales data.' Bottom-up innovation may be important, but data on actual buyer behaviour is at least as important. A lot of marginal differentiation in fashion (as described in Section 3.1) takes place on the basis of detailed sales data of the previous year, possibly added with data on consumer reactions. Finally, I have added the third mechanism of trickle-across, which is most important in determining final clothing purchasing behaviour. Fashion is about marginal differentiation within the cultural rules of one's relevant peer groups.

The next step in mapping a selection environment is presented in Figure 6.3. In this model, selection in fashion is presented based on the interaction between two related value systems: that of fashion firms and that of fashion magazines. When we look at the fashion buying behaviour of end consumers, we can see that they are influenced by their peers and also by critics and magazines, but to some extent they select on their own who they want to be influenced by. Consumers buy clothing and fashion magazines, and they may have a preference for certain designers, fashion brands, critics and some of their peers whose valuation they particularly appreciate. As we have seen, market selection does not entail buying alone. It includes all kinds of trickle-up and trickle-across processes: there is continuous change and innovation at the level of lifestyles—to a large extent also stimulated by innovation in other industries such as film or interior design—which influence customer preferences in the realm of fashion.

To some extent, experts influence buying in fashion, but there is also the market selection of experts by consumers (and to some extent by fashion firms who are an important source of income for fashion magazines). All of this illustrates co-evolution, the fact that consumers, fashion firms and magazines mutually select each other to an important degree. They are part

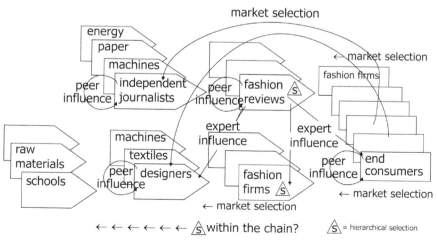

Figure 6.3 Value systems and selection in fashion

of at least related subcultures and subsystems. Even a complex diagram such as Figure 6.3 does not show all such interactions. For example, fashion firms in this figure include manufacturing firms as well as retailers, and buyers from the retail side especially play an important role in selecting from the offerings of the manufacturers. Because of this, we see complex interaction between all kinds of selectors, continuously influencing or trying to influence each other. In the language of complexity theory, this is a clear example of co-evolution within a complex adaptive system (CAS) (Holland 1995).

I can imagine that a diagram such as Figure 6.3 looks quite intimidating. In practice, however, for most firms the relevant selection environment will not be that complex. It all depends on the precise market and related tribes (subcultures or style groups) one is functioning in. Even in the growing subsector of outdoor sports fashion (hiking, biking, skiing, mountaineering, canoeing, etc.), the amount of relevant players, outlets and magazines is much smaller and more transparent than fashion in general or even leisure wear. For tribes such as the gothic scene, the system is of course even smaller.

Co-evolution and coselection in these smaller systems are, however, part of an even broader comprehensive CAS than represented in Figure 6.3. All valuations occur within a broader cultural context. For this reason, in Figure 6.4, culture has been added to the picture, from peer subcultures and neotribes[16] (Bennett 1999; Weinzierl & Muggleton 2003), to the cultural realm of the industry (with its paradigms, worldviews or recipes), to the broader culture at different possible levels: local and global, temporary (the zeitgeist) and longer lasting. In this way the cultural value side of value systems[17] is highlighted. From experience I know that probably no industry tries to track developments in values, tastes, moods and even the comprehensive zeitgeist as the fashion industry.

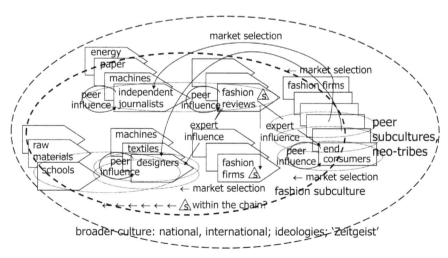

Figure 6.4   The value side of value systems

From this comprehensive understanding of selection, we can move down again to other fields which may be connected with parts of the fashion system. The fields of sport, movies or music, for example, could also be added to Figures 6.3 and 6.4 as they provide stars who may endorse (often on a contract basis) some of the fashion products (think again about expert influence and trickle-down). An example is the increasing importance of product placement in movies, music videos, games and television series. Quite a few movie or music stars receive expensive couture dresses for free as designers hope they will wear them to the Academy Awards or similar occasions which attract a lot of attention.

New channels and business models—possible arenas for selection—are being developed based on such interactions with other sectors, in which the borders of and overlaps between industries are explored. Some commercial television stations, for example, not only earn money because of product placement but also try to exploit related e-business sites, together with manufacturers: 'Did you like what Lady Gaga was wearing? Buy it directly by clicking on this button, inserting the desired size, together with your address and credit card number!' The market for product placement has even led to the development of its own brokerage industry (Caves 2000: 286–294).

6.6 MAPPING HYBRID SELECTION

In a similar way to the mapping of fashion in Figure 6.3, it is possible to map the selection systems of other sectors. In some industries, suppliers of crucial components (e.g., microprocessors) may play a relatively important role. In other industries (e.g., music) the role of preselectors such as experts (DJs, VJs, critics from music magazines or websites, bloggers) may be more prominent. Diagrams such as Figure 6.3 help us to understand a whole chain of activities or a value system, possibly with its related cultural value system (Figure 6.4). However, such diagrams may be so complex that it may be more helpful to concentrate on the key players in the more immediate environment of the firm, as in Figure 6.5. Who are the key players, the most important preselectors, the crucial opinion leaders or media? What are important subsidy schemes? Which are the most relevant, differentiating subcultures?

Based on such a diagram, it is possible to strategically concentrate marketing endeavours on the key players in the field, and perhaps develop new business models based on these. There could be new social media where important customer groups discuss the offerings of the various competitors in an industry. Firms can take part in these discussions, as well as use them to advertise attractive bargains or perhaps set up such forums themselves. Maybe some customers are prepared to reflect on the firm's innovative ideas and contribute to these. This brings us to the issues of open innovation and cocreation.

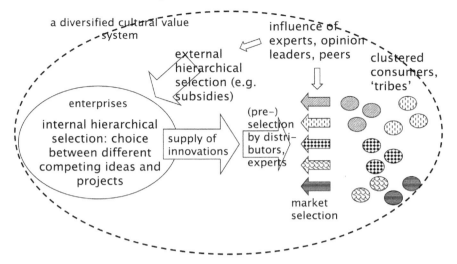

Figure 6.5   Hybrid selection from the perspective of enterprises

6.7   FROM MARKET RESEARCH TO COCREATION WITH CUSTOMERS AND VOLUNTEERS

'Open innovation' is the concept Henry Chesbrough (2003) proposed a decade ago for an older but increasingly important practice: innovation through cooperation with external partners. This can take place with different kinds of partners in value systems such as those depicted in Figure 6.3: suppliers, competitors, retailers and consumers. It can also entail crossovers with partners from totally different industries. There still exist enterprises which try to organize the whole innovation process as much as possible in-house. However, they are becoming increasingly rare, as most firms try to concentrate on their core strengths and then flexibly cooperate with other partners possessing strengths of their own (Prahalad & Ramaswamy 2004). In the framework of this book, I only focus on open innovation from the perspective of selection of resulting innovations. Therefore, I concentrate on cooperation at the demand side of organizations, client firms or end consumers. I will also look at the new culture of innovation which is emerging from such cocreative practices with customers and even volunteers.

In general, we can expect that the chances for selection of innovations increase when firms receive valuable information from their customers. Traditional market and consumer researchers try to collect as much information as possible about a multitude of consumers in order to adapt their products as closely as possible to the needs and preferences of their customers. Sales data and consumer surveys have been the most important sources for this.

Understanding, and especially forecasting, consumer behaviour has, however, remained quite difficult. For some time already, marketing professionals have complained that consumers have become fickle, unpredictable and as a consequence difficult to satisfy or to hold on to even when satisfied. To summarize the main problems of such research (Wouters 2005):

- People don't say what they think.
- People don't do what they say.
- Interviewers are not always able to register what people say.
- People are not able to think about or evaluate new things.
- Market research only measures the past.
- Consumers are increasingly sophisticated and know about most marketing tricks.

I certainly do not want to dismiss all endeavours with hypermodern marketing techniques. In the United States especially, crunching big data, sometimes combining a multitude of data sets, has become an important subsector of the information and information technology industries. For example, in election campaigns such data sets have been used to microtarget different audiences in a customized way. These campaigns have, however, also shown that it remains necessary to combine such an approach with genuine communication with living human beings. For this reason, another, postmodern marketing flavour has emerged in which real interaction with customer groups is key (Jacobs & Mossinkoff 2007; Mossinkoff 2012). As already said a few times, people are in continuous conversations about everything that surrounds them and through these discussions value is added to or subtracted from products and brands continuously. Increasingly, firms try to be part of this ongoing dialogue, for example, through the social media.

This is also the reason why open innovation, in which customers are not purely passive recipients of new products and services, has received evermore attention in recent decades. Chances for selection of innovations probably grow when customers are prepared to invest time or money in the innovation projects themselves. Especially in the framework of business-to-business (B2B) cooperation, it is much easier for a supplier to be successful with its innovations when these are thoroughly discussed and designed in close cooperation with customers. Big construction or automation projects are obvious examples of this. In the first pages of the first chapter, I already brought up the case of the development of new airplanes such as the Airbus A380 which takes places in close interaction with committed clients. Even then, the process is not straightforward. As a rule in such projects, a lot of improvisation, trial and error, bricolage (tinkering) and drifting takes place because many customers only learn what they want through what they learn during the project itself. According to Ciborra (2002: 94), in novel situations this is quite normal and even intelligent: 'Drifting stems from those mundane, invisible practices that, compared to the crisp world of procedure and method, in a way represent the dark, nocturnal side of organizational work. They are intelligent practices: the expression of practical intelligence.'

Cocreation with end consumers (business-to-consumers, or B2C) or even plain creation by consumers is also back in the interest of innovation research, as new technological opportunities related to information technology provide new opportunities in this field. Sometimes it is forgotten that most people *are* creative in one way or another and also continuously provide small free goods and services to each other (Benkler 2006: 117–118). As a consequence, many observers were surprised when apparently competent hackers (Levy 1984) and pirates (Lessig 2003) emerged and changed the rules in quite a few industries. Increasingly a free culture in the double sense of the word developed, and only slowly larger organizations have learned how to take profit from this. Comparable with what I proposed in Chapter 3 about incremental and radical innovation, here, too, we can apply a fuzzy approach to categorize cocreation:

- At one side of the spectrum we see firms providing clients with design software tools or even customer experience centres to help them personalize their products, from sneakers to cars (Dodgson et al. 2005: 131–133; Marsh 2012: 56–62). This is quite interesting, even when it mostly looks like a form of marginal differentiation, which only slightly increases the chances of market selection. First, one has to choose a certain model of car or sneakers, and then one is able to adapt it marginally according to one's tastes.
- At the other side of the spectrum, we see new forms of do-it-yourself practices—for instance, people making their own products with 3-D printers. This also leads to normal market selection, but now people choose the materials and tools for making their products instead of the products themselves.

Most interesting are, however, the practices in between these extremes. In many cases, they have led to new combinations of market and nonmarket activities. The clearest examples of these can be found in the realm of software development, where a large corporation such as IBM had to learn to cooperate with the volunteers of the Linux community. As a consequence, volunteers who work for free just for the fun, young programmers who see this activity as an opportunity to gain experience to increase their chances for employment and well-paid programmers together develop free software in the interest of both the larger community and the participating firms (Benkler 2006: 102).

Through such private-collective cooperation, a new culture of innovation has emerged. The traditional private innovation model was based on intellectual property rights. However, these rights increasingly have been hampering innovation (von Hippel 2005: 113–115). One moment Apple and Samsung are cooperating, but the next moment they are fighting with each other in different courts when the results of such cooperation lead to competing products. Beside this private model, there is the equally traditional public innovation model of publicly funded scientific research as a public good with free publication and right of use. Now a third private-collective innovation model has emerged, based on the assumption that the free revealing of proprietary innovations increases rather than decreases the profits of participating organizations. This model also proposes that contributors to this public good will obtain greater benefits than free riders because they learn more and more rapidly as they are involved in the process and because they receive more information as they are more trusted than outsiders (von Hippel & von Krogh 2006). Managing these private-collective forms of cooperation remains, however, tricky and full of ambiguities. In order to be credible partners, firms such as IBM and Nokia had to contribute hundreds of patents to the Free Software Foundation or openly license them to the software development community. Moreover, just as is the case of any other public space, the organization of these new commons requires the establishment of new formal rules beside the more informal, cultural ones (von Hippel 2005: 89–91, 106; Benkler 2006: 120–127, 143–146, 394–396).

Cooperation in the field of free software can still be viewed as cooperation on the supply side. More interesting and promising from the perspective of selection is, however, cooperation on the demand side. A few years ago, the Danish toy company Lego started Lego Mosaic, an online tool that allows users to calculate the number of bricks necessary to make a mosaic of different colours on the basis of pictures they could upload. On the basis of the success with this, Lego Factory was launched, a platform where users can calculate the number of bricks and other components required for their own designs. In a third move, Lego established Design by ME, a service through which the necessary blocks could be sent to these creative consumers. It appears, however, that this latter service was too successful ('several million per year') and that Lego got overwhelmed by it, so that it was finished in the beginning of 2012. Anyhow, the design software is still available on the Lego website, as well as a sharing platform through which consumers can download models made by others.[18]

In between cooperation with volunteering professionals and cocreation with end consumers, there is the realm of cocreation with lead users. Von Hippel (2005) has documented interesting cases in the realm of special sports such as mountain biking or kite surfing which were actually developed by such lead users. Such users in a way embody most of the traditional R&D function of the manufacturers with whom they cooperate, as they continuously develop new ideas and test the prototypes ensuing from these. However many of these user-innovators do not really cooperate with the manufacturers. Kite surfers were already designing and improving their equipment through Internet exchange long before any larger manufacturer stepped in. To the contrary, manufacturers gradually learned from these Internet exchanges and cherry-picked the best of the different proposals—which is not real cocreation (von

Hippel 2005: 103–104, 124–127). In the more popular field of mountain biking, which became a mass production industry, many user-innovators just start implementing their ideas themselves (von Hippel 2005: 34–37, 72–75). Thus basically von Hippel suggests that more productive cocreation could and should be organized, as user-innovators generally are lead users who are expert in the field or activity in which their new needs and ideas emerge. Frequently they have professional experience in a certain field (e.g., design, manufacturing or science) which they apply to their leisure activities (von Hippel 2005: 74–75, 94–96, 145). Therefore, just as in the case of software development, manufacturers could use such inputs in a more structural way, for example, by providing these users with specialized design tools. An important difference with software development or the creation of information products such as music or gaming is, of course, that for the production of material products the knowledge, experience and machinery of manufacturers remains necessary. That's the reason why a new relationship with these innovators should be established.[19] Of course, these amateurs can also become real entrepreneurs, as has sometimes been the case (von Hippel 2005: 121–131).

In Table 6.1, opportunities for cocreation are summarized with the help of two dimensions: vertically, the product categories as presented in Section 1.2 and, horizontally, the amount of actors on the supply side (S) versus those on the demand side (D).

In the realm of material products, we saw that the most genuine form of cocreation takes places in the realm of one-to-one B2B. Shipbuilding is a traditional example of this. Personalized services such as hairdressing, tailoring, architecture and interior design are quite similar to this. In such cases, cocreation takes place through personal interaction between supplier and customer.

When we look at the situation of one supplier related to many customers, nowadays the Internet plays an important role. In B2C manufacturing,

Table 6.1 Cocreative activities in different kinds of industries

	material products	information products	services
one S to one D	B2B manufacturing	B2B customized software projects	personalized services, B2B projects in automation or construction
one S to many D	mass customization, marginal co-design, focus groups	interactive blogs, crowdsourcing, beta testing	focus groups, crowdsourcing
few S to few D	cooperation with lead users		demand cooperatives
many S to many D		initiatives such as Wikipedia and Linux	

the supplier is taking the initiative providing customers opportunities for co-design by providing software which helps customers customize their products, from toys and sneakers, to personal computers and trucks. A firm may also ask consumers to provide ideas for new products or concepts (crowdsourcing, e.g., through Internet communities) or for instance to test beta versions of new software or games. In the marketing realm, focus groups have been a common tool to test and adapt ideas for new products with representative groups of selected consumers.

In the case of a few suppliers with a few actors on the demand side, we have the lead consumers as volunteers or amateurs who develop and test new product ideas which are possibly adopted by a few manufacturers; think of the mountain bikers who provide information to the bicycle manufacturer. In the realm of services especially, such as electricity, we see the emergence of demand cooperatives which bargain with different suppliers, be it mostly on the price.[20] Something similar can be observed when health insurance companies bargain with different suppliers of health services (hospitals, pharmacy chains).

Many-to-many is typical for big information projects such as Wikipedia or open-source software development. In such cases, we observe a kind of double network effect: the more people use the product, the more volunteers are enticed to participate on the supply side.

6.8 NICHES, TRIBES AND NETWORKS

Cocreative initiatives illustrate how firms are increasingly trying to move away from the traditional innovation-push model and have at least an awareness of the need for a better understanding of customer needs and of the complexities of the networks in which they operate. However, especially in B2C manufacturing (one-to-many), economies of scale remain important. As a consequence, not all individual preferences can be taken into account. Related to the concrete economies of scale and scope in each industry (from pharmaceuticals and computers, to apparel and furniture), firms will try to establish preferred relationships with different sizes of customer groups. Some firms will address the larger public; others will look for smaller subcultures or neotribes (from punk rockers to kite surfers and Moroccan immigrants) by establishing real or more imagined communities with related activities—think of Harley-Davidson, Innocent or Diesel.[21] Diagrams such as those presented in the Sections 6.5 and 6.6 may help to strategically position one's firm within these networks.

Probably no such initiatives will be decisive in making innovations succeed, as many frustrated marketers experience every day. What is attractive to one customer group may be appalling to another one. Moreover, even when intelligent marketers know an increasing amount of information about consumers, this is counterbalanced by many consumers' increasing sophistication and knowledge of marketing methods (Brown 2003: 36–37, 51–53) and their increasing knowledge about the qualities of different products through product-comparing websites. Marketers have been trying to segment consumers along a multitude of dimensions, but have found that it was not easy to make such segmentations work in practice. With the coming of the Internet and mobile telecommunications, however, opportunities have improved for consumers themselves to show their interest for certain innovations, and for firms to take profit from this. Moreover, certain firms appear to be quite popular. Some people genuinely want to adhere to their realm and even contribute to them—as examples like Harley-Davidson, Apple, Ben & Jerry's, and the Lonely Planet demonstrate (Mossinkoff 2012). Let us therefore turn the issue around and look more closely at the people's side of actual selection environments. As highlighted before, our species is a supersocial one. Mapping selection environments means also mapping our clustered social world.

A traditional concept to start with in this respect is that of 'niches.' In all ecological systems, including human ones, we observe a co-evolutionary development in the direction of ever more fragmentation and differentiation[22] (Jacobs 2000: 16–17). Many species find or construct niches into which they fit best. Other species have their own niche, and as a consequence, different species compete for the same resources only to a limited extent. In Chapter 4 I clarified that, as a consequence, fitness is not a one-size-fits-all criterion. Traditional mass markets have also increasingly become more differentiated, hence the emergence of concepts such as 'mass customization' or 'mass personalization' which help manufacturers and service providers try to reconcile economies of scale at the back of their organizations, with customization at the front.

Recent developments in network theory are quite helpful for understanding the development of a clustered network world. In network theory, it is recognized that the worlds of most people are quite small—from two different perspectives. On the one hand, most people only know a limited number (about 150) of people, and these other people to a large extent share the same cluster of acquaintances within the larger network. On the other hand, a few people called connectors know many people in a variety of clusters and form connections between these. As a result, the world becomes quite small. In fact, we can connect with most people in the world in only six steps (Gladwell 2000: 34–56; Janssen & Jager 2001: 750–751; 2003: 77). This view of clustered networks is visualized in Figure 6.6.

It is at the level of such clusters—sometimes called tribes or neotribes— that people are most influenced by others (the peer influence discussed previously). However, the more people we know personally, the less influence each of them has on us—apart from a few whose valuation we especially appreciate, such as close friends and opinion leaders within peer groups. As a consequence, in small villages or small organizations there is a higher degree of monoculture than in larger ones.

People increasingly belong to a greater number of groups, which expands the basis for possible identities. Someone can be a woman, an adolescent, a

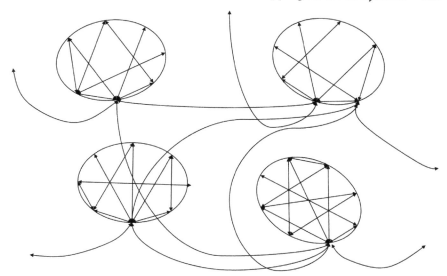

Figure 6.6   Clustered networks

Muslim, a psychology student, a lesbian, a punk rock fan and a scuba diver at the same time, but not all possible identities will have the same significance to her. Therefore, understanding possible customers to a large extent implies understanding which identity definitions are most important to each of them. Often observing them, how they dress (and the codes this expresses) and how they behave will provide important clues for this understanding. Many neo-tribes have their own dress codes, from accountants and architects to goths and punks[23] (Bennett 1999; Stahl 2003; Weinzierl & Muggleton 2003). For a long time marketers have not found it easy to deal practically with customer segmentation, but sometimes tribes have been organizing themselves sponta-neously around apparently popular firms. Firms such as Burberry or Lons-dale haven't even always been happy with their popularity.[24] It is obvious that as a consequence of spontaneous self-organization by different kinds of neotribes through the Internet, new opportunities arise for firms and other organizations in the field of co-evolution and even cocreation. In this respect, it is also necessary to look at a special aspect of our clustered world which is related to the possible speed of adoption of innovations: the appearance from time to time of hypes or information cascades.

6.9   HYPES AND INFORMATION CASCADES

Because connectors make the connections between clusters, they possibly play an important role in spreading information (or diseases!) and diffus-ing innovations through larger networks.[25] Most information, including selective adoption of certain innovations, remains within relatively small niches. However, when many connectors reinforce the same message, an information cascade or bandwagon effect (e.g., a hype or fad) may arise, through which—as in an epidemic—in a short time a lot of people are seized by that same idea: which movie to go to, which fashion item or Internet share to buy, which politician to vote for. Because this kind of cascade has similar features to epidemics, one sometimes speaks about social contagion.[26] There are, however, important differences between social contagion and the spread of diseases. Epidemics are stimulated when many people are connected to each other. Influence, however, works differently. As just mentioned, the more people we know, the less influence each of them has on us. As a consequence, social contagion works best in a social environment—such as the one which is most common—in which networks are highly clustered, but without too many people making the connections between these clusters.[27]

The clustered structure of networks also helps us to understand the tension between global developments and remaining local tastes. People are influenced by global trends and fashions, but this influence is filtered by their local culture and environment (Brand & Teunissen 2005). As a consequence, global fashions sometimes only reach clusters (various kinds of in-groups or peer groups) in a diluted way. In a similar vein, a few music styles and performers have become global, whereas many others have remained local.

Risks related to hypes

In the realm of movies or books, hypes are part of the blockbuster model and therefore actively sought. In other industries as well, as a consequence of sometimes unexpected positive feedback loops, hypes and rages occur, with opportunities for rapid growth. Such rapid growth opportunities may look very attractive but bear also important risks. One year a firm is world leader and expanding rapidly; the following year it may be out of fashion and having problems making ends meet. Therefore, it is quite understandable that firms react differently to opportunities for rapid growth. Some prepare themselves to be able to make a profit from hypes, for example, by establishing flexible networks with manufacturers around the world. Some even try to stimulate short-term hypes themselves. However, others opt for maintaining a consistent brand, even at the cost of missing temporary growth opportunities.

An interesting case in this realm is provided by the opposite reactions of the Tommy Hilfiger and Timberland fashion brands to opportunities provided by unexpected success in the American rap and hip-hop environment. Tommy Hilfiger, which previously had a more preppy image, jumped at the chance, immersed itself in this scene and adopted a more hybrid mix of preppy and urban street styles. When rap singers such as L. L. Cool J and Snoop Dog appeared on television wearing Tommy shirts, the rage was unstoppable. Tommy Hilfiger experienced a growth spurt which allowed it, around 1995, to finally catch up with its model and rival Ralph Lauren.

At about the same time Timberland was equally surprised to learn that its hiking boots and rugged outdoor gear were being bought by inner-city kids at a rate of three or four items at a time. Of course, it did not object but, in contrast to Hilfiger, opted to keep to its traditional brand image and customer group, even when at a later moment it decided to add a few colours to its range. Timberland did not experience the same kind of rapid growth as Hilfiger but later on it did not crash in the way Hilfiger did. At the end of the 1990s a number of hip-hop groups launched their own fashion label, and Hilfiger fell into a deep hole. Sales dropped and, even worse, the brand suffered from a kind of identity crisis. As a consequence, Europe, where Hilfiger kept its original identity, has become its main market (Agins 1999: 110–125; *Business Week* 27-10-2003; *Financial Times* 17-09-2004; Walker 2008: 84–87, 92–93).

A somewhat surprising consequence of network theory is that 'the structure of the network can have as great an influence on the success or failure of an innovation as the inherent appeal of the innovation itself' (Watts 2003: 244). Of course, the quality of the innovation plays a role, too, but at the same time we know that many—even attractive—innovations fail. Equally, we can observe that one moment nobody wants a certain fashion item like Ugg boots, and the following one it is the object of a craze. Even when innovations do not fail totally, in many cases they are unable to break out of restricted niches (Gladwell 2000: 35–46; Watts 2003: 217–244).[28] Therefore, even when an innovation reaches a larger network, this may remain a niche, be it a somewhat larger one. Howard Dean's campaign for the US Democratic presidential nomination in 2004, for example, took off quite rapidly on the basis of the Internet. At a certain moment it stopped, however, because it was not able to get out of its niche, as Dean enthusiasts mainly kept on merely talking to each other (Scoble & Israel 2006: 38–39, 134).

In these same clustered networks, some messages, however, break out relatively rapidly. In Chapter 5 (Section 5.3). I linked attractiveness of certain memes or cultural variants to a variety of basic instincts—more precisely, evolved psychological mechanisms related to important aspects of our survival within our environment. In communication literature, this attractiveness has been related to the stickiness of a message—both approaches do not have to be contradictory of course. For this reason, publicity specialists continuously search for sticky phrases and spectacular virals—you probably recognize the influence of epidemics as a metaphor and analogy? Similarly, politicians and their advisors look for catchy one-liners. Stickiness is, however, not easily obtained. Moreover, a tune for a commercial may be sticky, but its message or brand connection is easily forgotten. Subtle advertising, sometimes involving play, guesswork or reciprocation, is more effective in many cases than aggressive publicity (Gladwell 2000: 24–25; Mossinkoff 2012: 216–219).

Similarly, movies launched with great fanfare regularly fail. Quite a few celebrities' books have not been able to recoup the big advances paid to their writers. After the launch of a new product, word of mouth—or word of mouse on the Internet—in the clustered network appears to be more important than anything else in determining its success. In literature this is known as the 'nobody knows' property of innovation, especially in the cultural realm (Caves 2000: 138–142, 166–167). For this reason, marketers try to influence word of mouth and word of mouse as much as possible by mobilizing experts and opinion leaders in a multitude of networks.

There is, however, one important exception to the 'nobody knows' property of most innovation, and that is reputation. When Apple launches a new product, it receives a lot of interest. Similarly established authors or actors receive relatively more attention, and for this reason can secure higher fees.[29] For the same reason sequels are so popular with film producers.[30] That's why branding is so important and cannot be stressed enough. 'When an artist becomes branded, the market tends to accept as legitimate whatever the artist submits' (Thompson 2008: 14). This observation, of course, only begs the question: how does one establish a strong reputation? Again, quality may help but is certainly not enough. The central issue in this chapter therefore was, what are the fitness criteria in the different parts of your relevant selection environment and who is actually selecting (and influencing selection)?

Now that we have mapped selection environments and important mechanisms which regulate these, let us look in the next chapter at how we can actually influence these to make our innovations more successful.

7 Co-Evolution
From Description to Prescription

7.1 NEGOTIATING A DOMINANT DESIGN

In the framework of productive creativity, increasing the chances of success of an innovation means dynamically interacting with various possible customer groups and other allies—co-evolution in practice. This may sound like easy advice—which it is—but it is amazing how few textbooks really talk about process approaches, whether in the field of innovation or in the field of strategy.[1] In this respect, the kind of approach presented in the previous chapter may be helpful—that is, mapping your real networks and selection systems, including the related cultural value system. An important but not very surprising lesson from evolutionary theory is that people may influence their selection environment to some extent. More so than voluntaristic approaches like 'where there is a will, there is a way,' evolutionary theory may show us the strategic margins we have for this.

A historical example is the selection of the final dominant design of the bicycle mentioned in Section 3.4. Pinch and Bijker (1987) described how this selection at the end of the nineteenth century was the result of a complex interaction between completely different social groups. Women and older cyclists especially valued safety and comfort, whereas younger cyclists preferred the sporty aspects, such as challenge and speed. As a result, different bicycle designs were presented to a variety of groups, offering all kinds of real and rhetorical answers to the concerns of each. The basic design which finally won and which we now see as the normal (i.e., dominant) design of a bicycle apparently fitted the criteria of all of these constituencies best.

According to Bruno Latour (1987), for inventors to become innovators, they must continuously shift between their social and technical environment—as illustrated in Figure 7.1 (inspired by Latour 1987: 139). To start with, from a technical perspective, an invention has to work, to become an undisputed black box.[2] To realize this, inventors need to assemble many kinds of allies (human and nonhuman) in their environment and must 'translate' the interests and concerns of related social groups into the features of the technical design. The interests of others are continuously 'translated' into ours and ours into theirs (Latour 1987: 108–144; 2005:

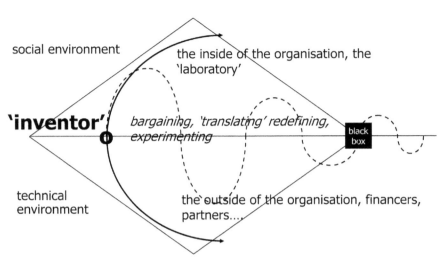

Figure 7.1   Negotiating between the social and technical system

106–109; Akrich et al. 2002a, 2002b). Returning to the bicycle, at a certain moment pneumatic tyres[3] became an important ally, helping to unite diverse groups of cyclists who valued comfort on the one hand and speed (younger and sportier cyclists) on the other. Gradually the design converged, as a result of both the search process and countless translations and negotiations. The end result is the black box, the dominant design with which bicycles since then are identified.

From the discussion in the previous chapters, we have learned that the social environment in Figure 7.1 will probably contain not only various social constituencies but also totally different selection systems with divergent rules. The technical environment also contains important nontechnical features such as the stylistic design and the values to which this appeals. In the case of the bicycle just mentioned, anticyclists, for example, found women wearing skirts or—even worse—trousers on a bicycle to be plainly immoral, whereas emancipated women especially appreciated this aspect. For the latter, the bicycle—at least when it was designed in a certain way—became an ally to their cause (Pinch & Bijker 1987: 32–41).

In Chapter 3, we saw that radical innovation leads to new sets of preferences or even to new sets of selectors. As a consequence, people aiming at radical innovation may almost automatically resort to rhetoric. The language of *selection* to some extent also suggests such an approach, as selection resembles a language of deliberate decision-making. Certainly, rational deliberation may indeed take place when we talk about hierarchical selection. However, decision-making is sometimes more emergent and intuitive. In addition, Latour's translation metaphor may suggest more rational strategizing than there actually is, but he himself tries to clarify that this is not what he means. Inventors becoming innovators may even perform these continuous translations in a more effective, 'natural way' when they naively ignore social groups and strategy: '*They do not know what society is made of,* any more than they know the nature of Nature beforehand. It is because they know about neither that they are so busy *trying out* new associations, creating an inside world in which to work, displacing interests, negotiating facts, reshuffling groups and recruiting allies' (Latour 1987: 142, Latour's emphasis). Most of these people see themselves as struggling with complex, mainly technical issues, not as strategists trying to make allies or win power struggles (Latour 2005: 88–93). As Latour says in a co-authored article: 'In the heat of action, there is no architect but several, no decision-maker but a multitude, no single plan but ten or twenty which confront one another' (Akrich et al., 2002a: 194).

Talking is not just a means of convincing other people;[4] it is also about trying to understand new realities. Section 3.2 clarified that especially the first stages of more radical innovation are about interpretative search and sensemaking—trying to understand totally new realities for which new concepts and categories have to be developed.

Linking innovations to existing categories

In Section 3.2, I clarified that linking radical innovations, which may not be well understood in the beginning, to existing product categories helps to decrease cognitive distance and thus to improve chances for successful selection. A recumbent bicycle is a kind of bicycle; from impressionism we moved to expressionism and even to abstract expressionism. Apple's Newton, which was sold as a 'personal digital assistant,' was not very successful. However, later on Apple successfully launched a similar product, the iPhone, as a new kind of smartphone.

Discussions amongst scientists and other professionals are, of course, not just value or interest free. Some of them possibly favour certain directions, and some of them may have interests (including intellectual capital invested in a certain theory or paradigm) in one of these. Some also have more power in certain selection systems. Therefore, Latour's translation processes are partly about understanding and partly about trying to win others over to one's own position. Both processes imply taking others' interests seriously, through genuine learning or at least manipulation. This is even more the case in relation to more comprehensive system innovations, such as those discussed in Section 1.8. The establishment of a new health or pension system calls for a great deal of bargaining and coordination, making it necessary to carefully map out the relevant parties, the extent of their interests and power bases and how these can be dealt with.

In a great deal of the literature it is stated that customers do not play an important role as far as more radical innovation in its initial state is concerned, as many of them may be too short-sighted (Veryzer 1998): 'If Henry Ford would have asked what customers wanted, they probably would have asked for a faster horse.' However, as we saw in Section 6.7, innovation on the customer side is increasing. In some cases, interested customers (professionals or other lead customers) have even taken the lead in this (von Hippel 1988, 2005). In addition, innovations will ultimately have to appeal to customers' values; at least these customers will have to be able to make sense of them. It is therefore wise to be genuinely interested in customers, especially their basic needs, their behavioural routines and their value connections, from an early stage (Rijkenberg 1998: 64).[5] Therefore it is certainly a good idea to give the people who are responsible for developing an innovation, sufficient external autonomy to interact with the relevant external actors in a productive way (van den Ende et al. 2003: 277, 282). As Akrich, Callon and Latour state: 'The stake in all cases is to identify the users who are in the best position to transform the innovation and to bring it to meet the demand of other users. To interest and to transform are two faces of the same reality' (2002b: 209).

In this respect, Hamel and Prahalad, in their famous book *Competing for the Future* (1994), talk about 'expeditionary marketing': 'When the goal is to create new competitive space, it is usually impossible to know in advance what configuration of product or service features, offered at what price point and through what channels, will be required to unlock the potential market. . . . If the goal is to accumulate market understanding as rapidly as possible, a series of low-cost, fast-paced market incursions, what we call expeditionary marketing, is imperative' (Hamel & Prahalad 1994: 237–238). The goal is, thus, to experiment and learn rapidly, integrating what one has learnt at one stage and using this as a kind of working hypothesis in the next one, and so on. As we saw in Section 3.4, 'The social-technical analysis underlines that the movement of adoption is a movement of adaptation' (Akrich et al. 2002b: 209).

7.2 PAYING FOR ATTENTION AND ADDED VALUE

From interacting with outsiders, it is only a small step to recognizing that these outsiders possibly play an important role in adding value and that, therefore, they should be paid. The smartest customers helping firms to innovate at least demand that these firms do not appropriate the intellectual property rights of these innovations but instead leave them to the *creative commons* (von Hippel 2005).

A next possible step is rewarding experts and peers. An important condition for the success of innovation is getting attention. Increasingly we live in an attention economy in which, as a consequence of oversupply, human attention is one of the scarcest resources. Firms and innovators literally have to pay for attention. Publicity is, of course, the clearest example of this (Davenport & Beck 2001: 2–10). However, in this respect we also have to look again at the possibly important role of outside observers, critics and other experts and preselectors. These may support an innovation by giving it more public exposure or by diffusing or creating new concepts and categories which allow broader audiences to see and understand innovations, connecting these to existing concepts, categories and values. In this way, experts may make an innovation—in Rogers's words—more compatible with existing culture.

Some of the experts and preselectors are paid for their contributions. For example, experts may be asked to reflect on certain innovations in a business magazine. Most of them will maintain their independent judgement—but at the same time, they can possibly be biased just due to the honour of being asked. Of course, some of them may be straightforwardly bribed. The clearest example of this is the practice of 'payola' in the music and other cultural industries. Payola is a kind of bribe, paid to influence the choice of experts and gatekeepers to bring a product to the attention of the public. The term comes from the music industry where DJs and VJs or their broadcasting stations are paid to give certain music airplay. Some DJs, VJs or programme directors may be bribed personally, but the practice can also be part of the business model of the radio or television station. These broadcasters are then paid for airplay instead of having to pay for the rights to this music.[6] In a similar way, bookshops may be paid by publishers to push certain new books by displaying large quantities of them in the shop or shop window. The market for product placement has already led to the development of its own brokerage industry (Caves 2000: 286–294). Worse and less acceptable, of course, are the practices in which stock analysts are paid to recommend certain shares.

In the meantime, there are now so many experts on the market that the value contribution of each is probably decreasing. The Internet with its many millions of blogs, platforms and chat rooms makes this situation ever more untransparent. The exception here is the superstars, the few programmes, magazines or experts that get most of the attention. It is said, for example, that even a bad review in the *New York Times Book Review* generates the sale of six thousand additional copies of a book. Even better can be Oprah Winfrey's endorsement, which easily leads to a few hundred thousand extra books sold. So it was understandable that Oprah established her own book club to capture some of the value she created (Green 2005). Similarly, DJs, VJs and news anchors who attract listeners and viewers to their stations exact a higher pay rate. These people, just like sport, rock or movie stars, have news value as such and may profit from the superstar effect (i.e., 'winner takes all') or the bandwagon effect through which only a few people receive most of the attention and payment, as a consequence of the additional value they hopefully bring to their employers or principals (Caves 2000: 73–77, 81–82, 109–110, 181). The difference is that an important asset of experts is their supposedly objective valuation. By accepting payola-like payments, they put their reputation at risk. A nice example of this was provided by the English conservative philosopher Roger Scruton, who was revealed to have been prepared to write protobacco opinion pieces in major newspapers and magazines in return for a fee of £5,500 from Japan Tobacco International (*The Guardian*, 24–01–2002).

Peers also create value by praising certain items they bring to the attention of their friends and colleagues. Our friends influence us more than any advertising or marketing campaign can ever dream of doing. Therefore, firms, political parties and other organizations try to get into our networks. One special type of peers is the connectors and opinion leaders discussed in Section 6.8. These have been regularly mobilized by policymakers, for example, to help encourage healthy practices in their environment, inter alia in the realm of AIDS prevention. In most cases, this has been quite effective in bringing about behavioural change (Rogers 2003: 321–325). In addition, modern viral marketing approaches have more or less successfully tried to involve these connectors in a commercial way (Rogers 2003: 313–314). As a consequence, at a certain moment, some of these peers are promoted into recognized and compensated experts. They may be paid to promote products (especially the ones they like themselves), to hunt for cool trends, to write reviews or to become paid advisers or brokers.

Since 2005, Procter & Gamble, through its Tremor and Vocalpoint programmes, has enlisted literally hundreds of thousands of connectors within peer groups to recommend its products by word of mouth. For this, P&G looks for women with larger social networks. Contrary to the policy advice of the Word of Mouth Marketing Association (www.womma.org), P&G does not require these connectors to disclose their P&G affiliation. This does not appear to be very smart, as people will start to distrust the peer recommendation of P&G products, or at the very least feel betrayed when they find out about this practice (*Business Week*, 29–05–06; Walker 2008: 172).

One step further are practices in the realm of stealth or undercover marketing in which a false impression is conveyed that people like something, for instance, by putting fake customer comments on the Internet. Regularly such actions are discovered and lead to embarrassed excuses from the firms in question. A comparable case was the action of consultancy firm CSC Index in 1995 to buy some ten thousand of copies of a book written by two of its top consultants (Tracey and Wiersema) in order to get it on the *New York Times* bestseller list (Micklethwait & Wooldridge 1996: 27–28). On an even larger scale, 'astroturfing' consists of faked bottom-up movements sponsored by firms.[7] An example is the Guest Choice Network, which opposes regulation of smoking in restaurants, bars and hotels and was actually created by tobacco firm Philip Morris.[8] Moreover, this practice, forbidden by most important public relations and communications associations, is not without risks, as nowadays quite a few people recognize such endeavours and publish them. Therefore, it is a tactic which may backfire. It is, actually, much more useful to monitor what customers are really concerned about and to act upon this, as many of them are well prepared to contribute. Nevertheless, we shouldn't entertain the illusion that most firms will not try to manipulate our valuation when they see an opportunity to do this.

In general, however, rewarding peers is still the exception.[9] If one gives away certain products for free, many people are prepared to carry them around. Personally, I have always been puzzled by the extent to which people are even prepared to pay for and walk around in T-shirts and jackets with big brand names and logos. It underscores the extent to which these brands and logos apparently add value (status) within certain groups. In the realm of marketing, at best some people receive a gift when they provide a firm with the address of a possibly interested peer. A few firms organize special activities for their more devoted fans. The more these marketing endeavours are personalized, the more it may be expected that these fans will be compensated for their share in the creation of added value.[10]

All of this illustrates the fact that there is no economic value creation without at least a reconfiguration of cultural values with the help of various actors outside enterprises. These actors are increasingly integrated into innovation and marketing approaches and, as a consequence, compensated to some extent. In the final analysis, doing this in an open and subtle way, playing fairly, seems to be the smartest approach.

8 Innovation Routines*

8.1 REPEATEDLY SUCCESSFUL INNOVATIVE ORGANIZATIONS

In Section 4.4, I clarified that as far as the economy is concerned, two units of selection are most important: organizations, on the one hand, and their products, on the other. As most studies in the realm of evolutionary economics have concentrated on the survival and growth of organizations, in the previous chapters I have tried to redress the balance by focusing on the selection of innovative products. Without successful products or services, in the end no organization survives. Even a giant with very deep pockets, General Motors, was not able to avoid bankruptcy in 2009. In Section 4.4, I also explained that routines are necessary for organizations to get really organized. However, such routines may hamper these organizations' adaptive capabilities later on—unless they also develop routines to adapt and innovate. With the examples of industries such as pharmaceuticals and fashion in mind, my colleague Hendrik Snijders and I therefore coined the concept of 'innovation routines.' Some firms and whole industries indeed innovate in a routine manner. Why are some organizations more successful in this respect than others?

As said, there exists already a whole literature on excellent or high-performing organizations which focuses on the survival and development of organizations as such. Organizations are then the unit of selection. In this literature, sometimes it is too easily concluded that an organization is well managed because it has a successful product. Indeed, such innovative success may also be the result of plain luck. In order to know whether an organization really excels in innovation management, it has to be *repeatedly* successful in this field. When organizations are repeatedly successful with their innovations, we can assume that there is a peculiar management system, an innovation routine, behind this success. Therefore, this chapter addresses the relationship between the two levels of selection: selection of innovations

---

*Apart from the last page, this chapter is coauthored with Hendrik Snijders, based on Jacobs & Snijders (2008; 2012).

related to the selection (i.e., survival and growth) of organizations. Why are certain firms better at making their innovations successful?

In 2008, with the help of a study commissioned by the Dutch Management Studies Foundation,[1] Hendrik Snijders and I were able to research this issue. We focused on twenty Dutch organizations with repeated success in innovation in a wide variety of industries (a short description of the cases is given in the box).

Our twenty cases

Besides the usual suspects in innovation studies (the Dutch based multinationals Philips, Unilever and Shell), we have included in our study industrial firms that outperform their competitors in their niche, such as ASML (wafer steppers), Intervet (market leader in the animal health industry), Ten Cate (amongst other things, manufacturing artificial grass used in major sports events) and MEXX (fashion). Other industrial cases in our study were DSM (specialty chemicals), Siemens Nederland (electronics) and Koning & Hartman (a niche player in telecommunications equipment).

We also selected organizations which are market leaders in service sectors and the creative domain: Rabobank, Achmea (health insurance), HEMA (department stores), Albert Heijn (supermarkets), Stage Entertainment (market leader in the musical industry on the European mainland) and the Efteling (the largest theme park in the Netherlands). To avoid a narrow scope on large firms, we included small and medium-sized firms, such as the advertising agency KesselsKramer, Effectory (a consultancy in the realm of HRM) and two museums, the Rotterdam Kunsthal and the Groninger Museum. The latter are museums which have been regularly successful with temporary expositions, as we did not want to include museums, such as the Van Gogh Museum, which are successful because of their permanent collection.

A Strategically Necessary Innovation Pipeline

We studied all these cases carefully in order to identify the features which were common to them and which differentiated them from their close competitors. Indeed, we found forms of routinization—a kind of innovation pipeline—even when these were different from sector to sector. Even the two museums in our sample, which to some extent retain—in Mintzberg's terms (1989)—the features of 'adhocracies,'[2] have such a pipeline in which ideas for new exhibitions are regularly discussed, selected and implemented. In Figure 8.1 (already presented in Chapter 5), the main elements of such a generic innovation pipeline have been brought together.

This figure resembles, of course, the innovation funnels or stage-gate models which can be found more often in literature, in which innovative proposals are selected through a series of stages after which only a part is further elaborated (e.g., Tidd et al. 2005: 89). There are, however, at least three important elements which sets our figure apart from those funnels.

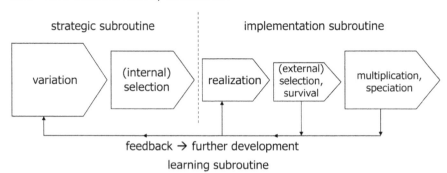

Figure 8.1   Innovation routines and subroutines

First, our figure helps to recognize the three important subroutines of successful innovation: the strategic and implementation subroutine and the feedback or learning subroutine. In order to have a successful innovation routine, all of these have to be present and related to one another. Later on, we will clarify that no less than ten essential disciplines are required for this. Our general message is one of continuous learning underpinning incremental innovation on a daily basis, combined with more radical innovation every now and then. Sometimes an important mental obstacle is viewing incremental innovation as not really innovative, whereas, to the contrary, as a rule organizing around incremental innovation helps to unify the different subroutines into one integrated innovation routine. As Tom Kelley from the American design firm IDEO states, 'Small observations lead to small improvements, but if you keep up that process continuously, you can find yourself at the head of the pack' (Kelley 2001: 47).

Second, the essential role of the strategic subroutine has to be recognized. In most approaches to innovation, the organization's strategy provides no more than the general framework. However, in order to realize repeated successful innovation, there has to be a *direct* link between innovation and strategy. Innovation then is necessary to realize the strategic objectives of the organization. For example, a few years ago, DSM (a firm that has made a successful transformation from coal—the original abbreviation stands for Dutch State Mines—to specialty chemicals and vitamins) said it wanted to grow 15% in three years organically. For this, it had to select no less than fifty promising innovation projects, as without these it would not be able to reach that goal (Jacobs & Snijders 2008: 75). When such a clear link between strategy and innovation is not present, innovation tends to remain incidental. Then organizing innovation on a routine basis is not likely to occur.

Finally, in the implementation routine the innovation is confronted with its external selection environment. Therefore, there is a direct link between the implementation and learning subroutines as, for example, was also the case with the discussion based on Figure 7.1 in the previous chapter. It is only because of continuous interaction and learning—co-evolution—that large-scale success becomes possible.

Indeed, all the organizations that we researched had established a kind of innovation routine, but they were not necessarily aware of this. During the interviews, the realization of this often gave sudden insights that led to new ideas about how to improve this routine.

Three mental obstacles

In order to make innovations successful, it is essential to leave behind a few traditional preconceptions. In our study, we stumbled across three possibly harmful mental obstacles that have to be disposed of.

Mental Obstacle 1: Absolutization of Innovation

As we saw in Chapter 3, more radical innovations are often considered to be the only real innovations. Moreover, emphasis is also often placed on technological innovation, which means that the many possibilities for the further development of successes (new versions, improvements and new styling) are under threat of not being completely exploited. However, such incremental innovation composes the lion's share of innovation. Incremental innovation bridges exploration and exploitation. Of course, the distinction between incremental and more radical innovation remains relevant, but even radical innovation often follows the course of a series of smaller steps. In this sense, we must aim to establish ambidextrous organizations—organizations with two right hands—that embrace both forms of innovation.

Mental Obstacle 2: Innovation and Routine Are Considered to Be Incompatible

All the organizations that we researched possess some sort of innovation routine, but only a few of them were actually aware of this. During the interviews, the realisation of this often gave sudden insights that also led to new ideas. Of course, this idea is not entirely new. As we saw in Section 4.4, according to Nelson and Winter (1982:133), Joseph Schumpeter said already that during the twentieth century big companies had routinized innovation. In sectors such as the fashion, automotive and pharmaceutical industries, we have known for a long time that organizing a pipeline of new products is crucial.

Mental Obstacle 3: Innovation Is Dependent on Leadership

Innovation is often seen as something mythical associated with visionary leaders. We actually did meet some passionate leaders who really sped up innovation. However, repeating their past success is problematic as long as innovation remains dependent on them. Visionary leaders are important for inducing an innovative culture, but they must ensure that this culture is structurally anchored within the organization and that it therefore does not remain dependent on them.

8.2 OPEN PROFESSIONAL BUREAUCRACIES

Part of the problem related to the establishment of innovation routines is the traditional connotation of innovation with creativity and serendipity. Look, for example, at Henry Mintzberg's characterization of the innovative organization, which he calls the 'adhocracy.' According to Mintzberg, sophisticated innovation requires a special form of organization that helps professionals with different backgrounds to work together in smoothly functioning ad hoc teams. The price of this, however, is a considerable degree of disruption or even chaos and waste; the innovative organization takes its effectiveness thereby from its ineffectiveness. Such adhocracies usually are young organizations or younger parts of large organizations. In his description of the typical development of such organizations, Mintzberg (1989: 208–209) makes a very interesting observation which triggered us: 'All kinds of forces drive the innovative configuration to bureaucratize itself as it ages. . . . As it ages, the successful organization develops a reputation for what it does best. That encourages it to repeat certain activities, which may suit the employees who, themselves aging, may welcome more stability in their work. So operating adhocracy is driven over time toward professional bureaucracy to perfect the activities it does best, perhaps even toward the machine bureaucracy to exploit a single invention. The organization survives, but the configuration dies.'

In our opinion, this describes precisely what happens when an innovation routine is established. Mintzberg considers this development from adhocracy to professional bureaucracy as somewhat tragic, but in our opinion that does not need to be the case. In innovation literature, it has been recognized that innovative organizations not only have to explore to profit from their innovativeness but also to exploit. Therefore, it is not necessarily bad when organizations standardize their successful innovative procedures and organize for the exploitation of their successes—simultaneously milking their cash cows and growing new ones. That may make them more conservative than they initially were, but ideally they remain innovative. The resulting innovations as a rule might be more incremental, but that need not be a problem.

Often such professional bureaucracies from time to time put together project teams which function in a similar manner as adhocracies. Mintzberg calls this alternative of the innovative organization a 'temporary adhocracy.' Specialists from several parts of the organization or even from different organizations are brought together in a project team which is dissolved after it has run its course.

In Mintzberg's organization types, we think that an increasing number of organizations meet the challenge to become an open professional bureaucracy, combining a creative learning culture in their innovation department with a clear organizational structure which provides reliable figures (focused management information) which helps support this learning culture.[3] Our addition of 'open' here is related with the concept of open innovation initiated by Henry Chesbrough (2003).[4] Innovative professional bureaucracies nowadays work more with people from other organizations and are more open than they were in the past.

Therefore, an interesting question was the extent to which the organizations we studied could be characterized as 'professional bureaucracies' in Mintzberg's terms, as was our hypothesis. As one can see from Figure 8.2, this was basically the case, with a few exceptions however.

The organizations with the longest tradition of having a separate innovation department (the black ones in Figure 8.2) could all be described as professional bureaucracies, even when a few had only recently moved there. Most of the organizations in white with a more recently developed innovation routine were still moving into this direction (from being a machine bureaucracy or an adhocracy). In addition, there were still a few real adhocracies (the advertising agency KesselsKramer and one of the museums). One of the black firms in black, finally, seemed to be losing its innovative edge and developing into a more traditional machine bureaucracy: the fashion enterprise MEXX, after being taken over by the American firm Liz Claiborne.[5] The MEXX example also illustrated another problem: organizations sometimes remain too dependent on their founder. Therefore, contrary to much literature, we see leadership as a potential trap.[6] From our study we conclude that smart leaders make their organizations independent of themselves by creating well-functioning professional bureaucracies.

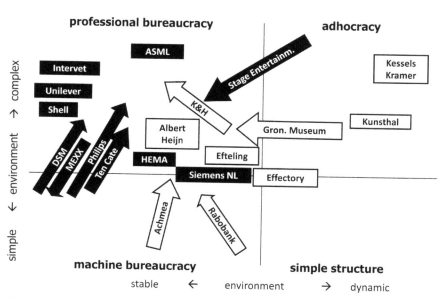

Figure 8.2   Our twenty cases in Mintzberg's taxonomy of main organization types

8.3   THE TEN DISCIPLINES OF THE INNOVATION DECATHLON

As said already, we have tried to understand as precisely as possible what differentiates our successful cases from less successful ones. More than expected, we found striking similarities between the practices within these quite different industries. The major difference was between organizations which had a longer tradition with a separate innovation department and the ones that had set up such a department more recently. Moreover, this department wasn't called 'research and development' in all organizations. Sometimes it was 'business development' or the group of curators in a museum.[7]

Our ultimate conclusion is that the success of innovation is more manageable than usually thought and that the differences between the separate sectors are of minor importance. Regardless of whether a separate innovation department does or does not exist, what is essential is that innovation is an integral part of the organization's basic routines. Moreover, we found that a strong innovation routine is a combination of ten disciplines in which organizations must excel in order to succeed in innovation. Surpassing the expectations that we had at the beginning of our study, we arrived at this success formula. For this, we employ the metaphor of the decathlon: ten disciplines in which one *must* excel. If you are successful in doing so, success is almost guaranteed! We use the metaphor of the decathlon because this precisely explains the logic: just as in the Olympic decathlon, it is possible to score somewhat less in one of the disciplines, but this relative weakness then has to be compensated for by exceptional strengths in the others. An athlete who is only strong in eight of his or her disciplines doesn't have a chance! Therefore, our message may seem to be simple, but it certainly isn't in practice.

The ten disciplines of the innovation decathlon

1. *A direct relationship between strategy and innovation.* As we already explained previously, the point of departure is a clear *strategic concept* (and related business model), in which innovation is necessary to realize its objectives. When there is no close connection between strategic objectives and innovation, there will not be enough urgency to keep the innovation routine in motion. In a way, this first discipline is also a kind of precondition. As a rule, innovation will take place in the areas in which the organization has built its competitive strengths and in which it sees further growth potential. However, an important qualification must be made: regularly new territories have to be explored as well, possibly in adjacent areas (the evolutionary law of *requisite variety*).

2 and 3. *Customer and societal orientation.* An important finding of our study is that customer orientation has to be split up into two separate disciplines. On the one hand, it is necessary to follow one's customers quite

closely, to learn what bothers them in your area and, of course, the possible complaints regarding your products. On the other hand, one has to look behind one's customers and their actual, recognized needs. Therefore, beside *customer orientation,* there is a need for a broader and more far-sighted *societal orientation.* We saw that in each of our cases mechanisms were put in place to safeguard that longer-term societal orientation too. Shell's scenario studies are probably well known (Kleiner 1996: 139–180; van der Heijden 1996). Another example is the department store chain HEMA, which invites different trend watchers twice a year to tell them about new social trends and what HEMA can possibly do with these.

4. *Ambition and daring.* Without these, the need for continuous innovation and improvement tends to come to a standstill. When MEXX had a turnover of 30 million guilders in the Netherlands, everybody was celebrating. But its founder Rattan Chadha said, '30 million is nice, but C&A is making 300 million. Why wouldn't we be able to do that?' (Jacobs & Snijders 2008: 112). In recent years, an opposite logic has taken over: Liz Claiborne, its new owner until 2011, looked at MEXX's figures and based on that decided to pull MEXX out of the United States and the United Kingdom.

5. *Incremental innovation.* There is nothing wrong with limited, incremental improvement. Many breakthrough innovations that have radically changed people's lives started out small. Successful innovators do not treat innovation as being something that is absolute. There appears to be no contradiction between large ambitions and taking small steps, as we saw in Chapter 3. To the contrary, we found that an important mental block hampering innovation routines lies in not recognizing incremental innovation as real innovation.

6. *Learning from real figures.* Previously we have explained that we view the most important challenge for innovative organizations to become professional bureaucracies: organizations that combine continuous innovation with clear agreements. Indeed, successful innovators establish a well-functioning management information system with which project leaders and managers can accurately follow the progress of their innovation projects. They analyze any possible setbacks they face based on this. They also develop a set of indicators (e.g., using a balanced scorecard) at a high level within their organization, which enables them to analyze their progress as an organization as accurately as possible and really learn from this. They do not shy away from recognizing their weak points and doing something about them.[8]

7. *Looking for the best people.* Successful organizations are continuously looking for the best people, even when these are possibly smarter than the managers themselves. When they do not have the required staff for a certain project which appears strategically important to them, they don't refrain from this project. They just look for the best people to implement it.

8. *Ambiance of an open culture.* This is the main element of the adhocracy which professional bureaucracies have to keep alive. They ensure that there is a climate of trust that allows difficult issues to be discussed.

> They keep the atmosphere fun but also keep people focused: commitments have to be kept.
> 9. *Integration into strong networks, inside and outside one's organization.* Whatever organizations want to achieve, it is increasingly difficult to do that alone. For this reason, they maintain strong links with the most (strategically) interesting networks.[9]
> 10. *Focus and commitment.* Finally, successful innovators keep their eye on the ball. They ensure as much as possible that project milestones are reached by the agreed points in time. Timing is quite important in innovation nowadays, as the competitors do not stand still. This does not mean that one should not be prepared to take the foot off the accelerator if it looks like things are going off course, but one should not put a stop to a project at the first setback.

We presume that most of these points look familiar. The danger is therefore that one thinks too easily that these disciplines are already taken care of. That's why we use the metaphor of the decathlon. Strength in eight disciplines is not enough to qualify for the Olympic decathlon. Therefore, organizations have to assess their performance in each of the disciplines as carefully as possible and especially work with priority on the disciplines in which they are not strong enough yet. They should also benchmark their performance in each of the disciplines with that of their strongest and most inspiring competitors, not necessarily to copy their practices, but to outperform them. Again, the success formula we came up with may perhaps sound simple, but it is by no means an easy one to implement.

Linkages between Disciplines Shouldn't Lead to Reducing Them

As we said before, the ten disciplines link to one another and together create one overall innovation discipline and related routine:

- Social orientation, for instance, relates to learning culture, as well as to networking.
- Finding the best people and building strong networks flow from a strategic focus on innovation but is also directly related to ambiance and maintaining an open learning culture.
- Learning from real figures fuels your strategic profile, helps with developing innovations and is itself propelled by being customer focused. It is therefore an essential component of the learning culture and the establishment of an open professional bureaucracy.
- The ambiance and open learning culture help to ensure that the innovation routine of the open professional bureaucracy does not degenerate into a rigid, inflexible machine bureaucracy.

We can imagine that these insights might result in the temptation to reduce the ten disciplines down to fewer, maybe even to three or two. There could seem to be a number of central disciplines that, when well met, include the others.

- The *strategy* offers the leading concept, fed by a real understanding of the organization's strengths and business model that are constantly innovated in new skills and products. Ambition leads to strong strategic objectives in terms of innovation, but the confrontation with the real figures protects the organization against reckless risk-taking. Smart strategic thinking also includes a thorough outside-in perspective and therefore leads to an anticipatory social orientation.
- Nothing is as strategic as selecting the best people. When everything goes well, they know how to maintain the ambiance and the open culture, but at the same time, they are prepared to continuously learn from the real figures. This confrontation with the hard facts helps them strengthen their customer focus, to understand and improve the business model and to monitor their innovation projects accurately.
- Continuously learning from the hard figures also filters through to several of the other disciplines: customer focus, understanding the business model and therefore the strategy, knowing where to develop innovations, monitoring innovation projects well and using this to make responsible decisions about whether to continue or to bring projects to a close.

Thus a number of core disciplines could emerge as candidates for reducing the model. A very old principle in science and philosophy is Occam's razor, which states that you should try to keep a theory or a model as simple as possible. Everything that is not strictly essential should be eliminated. So, is it possible to use Occam's razor to reduce the ten disciplines to fewer? We do not think that this is possible. Obviously, if several core disciplines are being well met, it is *possible* that the others are covered, too. The point is, however, that this is not necessarily the case, even in more successful innovating organizations. The advantage of the ten disciplines is that they are concrete and discrete and relatively easy to monitor. Part of the learning culture is working with real figures and for this it is necessary not to lump everything together.

If we were only concerned with a few general core disciplines, then our account would offer less concrete support as it would only open doors a little wider. Nowadays, every organization has a strategy, but it is not always based on knowledge of its precise strengths and business model. Moreover, is there a direct link between this strategy and working continuously on innovation? How many organizations work systematically on continuous learning and incremental innovation? How many actually put customer focus *and* social orientation centre stage? From our research, we have learned that it is only to the extent that all these concrete disciplines are discerned and developed that the organization can open the way to successful, repeated innovation. Therefore, those disciplines that are not so readily considered as core are more easily neglected. In addition, the business people in the advisory committee of our study tended to say that all of the disciplines were covered in their organization. When we started to question them about each of these separately, the image however became rapidly more differentiated. It appeared that probably a lot still had to be done. In analogy with the Olympic decathlon, the fastest progress is then realized by concentrating on one's weakest points in the most precise way possible.

The decathlon can also help to determine how well your organization scores in comparison with your competitors. When it comes to recruiting personnel, are you at the top of the list for graduates and people who wish to take a new step in their career? Do you know a lot of people at networking events and do they know you? Do you work together with other companies or knowledge institutes in challenging projects? Are you more advanced in this respect than your most interesting competitors? What do you know about the satisfaction levels of your customers? What do you know about societal developments which will possibly change their preferences? Which role do you play in changing customer preferences in your realm?

To illustrate how this can be done, let us first take a look at the overview table in the following section, in which all cases are scored on the basis of the disciplines.

8.4   THE SCORES OF THE ORGANIZATIONS IN OUR STUDY

The total scores for our cases are presented in Table 8.1. Not surprisingly, the majority of the scores are high or very high, as we selected organizations with repeated innovative success. However, these organizations had their relative weaknesses as well. We didn't find a champion with the maximum decathlon score.

Just like consumer organizations comparing different products, we worked with a simple system of crosses: good (+), very good (++) and almost no further improvement possible (+++). To be sure, these are relatively subjective scores. The scores are less unambiguous than in a real decathlon, where the tape measure and the stopwatch serve as accurate judges. With the innovation decathlon, it is much closer to judging an all-around gymnastics competition. As our scores are not being determined using exact measurements, the ranking only provides a relative indication. The competitive dynamic places increased pressure on innovation and on certain disciplines in several sectors, which is comparable to natural aptitude in sport; the starting conditions are not exactly the same for anyone. We have used ordinal ranking in the table, as this helps us to make certain conclusions clearer.

Table 8.1 Scores of our twenty cases on the ten innovation disciplines

	1. strategy and innovation	2. societal orientation	3. customer orientation	4. ambition and daring	5. incremental innovation	6. learning from real figures	7. the best people	8. ambiance of open culture	9. strong networks	10. focus and commitment
ASML	+++	++	+++	+++	+++	+++	+++	++	+++	+++
Philips	+++	+++	+++	++	+++	+++	+++	++	+++	++
Stage Entertainment	+++	+++	+++	+++	+++	+++	++	+	++	+++
HEMA	+++	+++	+++	++	+++	++	++	++	++	+++
DSM	+++	++	++	++	+++	+++	++	++	+++	+++
MEXX	+++	+++	+++	++	+++	+++	++	++	++	++
Albert Heijn	++	+++	+++	++	++	+++	++	+	+++	+++
KesselsKramer	+++	+++	++	+++	+	+	+++	+++	++	+++
Efteling	+++	++	++	++	+++	++	++	+++	+	+++
Intervet	+++	+	+++	++	++	+++	++	++	++	+++
Shell	+++	+++	+	++	++	++	+++	++	++	+++
Unilever	+++	+++	++	+	+++	++	+++	++	++	++
Koning & Hartman	++	++	+++	++	+++	++	++	++	++	++
Effectory	++	+	+++	+	+++	++	++	++	++	++
Siemens NL	+	++	+++	++	++	++	++	++	++	++
Ten Cate	++	++	++	++	++	++	++	++	++	++
Groninger Museum	++	++	++	++	++	+	++	++	++	++
Kunsthal	++	++	++	++	+	++	++	++	++	++
Achmea	++	++	++	++	+	++	++	+	+	++
Rabobank	++	++	++	+	++	++	++	+	++	+

A few of these organizations were not glad to appear relatively low down in this table, but we could reiterate our Olympic metaphor. There is no shame in being the last in an Olympic final. In addition, no organization had a minus symbol, which we expect quite a few other organizations to have.

Looking at Table 8.1, we can observe that the companies listed in the black boxes—organizations with a longer tradition of innovation and at least a medium-sized innovation department—score on average higher than organizations listed in the white boxes. This definitely applies to the manufacturing companies, where separately organized innovation departments have existed since the first generations of technology management. Outside the industrial sector, 'black box' companies with their own substantial innovation departments also score relatively high. It seems that on this point, *no* structural difference exists between a company with a technical focus and one with a nontechnical focus. ASML (supplier to the microchips industry) and Stage Entertainment (musical industry), Philips (consumer electronics and medical equipment) and HEMA (retail) all operate in different environments, but we see little difference in repeated innovation success, and where differences emerge, they are not significant but rather like a photo finish.

In Table 8.1, we have made a split between two groups: the leading gold companies, and a second silver group which had a total score at a somewhat lower level. The leading group is characterized by outspoken and numerically based ambitions, such as with ASML and Stage Entertainment who go for growth and market share. Again, we can imagine that people, who know a certain company to be a front-runner in innovation, will be surprised to see this organization in the second group. For starters, we repeat here that all these companies are finalists.

Let us, for example, take a look at the last in our list. Rabobank has often been a trendsetter in the financial sector. It was also only weakly hurt by the recent financial crisis. In the interviews we had with its managers, it was stated that they did not develop products that had no added value for their customers, even when these products were expected to be profitable for the bank.[10] Rabobank's initiatives surely signal ambition and daring and also a long-term societal orientation. That is why the score for these components is also high, but compared with the other finalists, not the top-ranking score. With respect to societal orientation, Shell, for instance, goes much further with its scenarios and HEMA with its trend watchers. In terms of ambition and daring, ASML really did more with extending its share in the world market from 65% to 70% and daring to take on two parallel development lines leading to a €100 million write-off in an innovation project before it is even ready for production. This final point is definitely on a world-class level.

To be honest, we were also surprised when studying our cases. We had obviously looked for innovation champions from a wide range of sectors, but we had not expected that the innovation routines at musical firm Stage Entertainment and department store chain HEMA were so deeply rooted. This leads us to the conclusion that the exclusive association of the topic of innovation with the manufacturing domain is really a thing of the past or, even better, must be relegated to the past, as the majority of the books and reports that we see still place the emphasis on manufacturing industries when it comes to this point.

Attention to innovation and management of innovation outside the manufacturing sectors is a relatively recent phenomenon. Innovation networks now exist in many organizations with specially appointed innovation managers, but quite a few have a relatively recent origin. We therefore see the fact that service companies are now doing well in the realm of innovation, despite their short tradition, as an important finding from our study. It shows that notable results can be achieved quickly with a sharp innovation focus and a strong anchoring in organizational routines.

However, the opposite is also true: results from the past are no guarantee for the future, even when we may expect that routines are more deeply rooted than, for instance, the leadership style of one CEO.

8.5 CO-EVOLVING FIRMS WITH A STRONG INNOVATIVE FOCUS

The metaphor of the decathlon is widely applicable, but obviously the exact same decathlon is not held everywhere. In many respects, each sector has its own game rules. Is emphasis placed on technical innovation or on the non-technical aspects? Does it concern a business-to-business (B2B) or business-to-consumers (B2C) market? Is there an emphasis on product or process innovation or is it mainly concerned with transactional innovation or combinations of these? Is the market global, national or rather more local? These are all relevant distinctions if you are competing within your sector, but the striking fact is that they really do not suffice if we are looking for the rules of repeated innovation success. From the comments we received on our book on innovation routines (Jacobs & Snijders 2008), it emerged that this conclusion is anything but obvious. Do the same rules for repeated innovation success really apply everywhere?

Not completely, of course. Let us take the simplest example: we can imagine that in B2B sectors—those that are aligned to business customers—the pressure on discipline 2, societal orientation, is less extensive. This can also be deduced from several of the scores in Table 8.1. But be careful on this point. If you innovate, do not just focus on your direct customer; also focus on your customer's customer. Companies that make yarn and material and supply to the clothing industry also follow the fashion trends or try to influence them. A company such as Philips has realized to its great cost that it can better concern itself relatively more with lifestyles than with technologies. The lesson is therefore rather that the dynamic and competitive pressure in a specific sector increases the pressure to pay relatively more attention to certain disciplines. Ultimately, they are all important to the continued success of innovation.

More innovative companies are strongly aware of this, which allows them to be inspired by what is happening in other sectors. This sometimes leads to surprising collaborations. Therefore, we want to encourage people not to revert to the reaction of 'it may be true elsewhere, but not with us.' Competitors need to keep an eye on each other, but they must also allow themselves to be inspired by innovative practices elsewhere.

So, when you are in the field where you compete on innovation, where innovation is strategically necessary to survive and grow (discipline 1), then the first thing to do is working on discipline 6: how good are you at learning from real figures? That is what we have to do now for all disciplines: look very critically at the performance of your organization and that of your close competitors. Three pluses mean world class, so only fill this in when you are sure you're in the top of the global league. Even one plus means *really* good, not just good. When we try to score some organizations, we really have the impression that even with a minus sign we would be too positive already! Look, for example, at customer focus. How seriously are organizations taking their customer needs, really? When you are recruiting personnel, are you sure you are not afraid of smart, creative or critical people? On the positive side, appreciate real innovativeness when it is present, too—for example, in the realm of continuous improvement. Identify your most important and inspiring competitors as well and try to score them in order to compare and learn. Of course, we are not talking about imitative benchmarking but about innovation. Copying is only possible when you're not first. Learning from competitors is not bad, particularly when these outperform your organization, but the challenge is to overtake them eventually with your creativity and understanding of markets—and therefore society. To summarize, do not try to look for reasons for not taking part in the decathlon. In doing so, you would only be helping your competitors.

8.6   INNOVATION SQUARED

A conclusion by many authors, including myself, is that management, and primarily management of innovation, is increasingly about dealing with paradoxes, where managers have to foster both sides of the paradox at the same time (Jacobs 2010: 197–213). In this chapter, the paradoxes of exploration and exploitation, and of course of innovation and routine, are key. In our study on successful innovation routines, Hendrik Snijders and I found a few other paradoxes which led to what we called 'Janus truths' (see Figure 8.3 for one of these): apparently opposing theses which are both true:

- *Do not make it too difficult.* Reap low-hanging fruit in the realm of incremental innovations. *Do not make it too easy.* From time to time, more radical innovations are necessary (related to discipline 5 of the innovation decathlon).
- *Concentrate on your core competences.* Most innovation builds on your actual strategic profile. *Concentrate on the edges of your competencies.* Most interesting developments happen not in your core, but on the edges of your organization. This reminds one of the evolutionary law of requisite variety: without variation, there is no evolution (related to discipline 1).
- *Be myopic.* Look at your actual customer needs quite closely. *Be farsighted.* Look ahead of your actual customer needs (related to the disciplines 2 and 3).

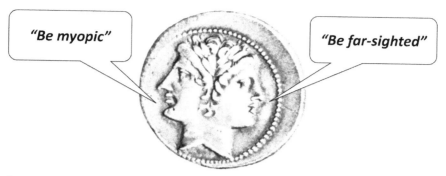

Figure 8.3 One of the Janus truths of successful innovation routines

- *Do not give up too rapidly,* but when it is really proving to fail, pull the plug out: *Don't be a hopeless stalker* (discipline 10).
- *Be disciplined. Cherish chaos* (the main paradox of professional bureaucracies).

There are more paradoxes like these. A decade ago, together with another colleague, I found out that quite a few companies are able to combine opposite elements of paradoxes when organizing innovative activities, for instance, when combining centralization *and* decentralization, globalization *and* local responsiveness, competition *and* cooperation, technology push *and* market pull (Jacobs & Waalkens 2001: 31–48, 82). Therefore, firms are not simply organizing innovation; increasingly, they do it in innovative ways. That's why we called it 'innovation²' ('innovation squared').[11]

Pharmaceutical firms, for example, to some extent have large R&D programmes which are managed in a traditional, programmed way, but at the same time, they have been organizing competing internal R&D labs to foster rivalry. In other fields, they cooperate with competitors or outsource activities. In addition, corporate venturing has become an important tool to stimulate creativity, innovation and related entrepreneurship and commitment. In the Netherlands, DSM and Shell probably have been the most active in this field. Shell, for example, set up its GameChanger initiative in 1996. Employees are invited to submit innovative proposals which, after a short presentation by and a discussion with the originator, are assessed by a small panel. A possible first evaluation is then followed by a somewhat more extensive elaboration of the idea and based on this a possible further increasing commitment. This approach has already led to a substantial amount of important new projects within Shell (Jacobs & Waalkens 2001: 71–78; Jacobs & Snijders 2008: 84).

I suspect that such practices are still more the exception than the rule. But as appears from increasing competition in more and more sectors, including the creative industries themselves, creativity becomes an ever-more important factor in this competition—as will be further clarified in the Bonus Track. When companies increasingly have the same standardized technologies at their disposal, they have to make the difference by innovative approaches in other fields. As a consequence, creativity becomes a kind of necessary hygiene factor all firms have to deploy to some extent.

I can imagine that some readers may see a contradiction or at least a paradox in the main logic of this book. I have been describing Darwinian evolution as a mainly blind process and now I am predicting innovative success. I certainly do not want to fall in the trap of voluntaristic approaches. People like to believe that when they try hard enough, they will succeed: 'Where there's a will, there's a way.' As in my book on strategic management (Jacobs 2010), I follow a more modest logic. Try to map your selection environment as closely as possible and continuously learn by doing. When you're not powerful, you have to be smart. Following such logic in this and the preceding chapters, I have provided a variety of clues as to how selection processes of that kind may be influenced, even when no final guarantees for success were given. This logic is more dialectical than voluntaristic, even when from a very long time perspective there is some reason for hope. As we saw in Chapter 4, for millions of years evolution has been a totally blind system in which new species continuously emerged that mostly disappeared again after some time. Through this process, gradually a few—really not many—more flexible species came into being. Out of these, modern humans developed, who after more than one hundred thousand years learned to learn ever more rapidly. Developments are taking place more and more swiftly. As a species, we are now able to influence our selection environment to quite some extent. Even when the success of innovations has remained mostly a blind system, we gradually learn to improve the success ratio of innovations, too. This is the optimistic side of the dialectics in this book. When voluntarism is not rooted in just a naive belief in 'where there's a will, there's a way,' but in the will to learn and improve continuously, the chances for success are greatly improved.[12]

9   A Never-Ending Dance

We have now come to the end of the systematic exposition of my argument in this book. In the introduction, I promised to provide an analytical basis for the idea of productive creativity. Let me conclude by referring again to the main theses and building blocks of this book:

1 It is important to make a clear distinction between technical and non-technical aspects of innovation. The technical aspects of innovations mainly relate to relative advantage that to a large extent can be objectified and measured by machines. With the nontechnical aspects, we address the relative compatibility of innovations with the (continuously changing) norms and values in society, and thus culture. Moreover, technical aspects are also subject to changing values as our opinions about the importance of certain technical aspects change over time.

2 As a rule, authors who do not make this distinction between technical and nontechnical aspects have neglected or at least underestimated the cultural side of innovation and, by doing this, hampered their success potential. Moreover, as a consequence, innovations in the field of services—including experiences and transformations—as well as industrial design, fashion and content, have been neglected to a very large extent. Without the multitude of mainly incremental innovations in these fields, economic life would come to a standstill.

3 It is true that especially in the realm of technological research, there is a danger of underinvestment because early followers may profit from the investment by the original pioneers without paying for this. For this reason, government subsidies to these pioneers have been legitimized by this possible market failure. However, the consequence of this logic has been that in the discourse of innovation policies the emphasis has always been on technology, leading to a neglect of the cultural aspects. This, in turn, endangers the success of private and public investments in innovation. Moreover, overconcentration on the technical aspects of innovation, and investments in research and

development—which to a very large extent are related to these—has led to an underestimation of overall innovativeness in the economy.[1]

4 Discussion about what constitutes real innovation is useless and hampers attention for incremental innovations and related learning that constitute the overwhelming majority of all innovations. For this reason, I have defined innovation as 'something new which is realized, hopefully with an added value.' Only from time to time do sudden radical innovations take place in which new concepts or new technological findings play a role. Many innovations which we now see as radical were the result of a succession of smaller, incremental innovations.

5 The technical aspects of innovations may be more important in the early stages of the life cycle of new product categories, especially when these are based on new technological opportunities. The more a product category is technologically standardized, the more important the cultural value side of the products within the category becomes, including the brands under which they are marketed.

6 The successful selection of innovations is a necessary element of the survival of organizations. Therefore, when we look at the economy from a Darwinian perspective, it is not enough to look at the routines of organizations—which has been largely the case in evolutionary economics. It is also necessary to consider innovations, as well as the products and production and transaction processes to which they lead, as units of selection as well.

7 Fitness of innovations in economic environments can best be defined as added value to various kinds of selectors in their relevant selection system. Value entails a quantitative and qualitative evaluation related to a culturally determined set of preferences. Some of these preferences are translated into explicitly ratified selection criteria, whereas others remain more tacit—especially when they are rooted in instincts which came into being through long evolutionary processes.

8 Creating economic value through innovation always entails at least a marginal reconfiguration of cultural norms and values leading to a reconfiguration of customer preferences. The more radical an innovation is, the greater its cognitive distance from the prevailing cultural value system of selection. The most radical innovations change not only the relative importance of preferences but also the selection system itself, if not the whole world.

9 Before innovations can be externally tested, they are the object of internal selection within organizations. Selection of an innovation, external to the place where it originated, takes place through market selection and external hierarchical selection but usually in hybrid combinations of these—all of them with their own criteria of success or fitness, or value. When being introduced in a market, innovations may also be the object of preselection, for example, by buyers for

supermarkets and large retail chains or by gatekeepers in the media. Moreover, experts, opinion leaders and peers influence selection to a large extent and in this way contribute to the cultural creation—or denial, if not destruction—of economic value. Increasingly, these actors are rewarded for this.

10 Innovation does not take place in isolation but is an element in a co-evolutionary system in which a multitude of firm innovations and social changes interact. In this co-evolutionary system, the importance of innovation initiated by consumers is growing. Firms increasingly have taken notice of this latter development and are integrating it into their business models.

11 It is useful to map the complexity of interaction between the different selection systems of industries in order to concentrate strategic and tactical endeavours on the most important links within these.

12 The reconfiguration of cultural norms and values is a social deconstruction and reconstruction process through never-ending conversations and changing practices that nobody controls—to the frustration of many innovators and marketers. Therefore, an important capability of innovators lies in a strong societal orientation and the continuous translation of others' interests and perspectives into their own innovation endeavours. Such translation processes are partly rational and strategic but to a large extent remain tacit exchange processes.

13 'Co-evolution' not only is a concept which helps to map and understand innovation processes but also continuously be a focus of attention for innovators. Co-evolution is not only about passively following social trends; it is about understanding these in order to be inspired by them to be able to surprise customers with one's innovations. Innovation is therefore like a dance, a co-evolving interplay between leading and following. Some organizations with strong innovation routines—summarized in the ten disciplines of the innovation decathlon in the previous chapter—are better equipped for this never-ending dance marathon than others.

Bonus Track
Creativity and the Economy—A Somewhat Uneasy Relationship

In this chapter, the importance of creativity as a competitive factor is critically reviewed based on different studies. First, it is stated that creativity doesn't have the same importance in different industries. In most cases, pure creativity is not an asset. It has to be combined creatively with accepted professional and scientific insights and with a sense of purpose and discipline in order to lead to what could be called 'productive creativity.' The extent to which the role of creativity in the economy is increasing is assessed on the basis of different approaches, one of which is totally new. To a large extent, this analysis is based on data for the Dutch economy which is similar to other countries in Northwest Europe. For the new approach I present in Section 8, unfortunately, no comparable data exist for other countries. From this assessment, it becomes apparent that the role of creativity in the economy is indeed increasing, but not in an unequivocal way. Dealing with creativity certainly is a new example of dealing with uneasy paradoxes. At the end of this chapter, the possible role of government in this respect is discussed.

1 INTRODUCTION: A SOMEWHAT UNEASY CASE

Since the publication of Richard Florida's *The Rise of the Creative Class* (Florida 2002), the issue of the creative economy has been discussed intensively. Many countries published policy statements in the field (e.g., Leadbeater 2004), the Flemish ministry of Economic Affairs launched the programme Flanders D.C. (District of Creativity) and its Dutch counterpart devoted its 2005 Innovation Lecture to the theme of 'Competing with Creativity.' The European Union declared 2009 the official European Year of

This essay is an updated and extended version of a paper commissioned by the Dutch Ministry of Economic Affairs in preparation of the Innovation Lecture 2005 'Compete with Creativity.' I thank Theo Postma and Andreas Stockert for comments on that first version. An earlier updated version was published in Dutch in *Holland Management Review*, 107, May–June 2006.

Creativity and Innovation, and different policy documents and manifestos were published related to this. These have been followed by a lot of initiatives which are still going on. So does everybody now agree that creativity is economically relevant? At least a lot of lip service is given to this idea. Creativity—just like innovation—is important for the economy, as it is important for just about everything, isn't it? In this contribution, I try to avoid this trap of stating the obvious, as the issue is surrounded by more paradoxes than many would probably think.

To make this chapter somewhat less comfortable, let me start by looking at a somewhat uneasy case, which shows that creativity doesn't come straightforwardly and is never totally acquired or secured. Endemol, the television producer which has often been hailed as *the* pioneer of the Dutch creative entertainment business, has been in a kind of creativity crisis for some years. Since *Big Brother* in 1999, it took a long time before it scored another major hit, *Deal or No Deal*. Partly as a result of this, at some moment it had to lay off half its workforce. Moreover, as a consequence of the takeover in 2007 by the media groups of Berlusconi and founder John de Mol, it was loaded with a lot of debt (in 2011, estimated at more than $4.1 billion), which it had difficulties repaying. Endemol certainly has been as much a case of business model innovation[1] as of innovation in the realm of its products.

Looking at Endemol's history, even *Big Brother* wasn't an easy success. For years, the firm searched for a successor to its 1995 hit *All You Need Is Love*. On the positive side—not for Endemol however—we can observe that in 1994, after the merger of Joop van den Ende TV and John de Mol Produkties, Endemol was a kind of a monopolist, whereas nowadays in the Netherlands there are about three hundred television production companies. The Endemol case is even more complex than that. Many of the observers attribute Endemol's creative problems to the fact that its founders, of whom van den Ende left in 1998 taking the live entertainment department of the firm with him,[2] surrounded themselves too much with yes-people—quite creative, isn't it? Nobody will deny that Endemol has played an important role in the development of the Dutch creative economy, but this case already highlights some of the paradoxes related to the coupling of creativity with economy, to which I will come later on.

Another part of the problem is that Endemol's most important customers in the broadcasting industry have become thriftier. They want to get more products for the same amount of money, partly because in this industry, competition has increased as well (De Bruijn 2005).

Industrial economists will recognize this last observation as a typical feature of an industry becoming more mature after an initial phase of rapid growth with little competition. Rapidly growing industries with relatively high profit margins always attract newcomers, and as a consequence, in the next phase competition increases, productivity is enhanced and profit margins get thinner.

Therefore, this case already highlights a few issues I want to address in this chapter:

- The importance of creativity and the growth of creative industries in advanced economies (Sections 2, 4 and 5)
- The contribution of creativity to economic growth, innovation and productivity in general, for which I will compare different statistical data, mainly from the United States and the Netherlands, which help to form an opinion about other advanced economies as well (Sections 3 and 6–8)
- The (not always creative) tension between exploration, exploitation and execution—for example, the relation between innovative or improvising professionals on the one hand and routine professionals on the other (Section 9)
- Based on these, a few recommendations in the realm of public policies, partly relating to education and the relationship between universities and business (Section 10)

But let us first deal with the question of what creativity is.

2   WHAT IS CREATIVITY, AND HOW IS IT DIFFERENT FROM INNOVATION?

Taken literally, creativity is the ability to create, but mostly we understand it as the ability to see issues or situations in a novel way. In this sense, the relation to inventing (and by extension, to innovation) is obvious. Edward de Bono therefore understands creativity as breaking through accepted truths or patterns. As a consequence, Richard Florida (2002: 31) also relates it to self-confidence, the ability to take risks and the subversive departure from the conformist ethos of the past. At the same time, we should not forget that invention and innovation require at least as much intelligence, accepted knowledge and purposive search as this creative art of seeing something in a totally new light.

Many people view creativity as elusive or intangible, driven by luck. To a large extent, this is correct. But isn't it also true that luck helps those who are most prepared? And who are these persons? They are especially the more curious, inquisitive people with *a broad interest,* as it is recognized that creativity is mostly stimulated by the combinations or spillovers of ideas and insights *between totally different fields.* De Bono (1992: 61–62) therefore identifies creativity with lateral thinking, thinking which—just like humour—'moves sideways across patterns' and shifts between perspectives in an unexpected way. Joseph Schumpeter saw innovation mostly as the art to establish 'new combinations,' Einstein summarized his own scientific work as 'combinatory play' (Florida 2002: 31). In organizational science, the important role of 'boundary spanners' has been recognized for a long time (Daft 2004: 145, 414). These are the people who establish and maintain the key links with the external environment or just with other departments and functions within their own organization.

Moreover, creativity is not always an asset. As we will see in Section 6, sometimes we have to deal with interpretative uncertainty, which means that we don't know to what extent the situation asks for a totally new approach. Sometimes, old habits work; sometimes they do not. As a result, creativity may also destroy value. Artists may produce rubbish, business consultants may provide destructive advices (Pinault 2000), scientists may spend time on worthless papers, policemen may increase tensions in a neighbourhood by just saying or doing what they shouldn't and advertising agencies may be so creative that their campaigns fail completely (Rothenberg 1994). Therefore, creativity is not a virtue in itself. It has to be combined with professionalism and a sense of purpose in which—where possible and necessary—professional or scientific insights are integrated. But, of course, in many cases we don't know to what extent this is necessary.

Concluding, creativity is about breaking through existing patterns and establishing new combinations. This happens at the level of individual people, of teams and of whole organizations. It is a necessary but not sufficient condition for invention and innovation. It requires at least some tolerance for exceptional or even subversive people and ideas (Sutton 2001) and for living with contradictions and ambiguities. In this way, it is related to a democratic and tolerant culture.[3] Of course, one will also find creative people in oppressive regimes, but the chance that they will contribute to innovation will probably be restricted. I will come back to this at the end of this contribution.

3   THE RAPID GROWTH OF CREATIVE INDUSTRIES

When we talk about the economic relevance of creativity for the economy, we can distinguish between three levels:

- *The micro level.* Innovating within organizations, which in this chapter, I take for granted—as it was the main theme of the rest of this book
- *The meso level.* The importance of creative sectors
- *The meso-macro level.* The importance of creativity in all industries, but not to the same degree, which is the basis for my presentation of a new, fuzzy approach in order to assess the overall importance of creativity in the economy

The easiest way to start this discussion is beginning with the meso level because it seems easiest to measure. When we talk about concrete, recognizable creative industries, their value added and employment can be calculated relatively easily. Many authors writing about innovation have talked about the economic relevance of creativity before. It was, however, Richard Florida who really put creativity on the agenda with his book *The Rise of the Creative Class*. According to Florida, in 2010 no less than forty-one million Americans, 32.6% of all employed, belonged to this class. This contrasts with—already—12% of the workforce in 1800, 16% in 1960 and 24% in 1980 (Florida 2012: 45–46). Around the turn of the century, the United Nations estimated that creative and cultural industries were growing at 10% a year, more than twice the rate of the whole world economy (Leadbeater 2004: 9). It was, however, not clear which definition of creative industries was used for this assessment. In general, we can say that the narrower these industries are defined, the more rapid growth can be observed.

Even when the recent crisis unemployment affected creative jobs, on balance between 2000 and 2010 in the United States, 2.8 million creative jobs were added, whereas the working class lost 6.2 million positions. Some creative industries experienced very large job losses: from 2008 to 2010, news analysts and reporters lost 22.9%, musicians and singers lost 16.9%, photographers lost 16.5% and editors lost 4.9%. However, some professions still experienced tremendous growth: art directors gained 45%, graphic designers gained 45% and audio and video technicians gained 40%. At its top in 2009, unemployment rose to 4.4% in the creative class, compared with 9% for the service class and 15.2% for the working class (Florida 2012: 49–54).

In the Netherlands, Paul Rutten's definition of creative industries (Rutten et al. 2004) has been mostly used for drawing up statistics. These industries are then the amalgamation of:

- the arts, including creative arts, museums, art galleries and theatres;
- media and entertainment, including publishers, news gathering, music companies, broadcasting, TV and film production, photography and cinemas;
- creative professional services, including advertising, fashion and interior design, architects and technical design, and town and country planning.

According to the latest calculation based on this classification, in 2011 in the Netherlands some 280,000 people worked in creative industries. From Table 1 (based on Rutten et al. 2012: 25–27), it emerges that employment growth in creative sectors in the last decade has been about three times as fast as in the whole economy. Design especially has grown tremendously.

According to KEA, an international consultancy specialized in creative industries, in Europe (EU 25), 5.89 million people worked in these sectors in 2004 (nearly defined in the same way as Rutten, excluding related manufacturing and trade, but including cultural tourism).[4] This is about 3.1% of total EU employment. Defined in this way, creative employment in the

Table 1 Jobs in Dutch creative industries (2011)

	jobs	% of Dutch employment	% growth/year (2000–2011)
arts and cultural heritage	98,874	1.23	4.8
media and entertainment	89,296	1.11	0.8
creative professional services	92,280	1.14	3.8
■ communication and information	66,080	0.82	1.9
■ design (including fashion and architecture)	26,200	0.32	12.7
total creative industries	280,450	3.48	3.0
total Dutch economy	8,065,110	100	0.9

Netherlands in 2004 did amount to 4.2% of the total, the highest percentage in Europe (KEA 2006: 73–82). Creative sectors in 2003 contributed 2.6% to European gross domestic product (GDP),[5] more than, for example, the food and beverages industry (1.9%), the chemical industry (2.3%) and even twice as much as the car industry. Between 1999 and 2003, creative industries grew by 19.7%, compared with 17.5% for the whole economy (KEA 2007: 6, 61–69).

4 MESO-MACRO: FROM CREATIVE INDUSTRIES TO A CREATIVE ECONOMY

As can be observed, the collection of sectors I just mentioned already lacks important creative *functions* like those in the field of science or research and development.

Therefore, a simple way to approach the issue of creativity and the economy is to work with a range of expanding concentric sets, as we can see from Figure 1.

- At the core, there are a few industries for which the creation of innovation (including content) is the work itself: the arts, the fields of scientific and technological research, the media, gaming, photography, town and country planning, amounting to most of the sectors in Rutten's first two categories and a few of his latter category, plus research in its different forms.
- Beside this, there is an (increasing) number of industries for which the products must have a creative design to a large extent: fashion, furniture, cars, architecture, entertainment parks, but also mobile telephones,

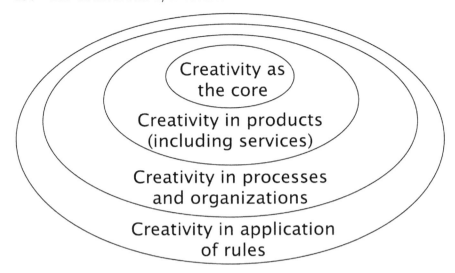

Figure 1   Creativity in the economy

kitchen tools, software programmes, machine tools, larger machines (including medical), the interior of shops and packaging. The more technology is standardized in a certain area and therefore *not* a differentiating factor between firms, the more these firms have to make the difference with products with a special look and feel. Without this, economic growth would slow down to the level of replacement of worn-out products. As a consequence of product differentiation, many people in the Netherlands now own two or even three bicycles where before they had only one! But to be sure, when we talk about design, as a rule not only the outside appearance but also functional design (including the design of parts and, in this way, design for manufacturing), ease of use and related elements like software design should be included.[6] In this way, design also plays an important role in productivity growth, not only at the level of the producers, but also at that of their customers!

- Beside this, in all kinds of sectors of the economy, people increasingly have to think about new ideas, new ways of organizing and new concepts. It is probably obvious that there is a direct link between creativity and innovation in its many forms. As said in Section 2, creativity is a necessary but not sufficient condition for invention and innovation. I will come back to this in Section 7.
- Finally, also in relatively basic or traditional jobs (teachers, health workers, police, social workers), employees increasingly have to think about the creative adaptation of rules to a certain situation. In recent years, awareness has grown about the important role these professionals play in dealing with social tensions between people from different backgrounds or religions. The behaviour of these professionals may

make the difference between increasing these tensions and a better mutual understanding and respect.

Looking at these concentric sets, we could say that the inner ones are more about product innovation in different ways—innovations in content, products, technologies, experiences, concepts and styles—and the outer ones more about innovations in production and transaction processes, in organizing, or just intelligent approaches in general. However, we also saw that intelligent product design plays a role in productivity growth and therefore process innovation as well.

Another way of addressing the issue is understanding that more functions boil down to symbolic-analytical work: problem identifying and solving activities which require the manipulation of symbols, data, words and oral and visual representations. Robert Reich (1991: 177–180) in this realm enumerates, beside creative jobs like the ones just mentioned by Rutten and others, functions like research scientists, all kinds of engineers and consultants, public relations executives, investment bankers, headhunters, system analysts, lawyers, real estate developers, 'a few creative accountants' 'and even university professors'! All these functions together grew from about 8% of American workers in 1950 to 20% in 1990. As a rule, these functions demand a high level of education, although Reich concedes that functions at lower levels—like secretaries or salespeople—require similar kinds of symbolic-analytical skills. Personally I would add quite a few jobs in the field of personal services, where applying rules *in an intelligent way* requires the same kind of skills and the capability of dealing with ambiguous situations: think of social workers, teachers at all levels of education, police officers, ticket collectors in public transport.

In a not totally similar vein, Florida divides his creative class into two groups. Around the turn of the century, fifteen million Americans (12% of the workforce) composed the 'Super-Creative Core,' whereas twenty-three million (18%) were labelled as 'creative professionals.' The core creatives are the most innovative. They work in the field of 'science and engineering, architecture and design, education, arts, music and entertainment,' and create new ideas, technologies or forms of content. The other creative professionals engage in complex problem solving that involves a great deal of independent judgement and requires high levels of education or human capital. 'Both groups share a common creative ethos that values creativity, individuality, difference and merit' (Florida 2002: 8–9). Interesting to notice is the fact that the supercreative core earns less on average than the creative class as a whole: in 1999 only $20.54 per hour compared with $23.44 for the whole creative class (Florida 2002: 77). In the new edition of his book, Florida does not mention average income for these broad subcategories, but from the data for different professions, it emerges that creative professionals are still better paid. It is striking, however, that in 2010 even the lowest paid creative categories earn much more than working- or service-class people: arts, design, entertainment, sports and media ($52,290); education, training and library ($50,440); working class ($36,991); service class ($29,188) (Florida 2012: 42). Therefore, creation (exploration) is still valued less economically than exploitation and execution. The economy doesn't yet appear to be convinced of the value of the purest form of creativity that much! It could, of course, be the case that so many people desperately want to work in creative functions that oversupply leads to a relatively lower remuneration.

5   CREATIVITY IN MANUFACTURING AND SERVICES

Florida's definition of the creative class is very broad. Despite this, people in Florida's two remaining classes—the traditional working class and the service class—also increasingly have to work more creatively, at least in the way Florida's second category of creative professionals does. I already mentioned dealing intelligently with ambiguity in personal services. Moreover, Florida talks also about creative factories, like the ones pioneered by Toyota and Matsushita, 'where factory workers contribute their ideas and intellectual talent as well as their physical labor.' In the first edition of his book he also quoted Akio Morita, founder and former chairman of Sony who once said, 'A company will get nowhere if all the thinking is left to management.' In addition, the contributions of specialized subcontractors within these manufacturing networks may not be neglected (Florida 2002: 52–53; 2012: 10, 32–33, 48).

A similar observation can be made about service workers. Florida seems to have the lowest esteem for this group. In the first edition of his book, he saw this service class—in the United States now about 47% of the workforce—mostly as 'a growing pool of low-end service workers to take care of them [i.e., the Creative Class] and do their chores'! Think of food-service workers, janitors and groundskeepers, personal care attendants, secretaries and clerical workers and security guards, as well as computer support specialists and systems analysts (Florida 2002: 71). Of course, as in factories, there is a lot of repetitive work in this realm, but many service workers have a lot of interpretative work to do as well. The fastest growing service functions are nowadays personal care aids and home health aids. As a consequence, service jobs also have to be 'creatified' ever more (Florida 2012: 46–47, 388). From other literature, it appears to what extent this development is already taking place. It has, for example, been recognized for a long time that the strength of the low-cost Southwest Airlines—the only profitable US airline for a long time, even during crises—has been found in the good atmosphere, creativity and empowerment of its employees, from the lowest to the highest levels of that organization. Of course, there is a lot of standardization implied in this, which leads to the highest levels of productivity in this industry. However, an important part of the deal has been Southwest's commitment to never dismiss employees. Therefore, the employees know that with their creativity they are not rationalizing away their own jobs (Parks & Noer 1993; Peters 1994: 164–166). I dare say that when we talk about competing with creativity, these kinds of employee contributions are essential. Not tapping into this creativity brings the company to a lower level of competitiveness, as Akio Morita recognized.

Another way in which there is more creativity in the service industries than Florida realizes is related to the development of the experience economy. Think for example of the continuous innovation necessary in entertainment businesses like amusement parks, shopping centres or casinos. People who have ever experienced places like Las Vegas[7]—about which Florida (2002: 235; 2012: 204) doesn't have a high opinion either—will probably understand this. Here it appears that Florida, who has a background in the economic analysis of technological innovation, has kept a kind of moral vision on what real or unreal innovation is, a vision one encounters more in engineering milieus. As a rule, this kind of moral-technical evaluation of (un)real innovation has, however, hampered the understanding of innovation and its promotion. Of course, one can have moral judgements about innovations in fields such as armaments, crime, tax evasion, child pornography or aggressive gaming—in other words, all industries, including the creative ones, are concerned.

Therefore, the fact that service workers on average receive the lowest wages does not alter the fact that in their jobs a lot of creativity may be involved. People who understood this probably better than Florida are Joseph Pine and James Gilmore, who coined the term 'experience economy.' These authors, who before introduced the concept of 'mass customization,' make a further subdivision within the service industries between relatively simple services, experiences and transformations (Pine & Gilmore 1999: 166).[8] Economic activities become less tangible, but as a rule their added value increases. A normal product or service may be consumed and forgotten rapidly, but a nicely designed product is cherished, gets everybody's attention and may command a higher price. A special experience is not easily forgotten, whereas with what Pine and Gilmore call 'transformations'— think of education, a more healthy lifestyle, coaching activities and aesthetic surgery—the consumers themselves are transformed and in this way become the product of the process themselves! The result of this transformation— literally added value—as a rule is not taken away that easily.

Florida's creative class plays a role in most of these stages. Innovators may be active in manufacturing and devising new concepts or appealing products. As a result of these endeavours, relatively simple services (e.g., Southwest's) may become more like experiences. In the field of experiences themselves (theatre, travel, amusement parks) and transformations, continuous innovation is necessary as well. It is a known fact that when theme parks or zoos stop investing in new experiences, visitor numbers go down quite rapidly. Looked at this from the opposite side: the more products or services become standardized with just average quality, the more they will lose their appeal so that they will be downgraded.

Many economists and policymakers like to think in terms of productivity, as apparently this provides them with a general benchmark to compare the relative performance of industries or whole economies. They should, however, keep in mind that higher productivity equals lower added value, whereas customization to some extent decreases productivity yet adds value. The fact that specialists in the field of mass customization try to combine both logics doesn't take away this basic principle—they only try to deal with it creatively. Therefore, when we talk about creativity and innovation, we should remember that in general there is quite a difference between thinking creatively about new concepts, new products, services or experiences on the one hand and thinking creatively about more productive processes—technical and organizational—on the other hand. As a rule, the second logic also comes at a later stage, when successful new concepts are copied by competitors and competition increases. Moreover, in the field of services, sometimes the quality of the service—and its related value—disappears totally when one tries to increase productivity beyond a certain point.

In economic literature, this is referred to as 'Baumol's curse' after William Baumol who first raised this issue. The classical example is the playing of a symphony, but the same applies to many personal or transformational services. This brings us to the tension between exploration and exploitation and the relationship between creative and routine work.

6   A FUZZY APPROACH 1: CREATIVITY AND TALKING

All economic activities, even in the field of the most creative work, contain both more creative and more repetitive elements. Not all intellectual work is creative or requires interpretative activity. In most cases, people perform both kinds of work: employees in an amusement park or even in a fast-food restaurant to some extent work like actors in a theatre. And of course, university professors have to perform routine activities such as correcting exams. According to Pine and Gilmore, all workers become actors of a certain kind more and more. Some actors, however, play about the same character on the same stage every day, whereas others are part of a continuously changing improvisation theatre (Pine & Gilmore 1999: 123).

Such a gradual or fuzzy approach allows us to understand the dynamic tension in the economy between creativity and routine, sometimes called the tension between exploration and exploitation (March 1991; Nooteboom 2000). A firm which is only creative will never harvest. A firm which does not innovate will rapidly deteriorate and become obsolete. Florida, as well as Pine and Gilmore, helps us understand that increasingly all functions have creative elements. As a consequence, the managers who do not agree with Akio Morita's statement quoted previously, about the necessary thinking contribution of all employees, in the end are even dangerous for their firm—I will come back to this. But at the same time, firms have to be organized for harvesting, exploitation and execution. That this tension is not always easy to manage already became apparent from the Endemol case with which I started this chapter.

An inspiring approach in this respect is that of McCloskey and Klamer (1995), who proposed a gradual or fuzzy calculation from which it emerged for 1993 that 26% of the American economy boiled down to persuasion or 'sweet talk'—that is, the persuasive and judgemental part of transactions.

- Jobs that are 100% persuasion include lawyers and judges (813,000), public relations specialists (155,000), actors and directors (96,000), and social, recreational and religious workers (1.1 million).
- Jobs that are 75% persuasion include counsellors (222,000), editors and reporters (266,000), supervisors of different kinds (clerical, 778,000; construction, 735,000; protective services, 185,000; precision production, 220,000), teachers including professors (5.17 million), salespeople excluding cashiers (11.7 million), and managers (15.4 million).
- Jobs that are 50% persuasion include police and detectives (923,000), adjusters and investigators (1.37 million), teacher's aides (508,000), authors and technical writers (202,000), social scientists, economists and urban planners (399,000), and workers in health assessment and treatment (2.60 million).
- Finally the 25% persuasion jobs include natural scientists (531,000) and legal assistants (254,000).

Of course, again there is room for discussing this classification. Moreover, talking certainly is not only about persuading others but also about the interactive search for meanings and solutions. However, weighing these employment figures for 1993, McCloskey and Klamer came to 26% of the person-years involved, compared with 23% ten years earlier. In a country with a talkative culture like the Netherlands, these figures would even be higher.

People may find this approach too neutral or even cynical, as these authors do not give any positive or negative evaluation per se to the talking, judging and persuading activities. To what extent is all this talking constructive?

Richard Lester and Michael Piore from the Massachusetts Institute of Technology delve somewhat deeper into these judgemental and persuasive aspects when they emphasize that an important *and often neglected* part of innovative activities, even technological ones, is the *creation of new meaning*. Especially in the first phases (by other authors called 'the fuzzy front end') of really innovative trajectories, it is not really possible to search for solutions—even when many people try this—as in most of these situations it is not clear at all what one is looking for. Therefore, Lester and Piore do not refer to persuasion but to interpretation and what we could call 'searching conversation': 'In stark contrast with analysis and problem solving, interpretation plays in the space of ambiguity. When a conversation begins, the participants may have considerable difficulty even understanding one another. . . . From this perspective, ambiguity is the critical resource out of which new ideas emerge. It is ambiguity that makes the conversation worth having, not the exchange of chunks of agreed-upon information' (Lester & Piore 2004: 53–54). Think, for example, about the social use of new technologies. In most cases their inventors really have no clue how this will take shape, and many innovations have failed as a consequence of this. Thus there is a need for experiments and a lot of conversations to interpret and really understand these.

Lester and Piore conclude, therefore, that innovation needs both approaches: interpretative work in order to better understand radically new issues, and analysis and problem solving when it has become clear what one is looking for. In a way, these are two totally different forms of creative work which have to complement each other.

7   COMPARATIVE STATISTICS ABOUT THE CREATIVE ECONOMY

Inspired by McCloskey and Klamer, I developed a fuzzy approach of different degrees of creativity in different professions, which I will come back to in the next section. Together with researchers from Statistics Netherlands, I was able to make calculations of this for the Netherlands. But for the sake of methodology, let us first take a look at how other researchers have measured the extent to which a country like the Netherlands, for which a lot of statistical data are available, is a creative economy based on the human potential instead of industries (as in Table 1).

Richard Florida's overall assessment of creative economies, summarized in his Creativity Index ranking, is based on the composition of three T-indexes: Technology (R&D investment, researchers and patents per capita), Talent (education level, creative class) and Tolerance (attitudes related to gays and lesbians and to ethnic and racial minorities) (Florida et al. 2011: 28–30). In his latest Global Creativity Index, the ranking for the first twenty countries (out of eighty-two) is presented in the Table 2 (Florida et al. 2011: 49).

Therefore, from these calculations it appears that an assessment in terms of the creative economy leads to quite a different ranking than when using only the traditional technological yardstick.[9] This ranking leads to surprising results which raise some doubts about their validity. Greece, for example, ranks ninth in the Talent Index (third in human capital and twenty-ninth on creative class) and as a result in the overall rankings gets the twenty-second position, ahead of Japan with the thirtieth overall ranking, coming second in the Technology Index, but scoring low on Talent (forty-five) and Tolerance (sixty-one).

Table 2   First twenty countries in the Global Creativity Index 2011

GCI rank	country	technology rank	talent rank	tolerance rank	GCI
1	Sweden	5	2	7	0.923
2	United States	3	8	8	0.902
3	Finland	1	1	19	0.894
4	Denmark	7	4	14	0.878
5	Australia	15	7	5	0.870
6	New Zealand	19	5	4	0.866
7	Canada	11	7	1	0.862
7	Norway	12	6	11	0.862
9	Singapore	10	3	17	0.858
10	Netherlands	17	11	3	0.854
11	Belgium	16	12	13	0.813
12	Ireland	20	21	2	0.805
13	United Kingdom	18	19	10	0.789
14	Switzerland	6	22	20	0.785
15	France	14	23	16	0.764
15	Germany	9	26	18	0.764
17	Spain	24	28	6	0.744
18	Taiwan	—	32	21	0.737
19	Italy	26	18	23	0.707
20	Hong Kong	22	37	12	0.691

The main question, however, is, what do we really learn about the level of creativity from this table? What does a country need to do to become a more creative economy? Of course, creativity is also important for technology development, but what do we learn about the position of these countries in the realm of art, cultural production or competitiveness in creative industries? I dare say, not very much, as only one-half of one criterion (talent) is really related to this. If a country would invest a few billion euros in creative sectors or creative professions, it wouldn't climb much in this ranking. Isn't that remarkable?

Do Florida's data for the creative class maybe come a bit nearer to our understanding? In his latest calculations (Florida et al. 2011: 36), Singapore comes first with 46.3%, ahead of the Netherlands with 46.2% of the work-force, Switzerland 44.6%, Australia 44.5% and Sweden, Belgium, Denmark and Finland all above 43%.

In the Netherlands, Marlet and van Woerkens (2004) have used the same professional groups to make their calculations but in a more restricted way—they excluded, for example, people working in the public sector (but they included scientists) and managers and salespeople working in noncreative industries. This led to an estimation for the creative class of 19% of the Dutch workforce in 2002, up from 17.3% in 1996. More interestingly, just as with Florida's calculations for the United States (Florida 2012: 40–41), the presence of this group in different regions of the Netherlands did correlate more significantly with economic growth than any other category of employees (e.g., highly educated people).

When we compare these different estimates (including those in Section 3) for the Netherlands, we observe that they are in the range from 3.1% of the workforce to no less than 46%! Of most concern to me is, however, the basic black-and-white assumption included in all these calculations that workers either are creative or not. In the KEA and Rutten approach (Section 3), a janitor of a theatre is a 100% creative worker, but when working for a hotel he isn't that for 1%. Even Florida has some doubts about this assumption when he mentions—as we saw in Section 5—how, for instance, at Toyota and Matsushita, factory workers are also expected to deliver creative contributions. In the end everybody is, of course, creative to some extent. This is the reason I developed, together with researchers from Statistics Netherlands, a more fuzzy approach.

8   A FUZZY APPROACH 2: DEGREES OF CREATIVITY AND ROUTINE*

In my opinion, the obvious solution to avoid black-and-white approaches is to think in a fuzzy way[10]: all of us do to a certain extent—but in different degrees—both creative and noncreative, routine work. Together with Mies Bernelot Moens and Marco Mossinkoff with whom I developed this approach, I therefore propose to estimate the degree of necessary creativity for all jobs and then to aggregate these estimates to higher levels of the economy in order to really understand how creativity contributes to the economy as a whole. In a comparable way with the presentation in Figure 1 (Section 4), we see the realm of creativity in the economy as a range of expanding concentric sets:

1. In the core there are functions where the creation of innovation and content constitutes the essence of the job, but not 100%, as there always routine parts even in creative jobs. These include occupations in the realm of the arts, scientific and technological research, media, games design, photography, fashion and other product design, graphic design, architecture and technical design, town and country planning.
2. In a wider set in all kinds of sectors of the economy, people have to think about new plans, new ideas, new ways of organizing and new

*This section is based on Jacobs et al. 2008 and Mossinkoff & Jacobs 2009.

concepts. Think, for example, of consultants or people working in the realm of policymaking. In addition, education at different levels requires quite some continuous creativity.

3. In a still wider set, also in relatively basic or traditional jobs (health workers, police, social workers), employees increasingly have to think about the creative adaptation of rules to a certain situation. Awareness has grown in recent years how important a role people in such functions sometimes play in dealing with social tensions between people from different backgrounds . Just sticking to the rules in such situations may be quite counterproductive. Therefore, the amount of creativity and related flexibility in the behaviour of these professionals may make the difference between increasing these tensions and a higher degree of mutual understanding and respect.

4. The lowest level of creativity is required in pure routine jobs, but even here, no zero-level exists. Some form of pattern recognition and creative adaptation of rules will always be required.

Relaxing the black-and-white assumption of the traditional approach might lead to a more realistic view and less extreme estimates about the role of creativity in the economy. Therefore, we took the 'Standard Classification of Occupations' of Statistics Netherlands (Centraal Bureau voor de Statistiek [CBS])[11] as a starting point and estimated the required creative component for each of the about 1,200 included occupations. Of course, it was not possible to measure this precisely for all of these occupations. But with the help of the short description of necessary capabilities and tasks enumerated in this classification, we made a categorization of all occupations in different creativity categories: 1%, 2.5% and 5% creativity (group 4); 10%, 15% and 20% creativity (group 3); 25%, 33.3% and 40% (group 2); and 50%, 66.7% and 75% (group 1, the core). As creative tasks, we see all those involving the creation not only of something new, such as a work of art, but also of a strategic plan or project. In addition, parts of the jobs that require independency, abstraction and complex problem-solving capabilities are considered creative. On the contrary, jobs that imply more supportive tasks may be considered as requiring more routine or repetitive, least-creative tasks. Because every job requires at least some basic pattern-recognition capability—for example, 'is this tomato mature?'—we see 1% creativity as the minimum level. At the other side of the spectrum, we think that even the most creative people spend at least a quarter of their time in a more routine fashion, so 75% creativity is our top category. One can check the way we applied this approach in Table 3, in which a range of examples is provided for each of our categories. Of course it is possible to argue about these estimates, but we are pretty sure that this approach is more correct than the simple binary approach in which everyone is 100% or 0% creative.

On the basis of this subdivision, we have aggregated the data of all working people in the Netherlands and—taking into account the number of hours they

Table 3   Estimated degrees of creativity in different occupations

% creativity	examples of occupations in each category
1	Auxiliary workers in horticulture, simple machine workers in manufacturing, cleaners
2.5	Agricultural workers, cleaners of machines, bricklayers, welders, electricians, lift truck drivers
5	Couriers, house upholsterers, bus drivers, waiters, chemical laboratory workers, heating fitters, clockmakers, caretakers, arithmeticians
10	Flower arrangers, butchers, lorry drivers, secretaries, auxiliary nurses, plumbers, building inspectors, pattern designers
15	Pollsters, animal attendants, receptionists, sport instructors, most of the directors and managers of SMEs, network managers, teachers of practice courses, archivists
20	Maintenance personnel, bus drivers group transport, tourist guides, ship captains, directors and managers of SMEs in more complex industries, draughtspeople in the machine tool industry, beauticians, primary school teachers, dieticians, office managers, investment and credit analysts, tax consultants
25	Travel organizers, medium-level advertising copywriters, real estate agents, chefs
33.3	Sociocultural workers, nursery school teachers, special education teachers, prostitutes, physiotherapists, detectives, editors, public relations specialists, management consultants, system designers, educational advisors, course leaders, university teachers without research assignments
40	Policy officials; higher-level occupational, music and play therapists; higher-level advertising copywriters
50	Photographers; educational staff members; mechanical and structural engineers and design engineers; traffic planners; technical copywriters; higher-level and executive chemical, textile, food, etc., technologists; visual artists; choreographers; directors; scientific researchers
66.7	Architects, executive engineers and design engineers, industrial designers
75	Authors, higher-level editors, journalists

have been working—made an estimation of the average required creativity in the whole Dutch economy for two periods. Every year, Statistics Netherlands estimates the amount of people working in all occupations (and the amount of hours worked) on the basis of extensive sample surveys. However, especially for occupations in which relatively small numbers of people work, these estimates are less statistically reliable. For this reason, we haven't used data for single years. Instead, we have compared the data for two periods of three consecutive years: 1996–1998 and 2004–2006. Given the methodological limitations of our approach and of the survey, this was no more than a first kind of 'finger exercise.' Nevertheless, as rough as this may be, the consistency of our approach should gave us at least an idea of the amount of increase (or decrease) of required creativity in the whole of an economy and in this way test the hypothesis of increasing creativity. Of course, as our approach was based on actually performed hours, conclusions with respect to labour demand should be nuanced. There are always functions for which it is difficult to find the necessary people. When these people haven't been found, they haven't worked of course, so they haven't been counted. Thus, the required level of creativity could have been somewhat higher than what we found.

First, we have aggregated the numbers of persons and hours spent in total and those spent creatively (per week) for the different creativity percentage categories. After that, we added up the numbers for 1996–1998 and 2004–2006, respectively, to come to a general estimate of the average creativity of the Dutch economy. To start with the general conclusion, the contribution of creative work to the total amount of worked hours in the Netherlands increased from 13.8% in the period 1996–1998 to 14.7% in 2004–2006. This increase is due both to shifts between creativity percentage categories in number of workers and to changes in the amount of hours spent in different occupations.

Comparing our final 14.7% estimation of creativity in the Dutch economy in the more recent period with those of Rutten and others (3.5%), Marlet and van Woerkens (19%) and Florida (29.5% or 47%) (Sections 3 and 7) leaves us with the feeling of having found a more realistic estimation. First, our estimation is not extremely high or low. Moreover, even when it is relatively on the lower side of the spectrum compared with other estimates, our calculations lead to an increase of 0.9% in eight years (in absolute terms, 6.5% in relative terms) related to the total of hours worked in both periods. Therefore, our calculation supports the hypothesis of an increasing level of required creativity in the economy.

Table 4 shows the number of workers per creative category, as well as the amount of hours worked in the two periods (own calculations on the basis of CBS Labour Force Surveys).

In almost every category, both the number of workers and the total hours worked have increased, with the exception of the lowest 1% category. The highest relative increase of working people was in the 40% category. In relative terms, the highest creativity categories (50%–75%), the creative core, however, remained about constant. The average number of hours worked has decreased from 33.3 to 31.8 hours per week between the two periods, but the average number of hours spent creatively has increased from 4.60 to 4.67 a week.

In order to look more critically at the thesis of the emergence of a creative economy, we have done a second, follow-up exercise. For this, we

Table 4 Working persons and their working hours according to creativity percentage groups

creativity percentage of occupation	1996–1998 working persons average per year ×1,000	%	average hours	hours worked per week – hours of all people total %	creative hours	2004–2006 working persons average per year ×1,000	%	average hours	hours worked per week – hours of all people total %	creative hours
1	593	8.3	30.1	7.5	0.5	558	7.1	27.6	6.2	0.4
2.5	1,443	20.2	30.6	18.6	3.4	1,464	18.7	29.2	17.2	2.9
5	792	11.1	32.1	10.7	3.9	822	10.5	30.4	10.1	3.4
10	1,252	17.5	31.7	16.7	12.1	1,438	18.4	30.6	17.7	12.1
15	937	13.1	39.3	15.5	16.8	1,003	12.8	36.9	14.9	15.2
20	1,145	16.0	33.3	16.1	23.2	1,318	16.9	31.9	16.9	23.1
25	219	3.1	39.7	3.7	6.6	239	3.1	37.4	3.6	6.1
33.3	438	6.1	34.7	6.4	15.4	578	7.4	34.2	7.9	18.0
40	94	1.3	34.0	1.3	3.9	148	1.9	33.7	2.0	5.5
50	162	2.3	36.6	2.5	9.0	171	2.2	35.2	2.4	8.2
66.7	35	0.5	38.6	0.6	2.7	37	0.5	38.6	0.6	2.6
75	34	0.5	32.2	0.5	2.5	37	0.5	31.2	0.5	2.4
Total	7,144	100	33.3	100	100	7813	100	31.8	100	100

Table 5 Three new economies with examples of related occupational fields

knowledge economy (labour force 414,134[1])	creative economy (labour force 215,079)	experience economy (labour force 465,721)
scientific and technological research	artisanship	retail
higher education	design and fashion	entertainment
marketing and advertisement	media	theme parks
consultancy	figurative arts	performing arts
	photography	festivals and exhibitions
	architecture	sports
		hotels and catering

have zoomed in on three groups of occupations which are at the core of recent discussions about new developments in the economy. First, we have listed occupations which are typical for the knowledge economy, the creative economy and the experience economy, respectively. Then, for each of these, we have looked at the developments in terms of total employment (including independent entrepreneurs) and the required levels of creativity. An indication of the occupational fields included in the three economies is given in Table 5. As can be seen from this table, to reach clear conclusions we have avoided any overlap between these three new economies. Thus, for example, theatre is considered a part of the experience economy, whereas scientific research a part of the knowledge economy and therefore not of the creative economy in the strict sense.

Thus the knowledge economy includes all jobs related to the development and diffusion of knowledge which enhances innovation and efficiency (Jacobs 1999a; Foray 2004; Dolfsma 2007), whereas the creative economy relates to all activities for the creation of new cultural products in the realm of design, fashion, the arts, media and advertising (Rutten et al. 2004). The experience economy, finally, relates to the newest development in the service economy in which consumers are engaged in special three-dimensional settings in which something exceptional is staged (Pine & Gilmore 1999).

Creativity in Knowledge Economy Occupations

In the knowledge economy, people either create or diffuse knowledge meant to increase the international competitive advantage of a developed economic area (Jacobs 1999a; Foray 2004; Dolfsma 2007). One of the most obvious indicators for the development in the direction of a knowledge economy is the required competence level for all occupations in the whole economy. Table 6 shows an absolute increase in jobs at all competence levels, but

Table 6   Working persons according to level of occupation

competence level	working persons 1996–1998 (average per year)		working persons 2004–2006 (average per year)		% growth
	× 1,000	%	× 1,000	%	
elementary	656	9.2	780	10.0	18.9
low	1,917	26.8	2,012	25.8	5
intermediate	2,711	37.9	2,816	36.0	3.9
high	1,320	18.5	1,598	20.5	21.1
scientific	541	7.6	607	7.8	12.1
total	7,144	100	7,813	100	9.3

Note: Data processed based on CBS Labour Force Survey.

mostly in the occupations requiring the highest and lowest competences. The least growth is observed at the intermediate levels.

Concentrating on occupations typical for a knowledge economy, we found eighty occupational categories, for which the data are summarized in Table 7. All together, these categories occupied 414,000 working people in the period 2004–2006, an increase of about sixty thousand compared with 1996–1998. Among the occupations contributing to the knowledge economy, we considered researchers, consultants (private and public) and teachers. In the following

Table 7   Changes concerning persons working in knowledge economy occupations by creativity categories

creativity percentage category	≤10	15	20	25	33	40	≥50	total
working people 2004–2006	1,149	39,731	20,891	46,187	73,001	180,865	50,919	414,134
absolute change since 1996–1998	−341	+20,050	+1269	+11,308	+38,473	−417	−5,462	+59,399
relative change since 1996–1998	−30%	+50%	+6%	+25%	+53%	−0.2%	−11%	+14.3%
number of occupations	3	5	15	3	29	5	17	80

table, just as in the Tables 8 and 9, all occupations have been categorized according to the degree of creativity implied. The quantitative development of each of these categories between the two periods should help us to understand the development of required creativity from another perspective.

Therefore, looking at our creativity categories in knowledge-related occupations, we see a kind of opposite evolution compared with the required competence levels in the whole economy: the amount of jobs in the highest and lowest creativity categories are declining in favour of jobs in the middle-high and middle-low categories. Qualitatively, this shift is mainly due to a decrease of jobs in academic research and a growth of teaching, consultancy and automation-related functions, so there appears to be a qualitative shift from knowledge creation to knowledge diffusion. If we agree that knowledge development is crucial to a knowledge economy, this development does not look very promising. An optimist could, however, propose the hypothesis that now finally due attention appears to be given to the valorisation of knowledge, so that a traditional weakness of many knowledge economies—insufficient valorisation of investments in knowledge creation—is at last being addressed.

Creativity in Creative Economy Occupations

Reading Richard Florida (2002, 2005, 2012), one could ask to what extent there is a difference between a creative and a knowledge economy, even when his writings have led to quite different discussions about the development

Table 8   Changes concerning persons working in creative economy occupations by creativity categories

creativity percentage category	≤5	10–15	20	25	33	40	≥50	total
working people 2004–2006	13,939	2,104	44,622	13,201	33,287	7,690	100,236	215,079
absolute change since 1996–1998	−35	−448	+10,548	+2,252	+5,882	+357	+21,428	+39,784
relative change since 1996–1998	−0.01%	−21%	+24%	+17%	+18%	+0.5%	+21%	+18%
number of occupations	3	9	6	9	11	5	15	58

of the economy and related policies. Nevertheless, all important knowledge-related professions are part of Florida's creative class. Therefore, in the following we have used narrower definitions of the creative economy, again concentrating on occupations rather than on creative industries. In Table 8, a total of fifty-eight occupations are included which we consider representative for the creative economy. We have, however, excluded jobs in the realm of entertainment, as we consider these more related to the experience economy. Of the three new economies we look at in the second part of this paragraph, this one is the smallest with only 170,500 people occupied. Growth is however a bit higher than in the two other new economies.

Of the three economies under scrutiny in this part, the creative one is, not surprisingly, the fastest growing from the perspective of the hours creatively spent, twice as fast as the overall growth of the Dutch workforce. There is a decline in the lowest creativity categories, but above the 20% creativity mark, growth has been above 20%, except for the 40% creativity group, which grew quite slowly.

Creativity in Experience Economy Occupations

According to Pine and Gilmore (1999), the experience economy brings with it the newest development in the services sector where consumers are engaged in special three-dimensional experience settings. This involves jobs related to going out, such as restaurants, hotels, tourism and entertainment. In our calculations forty-five occupational categories are involved, but these are relatively crowded (see Table 9).

This is the biggest of these three new economies when it comes to the number of working people (465,721), although the distribution of the amount of hours creatively spent is skewed towards lower-creativity jobs

Table 9   Changes concerning persons working in the experience economy occupations in creativity categories

creativity percentage category	≤5	10	15	20	25–33	40–60	total
working people 2004–2006	195,944	21,062	138,261	93,009	2,826	14,619	465,721
absolute change since 1996–1998	+46,554	+4,534	+2,195	+14,957	−1,692	−987	+65,561
relative change since 1996–1998	+24%	+22%	+6%	+16%	−60%	−7%	+14%
number of occupations	9	4	8	19	2	3	45

when compared with the other two economies. Especially in the medium-creativity range there doesn't appear to be a necessity for many people. A renewed interest for entertainment and special experiences leads to a growth of jobs, but most of these involve relatively routine and execution tasks.

Concluding this section, the fuzzy approach to the creative economy I proposed confirms the increasing need for creativity—at least in the Dutch economy during the last decade. We found, however, for the whole economy (Table 4), the highest relative increase of working people in the 40% creativity category. In relative terms, the highest creativity categories (50%–75%), the creative core, remained about constant. Remarkably, in the most typical creative economy occupations in the strict sense (Table 8), we saw about 20% growth in all categories above the 20% creativity jobs, except the 40% category precisely. There are a few other conclusions we can draw from this follow-up exercise in which occupations were assembled that are representative of the three most commonly mentioned new economic developments: those in the direction of a knowledge, a creative or an experience economy respectively:

- Where the total Dutch workforce has been growing between 1996–1998 and 2004–2006 with 9.3%, the knowledge, creative and experience economies accounted for an employment growth of 14.3%, 18% and 14%, respectively. So growth in these sectors was between one and a half and twice as large as the average.
- The three new economies we looked at in this follow-up exercise show, however, quite divergent patterns related to the level of required creativity. As one might expect in the creative economy in the strict sense, the amount of hours spent creatively grew the fastest. More surprising was our finding that in occupations typical for the knowledge economy, those with a medium level of creativity grew most. In the experience economy, finally, jobs requiring the least creativity show the largest increase. These findings certainly qualify the hypothesis of a general development in the economy towards more creativity.

9 PARADOXES OF CREATIVITY

For about a decade now, we have been discussing the creative economy. For this reason the extent to which many firms still do not use the intelligence and creativity of their employees in the way Sony's Morita advised them many years ago (see Section 5) is alarming. In addition, Lester and Piore warn that the increasing emphasis on shareholder value and short-term financial gains risks smothering creativity ever *more*. Pressure in the United States in the direction of more efficiency has narrowed the space for necessary interpretative processes (Lester & Piore 2004: 119, 170–174). Sometimes, firms do not have sufficient patience to let new practices blossom. For example, in the beginning of the 1990s, many firms in the West experimented with Japanese-influenced quality circles in order to tap into the creativity of their employees. However, most of these experiments were finished when they didn't lead to the expected results rapidly enough. In addition, the Endemol case showed that too much emphasis on execution and control risks killing creativity. As competition has increased in many creative sectors, room for patient nurturing of talent certainly has decreased. Isn't it ironic that for all the talk about the creative economy, some music firms concede that nowadays artists such as Bob Dylan or Bruce Springsteen probably wouldn't receive the time necessary to develop their talent anymore?

Moreover, firms may invest in creative designs and successful approaches, but the macro result is not necessarily very stimulating. Competitors' successes are sometimes imitated so frequently that the end result is uniformity, not originality. A paradoxical consequence of the multiplication of uniform brand designs and franchise formulas is that shopping centres all over the world increasingly look the same, with bored shoppers and closed wallets as a consequence. Therefore, the final result is fewer genuine experiences as the consequence of creative investing in the experience economy! Thus this practice of continuous multiplication, imitation, and controlling of success formulas kills innovation and experiences in the end and, as a consequence, even leads to decreased sales (Jacobs 2004: 30). Again, it appears that competing with creativity is not an easy game and the story about it is full of possibly unexpected, uneasy paradoxes.

10   SAFEGUARDING A CREATIVE CULTURAL ENVIRONMENT

This brings us to the question as to what governments can do in this realm. In this chapter we have seen that there may be some tension between creativity and economy. Creativity increasingly is an important competitive resource but, at the same time, is continuously under pressure as a result of the requirements of exploitation and execution. Governments traditionally have played an important role in the safeguarding of a relatively autonomous cultural realm, not only in the field of the arts, but also—and increasingly—in that of safeguarding a healthy, attractive and tolerant environment. A result of the discussion about the creative economy is that we now understand that there is an economic basis for this as well.

Another important element lies in the field of discourse. Innovation policy has been nearly synonymous with technology policy for a long time.[12] Therefore, an important gain of the discussion on creativity and the economy is the broadening of the scope of innovation to all kinds of nontechnical innovation. Policymakers sometimes underestimate to what extent their discourses set the agenda and limit entrepreneurs' mental scope. For this reason, we can only hope that these policymakers will refrain from sanctifying creativity as the only way to heaven, as they did with technology before, but instead will frame the discussion about innovation in a more balanced way, as a necessary, always different creative combination of new technological opportunities with innovative concepts.

Related to this is also the fact that innovation requires more than technicians and people educated in natural and engineering sciences or informatics. We saw that creativity is especially about lateral thinking and boundary spanning, as well as about being able to live and deal with ambiguity. Beside analytical problem solving, there is a need for interpretation and searching conversations. For this reason Lester and Piore argue in favour of more humanistic studies such as literary critique, history, language and arts in undergraduate and secondary education. They also see problems with standardized multiple-choice testing that 'almost by definition . . . is antithetical to the cultivation of a tolerance for ambiguity. They do not teach the skills required to generate and live with alternative interpretations' (Lester & Piore 2004: 187). In the field of science itself, there also should be more conversations and cooperation *between* disciplines than is now the case (Lester & Piore 2004: 166–167). This monodisciplinary culture has been stimulated largely by the publish-or-perish culture stimulated by results-oriented science managers. It is probably not a coincidence that one of the most stimulating and productive initiatives in the field of multidisciplinary science development on the global level—the Santa Fe Institute in the realm of complexity sciences—has emerged outside the university system (Waldrop 1992; Regis 2003).[13]

When managing paradoxes, the issue is not to avoid the extremes but to learn to live with them, at the same time stimulating scientific autonomy *and* its involvement with social and business problems, stimulating creativity *and* discipline. In a similar vein, there is the defence of high (difficult) *and* low (entertaining) culture. A creative space needs both. Richard Florida taught us that creative, diverse, tolerant, cultural spaces are necessary for innovation and for attracting the best professionals—and the innovative firms which follow them—who want to live and work in such an environment. Defending such an open, diverse and challenging cultural environment is therefore an important factor in the competition to attract and preserve creative professionals and innovative firms.

For this reason, Florida himself for some time was worried about the direction of discourse in American society since 9/11: 'In the zeal to ensure homeland security, the nation also has placed tighter restrictions on immigration, foreign students and the flow of scientific information. If these trends continue, the U.S. may well squander its once-considerable lead. Consider this thought: The real threat to American security is not terrorism, it's that creative and talented people may stop wanting to come here' (Florida 2004: xxiv; Florida 2005: 109–132). Lester and Piore (2004: 185) add to this that firms employing people from different cultures learn to live with cultural ambiguity and profit from the fact that with the help of these people they can make the translation of their product and approaches to other places more easily.

In the realm of cultural policies, there are worries as well. Traditionally the cultural role of governments has been to deal with market failure or at least market paradox in the cultural realm. Governments have been supporting new directions in art which were not yet well understood or, on the basis of Florida's arguments, have been maintaining a cultural infrastructure in order to compete for the best professionals. However, in recent years, partly as a consequence of the financial crisis but also of populist movements, there has been a backlash against such public investment in culture. Even when in the cultural realm there were also forms of government failure and elitist forms of arrogance (van Klink 2005), we can only hope that such a simplistic backlash[14] will stimulate creative entrepreneurs to present their case in a clearer way.[15] I hope that my own contribution related to productive creativity may inspire such endeavours.

11   CONCLUSION: LIVING WITH AMBIGUITY, EVEN ABOUT CREATIVITY ITSELF

As I hope has been clarified in this chapter, creativity is an increasingly important factor within the whole economy, not only in the so-called creative industries, be it in different degrees depending on the professions and industries. Without productive creativity there can be no new concepts, products, technologies, production and transaction processes, or forms of organizing, and therefore no economic growth (or even ideas for more sustainable growth), as well as no increase in productivity and competitiveness. Is this more than stating the obvious? Yes, we saw, for example, that assessing the competitiveness of firms or countries on a broader set of indicators than only R&D statistics leads to a totally different picture. At the same time, we found that quite a few tensions and paradoxes remain. Creative people are not necessarily the most easy people to deal with. Investment in creativity and innovation is never secure, as many innovations fail. Creativity is not a virtue in itself. Many creative ideas are just rubbish. Creativity has to be combined with professional, accepted insights from different fields, but nobody knows to what extent precisely. New ideas and concepts have to be tested in the market. Disciplining these through the market, however, has its drawbacks as well. Sometimes talent doesn't get the necessary time to develop anymore as a result of short-termism. Therefore, creativity is never an efficient process, even when we can improve management of creativity and innovation.[16] In the final analysis, creativity depends on tolerance and the ability to live with contradictions and ambiguities.

Creative industries have been growing, but at the same time, many of them are in a crisis. A lot of investment in creative activities has not really been creative but rather has boiled down to attempts to imitate competitors' successes as rapidly as possible. This has led to increasing competition, lower margins, cost cutting, less room for really creative developments and predictability and boredom instead of surprise, refreshment and delight. Moreover, some creative industries (related to the Internet, gaming and consumptive elements of the experience economy) may be substitutes for traditional cultural sectors such as book and newspaper publishing. Even television nowadays experiences the well-known problems of a mature industry. In conclusion, the economy is ever more based on creativity, but creative industries themselves remain part of Schumpeter's creative destruction. Quite a challenge!

Notes

NOTES TO THE INTRODUCTION

1. A value system is here something completely different from Michael Porter's (1980; 1985) use of the term as a kind of supply chain linking different firms (each with its own value chain) into a larger whole.
2. An updated and extended version of this essay is included as a 'Bonus Track' in this book.

NOTES TO CHAPTER 1

1. These authors are by no means alone. A key Organisation of Economic Co-operation and Development (OECD) overview, based on discussions with a high-level international group of experts quotes, without criticising this aspect, the definition of (technological) innovation provided by the first OECD study in 1971 in the field was 'the first application of science and technology in a new way, with commercial success' (OECD 1992: 24).
2. Wijnberg (2004: 1472) restricts his definition to product innovation (including that within the realm of the arts), but I see no reason for this restriction.
3. I do not mean something radically new. In Chapter 3, I will clarify that most innovations are incremental or even marginal.
4. This definition also appears to be a shorthand version of Chakravorti's (2003: 23): 'A word on innovation: I am interested in the broadest possible definition. In the discussions to follow, innovation covers *new* products, technologies, business models, and other processes and ideas. It can even mean ways of organizing markets. As breaks from the status quo, all these innovations have the potential to add value in a market setting and contribute to what we would otherwise recognize as progress.'
5. As with many innovations, furniture to be assembled by the customers was not IKEA's invention. However, due to IKEA's early—and massive—adoption, this innovation is usually associated with this firm.
6. See also the box on dominant designs in Section 3.4.
7. 'Versioning' means to provide different versions of the same product (Shapiro & Varian 1999: 45, 59, 63–64).
8. See my discussion of the Encyclopaedia Britannica case in Jacobs (2010: 26–28).
9. Although this may seem obvious, in many analyses of the information economy, this feature of materialized information products has been neglected. Some authors, for example, have questioned the rationality of investments in material transportation infrastructure in the new economy, while forgetting

that e-business in most cases leads to more transport of material goods—and in most cases to smaller, individualized packages (Jacobs 1999b). As long as Amazon distributes material books and other products, it—or its suppliers—needs warehouses and mail services to handle its goods.

10. As we can see from this discussion, in the realm of services, product and process innovation are probably more intertwined than in manufacturing (van Ark & de Jong 2004: 31).

11. As we will see in Section 1.4, a transaction innovation such as the leasing of airplanes has radically changed competition in the airline industry, lowering fixed costs and as a consequence entry barriers to that industry.

12. See also Pine and Gilmore's statement (1999: 101–162) that 'work is theatre.'

13. As with all innovations, people may argue that an increase in real added value is not guaranteed. People may, for example, become addicted to cosmetic surgery, never being satisfied with their appearance. From an economic point view, these customers are, of course, the most interesting.

14. None of these developments are, however, unequivocal. Museums increase their visitor numbers by integrating more experiences. In many cases, their shops are the most crowded part of the museum. However, this does not mean that museums do not also have an educational value and, in a broader way, lead to a higher quality of life in their environment (Throsby 2001: 34–40; Florida 2004: 182). Related to this is the distinction drawn by Diane Nijs (2003: 24–25) between the 'sensation track' and the 'sentiment track' of what she calls the 'emotion economy.'

15. See the discussion of the technical and nontechnical aspects of service innovation on the basis of den Hertog's 6-D approach in the previous section.

16. Organizational innovation is clearly a form of process innovation. Therefore, I see no reason to make organizational innovation a separate category from process innovation, as some authors do.

17. My own PhD research was about such institutional trial-and-error learning in the Western European steel industry between 1750 and 1950, for instance, leading to a private international steel cartel in the 1930s which was replaced after the World War II by the public European Coal and Steel Community, the nucleus of what later became the European Union (Jacobs 1988).

18. Of course, transaction innovations may also increase overall productivity, as they facilitate the more smooth execution of transactions (den Butter et al. 2008), but the stimulation of transactions as such is their main function.

19. As has been clarified in a separate box in Section 1.3, there are also some process innovations related to the quality of products that lead to lower productivity.

20. Computer-aided design and manufacturing (CAD-CAM), radio frequency identification (RFID).

21. Christensen does not mention transaction innovation capabilities and sets aesthetic design in a category separate from what he calls technical and functional 'product application.'

22. In addition, this enumeration builds on Christensen (1995) but adds the final bullet, as well as the importance of aesthetic design in entertainment and hospitality industries.

23. See also the discussion in Chapter 2 of technology push and market pull models of innovation and that on co-evolution in innovation management in Chapter 7.

24. See the box 'Myths Related to Pioneers' in Section 3.2.

25. In the previous edition of this book, I still called these 'techno-economic paradigms,' following, amongst others, Chris Freeman and Carlota Perez (1988). However, I agree with Grin and others (2010: 19–21) that it is better to talk

about 'regimes,' as 'regime' is a concept with which it is easier to cover cognitive, regulative and normative levels of a system comprehensively. Paradigms, to the contrary, mainly relate to the cognitive level. However, a major weakness of the approach of Grin et al. is that they do not make the distinction between the two major forms of comprehensive innovation I make in this section. As a consequence, they think it is possible to pursue system innovation relatively bottom-up, extending experiences in different niches.

26. I will come back to this in Section 2.2.

NOTES TO CHAPTER 2

1. The latter four are examples of what I have called 'transaction innovations' in Section 1.4.
2. Thomas Misa is perhaps the author who has discussed the definition of technology most extensively (Misa 1992; 2003; 2004: 260–276), but in the end, he is not prepared to define it: 'Technological changes . . . generate a mix of economic, social, and cultural changes. I maintain that this insight is more valuable than having a simple definition of a complex term' (Misa 2004: 263).
3. Quite a concise dictionary: 1,682 pages.
4. See Section 1.3 on process innovation and Section 1.7 on business model innovation.
5. Think of (constructive) technology assessment (Smits & Leyten 1991) or focus groups in the realm of marketing. I will come back to this in Chapter 6.
6. Of course, some of our norms and values may be based on biological instincts or age-old habits, which some time ago and for a very long time since, were essential for our survival. I come back to this in the following chapters.
7. I will come back to more objective and subjective forms of valuation in Section 5.2.
8. See, for example, the discussion of the technical and cultural aspects of the value of industrial design in Section 5.6.
9. I will come back to open innovation and co-development with customers in Section 6.7.
10. The first thing I do when I see new book on innovation is look in the index for the entries 'fashion,' 'design' and 'lifestyle.' This is usually quite disappointing. Most literature on innovation is not very innovative.
11. Think, for example, of different approached related to demand chain management (Jacobs 2006a).
12. For an detailed overview of which elements of design fall within the *Frascati* definition of R&D, see the working document 'Design as a Driver of User-Centred Innovation' of the Commission of the European Communities (CEC 2009: 12–13). Basically, prototyping and the first industrial design are seen as part of R&D, but design for the production process is not.
13. The financial crisis which erupted in 2008 clearly illustrates that not all innovations increase welfare.
14. With this statement, I do not want to suggest that in modern Western economies manufacturing—or even agriculture—is doomed to disappear, as many authors contend. It is one of the paradoxes of the modern economy that because of its relatively lower productivity, the services part of the economy becomes relatively more important. The much higher productivity of manufacturing and agriculture leads to relatively lower added values and decreased employment in these sectors and their gradual disappearance from economic statistics. However, in many cases, the volumes these sectors produce do not change greatly.

NOTES TO CHAPTER 3

1. The added value of an innovation (see my simple definition in Section 1.1) therefore should not be given a moral interpretation. A large proportion of purchases is based on impulse decisions.
2. Following Christensen (1997: xv), disruptive innovation sometimes denotes a radical innovation that initially results in lower performance than would normally be expected at that moment. However, it may be, for example, cheaper, simpler, smaller or easier to use and therefore be attractive to some customers.
3. Apart from radical innovations, Markides and Geroski (2005: 5–7) distinguish strategic innovations, for which only this second characteristic applies. As examples of such strategic innovations, they suggest Internet banking, low-cost airlines, catalogue retailing, steel minimills and online universities. It appears to me, however, that nearly all of these necessarily require new consumer habits as well. For this reason, I see no point in distinguishing them as a separate category. In addition, I would rather reserve the term 'strategic innovation' for what sometimes is also labelled 'strategic renewal' for organizations. Such strategic renewal may be related to radical innovation, but not necessarily.
4. Of course, as we saw in Chapter 1, changes in techno-economic regimes may be the result of a series of incremental innovations.
5. This diagram is inspired by Geoffrey Moore (2005: 61), but I have changed his diagram substantially. It has been partially simplified and extended and also some of the terms are different (e.g., replacing 'disruptive innovation' by 'radical innovation'). Moreover, stylistic innovation and especially 'standardization or dominant design' have been added and part of the line between the second and third stage has been dotted to illustrate the idea that many firms try to prolong the life of a product category as long as possible. Many product categories (e.g., bread and clothes) probably go on forever. As is clarified in this section, after the first phase of radical innovation, the precise place of most of the other forms of innovation in this diagram should not be taken too literally.
6. As I have clarified in Section 2.2, it has long been recognized that in the realm of technological research there may be a danger of underinvestment in the early precompetitive phase, as many followers may profit from the investment by the original pioneer. For this reason, government subsidies to these pioneers have been legitimized by this possible market failure. The consequence of this has been that in the discourse of innovation policies the accent has always been on new technologies. However, new innovative trajectories can also start with new concepts, new business models or (scientific) paradigms.
7. Quite appropriately, the title of Moore's first book was *Crossing the Chasm*.
8. This does not mean, however, that all competitors are in favour of standardization. Some firms may have no interest in innovation at all, preferring the old status quo, whereas others may be more interested in the position they have established in certain niches—think of Apple (Shapiro & Varian 1999: 228–236).
9. These specifications lead, in Latour's (1987) terms, to a 'black box' which everybody takes for granted.
10. This case is nicely illustrated by the reproduction of old copies of 'De Kampioen,' the (still existing) publication of the Dutch cyclists association Algemene Nederlandse Wielrijdersbond (ANWB; which later on became the Dutch Automobile Association), from the end of the nineteenth century in de Vries (1973).
11. Beware, however, of line extensions which extend a successful brand to totally different product categories. In many cases this leads to the fragmentation of the brand and a decrease in the clear position it probably had in customers' awareness (Ries & Trout 1986: 101–125; Zyman 2004: 15).

12. As said before, not much meaning should be given to the precise position of each of these forms of innovation in Figure 3.2.
13. The share of disposable income spent on such categories may decline as an economy develops; this does not necessarily mean a decline in absolute terms.

NOTES TO CHAPTER 4

1. 'Generalized Darwinism' thus refers to a multidisciplinary Darwinian research programme and not a kind of one-sided biological imperialism or reductionism, a connotation which 'universal Darwinism' or 'ultra-Darwinism' sometimes have (Hodgson and Knudsen 2010: 10, 21).
2. Despite this, the scientific discussion as to whether we really have some degree of freedom in what we do is still going on.
3. Comparable with other mammals and birds, there is of course also individuation and personal recognition. More than a hundred years ago, the American sociologist Graham Sumner characterized human societies therefore as systems of 'antagonistic cooperation.' For this reason, human societies are less well coordinated than termite colonies or wasp societies (Lenski 2005: 37–39).
4. All primates may be social animals, but this doesn't mean that their social behaviour is necessarily similar. In this respect, all kinds of differentiation between different species can be found (Rowe 1996: 6–8). Moreover, the social behaviour and structure of our species does not necessarily resemble that of our nearest relatives such as chimpanzees and bonobos—do not forget that our common ancestor, *Pan prior*, is estimated to have lived no later than until about eight million years ago. For example, forms of reciprocal altruism in which humans keep track of what they give to and receive from others has only been found with smaller monkeys such as tamarins and marmosets. These monkey species are also known to be eager towards other adults, helping them to raise their offspring, a characteristic which is not found with other apes or monkeys, besides humans. The dark side of this cooperative breeding behaviour is that humans, marmosets and tamarins are the only primates where mothers sometimes deliberately harm their own babies or leave them to die (Hrdy 2009: 96–101).
5. As a sociologist by training, I regret that my discipline—contrary to, for example, the economics of innovation—appears to be one of the most hesitant to contribute to this research programme. In sociology Darwinism appears still to be associated with social Darwinism, which in its turn in most textbooks is incorrectly associated with Herbert Spencer. Social Darwinism is a somewhat simplistic adoption of Darwinism by many conservatives—even nowadays—who equate individualistic competition and socioeconomic equality with the Darwinian principle of survival of the fittest. Herbert Spencer, who coined that principle of survival of the fittest, would, however, never have called himself a Darwinian, as he supported the optimistic Lamarckian version of evolution. At the same time, even when Spencer supported the market system, he emphasized human cooperation more than typical social Darwinists would do (Hodgson 1993: 80–98; Leonard 2009; Hodgson & Knudsen 2010: 16–18, 102–103, 223). For a more general assessment of sociologists' aversion towards Darwinism, see van den Berghe (1990). Authors who have been emphasizing the cooperative elements in evolution and who could maybe help sociologists to overcome their aversion are Samuel Bowles and Herbert Gintis (2011) and Martin Nowak (2011).
6. Of course, there is not always agreement in this research programme. On the contrary, there are lively discussions and polemics continuously, so that it is not always easy for relative outsiders to see the forest for the trees.

7. Aldrich (1999: 21) mentions diffusion as a fourth mechanism, but diffusion is never static: it nearly always implies at least marginal innovation—that is, new variety—as we saw in Chapter 3 with the help of Figure 3.3 (Gold 1983: 107; Jacobs 1990: 11–12).

8. Eldredge and Gould (1972) introduced the concept of 'punctuated equilibrium' to emphasize that evolution in many cases only proceeds through sudden leaps which interrupt long periods of stasis. *Homo sapiens,* for example, have not changed much since its inception some 130,000 years ago.

9. In neo-Darwinian approaches, beside selection, the concept of 'sorting' is used. With this term, authors such as Gould, Vrba and Eldredge refer to relatively random survival as a consequence of sheer chance, contrary to selection, which implies causality: survival as a consequence of greater fitness in a given environment (Hodgson 1993: 46; Eldredge 1997: 393).

10. Sometimes this mechanism has been called Lamarckian, but strictly speaking, this is not correct, as cultural inheritance works through imitation, communication and learning and not via the genes (compare, e.g., Hodgson 1993: 40, 47, with Hodgson & Knudsen 2010: 61–88). Interestingly, Lamarckian inheritance has recently received a renewed relevance as a consequence of the epigenetics revolution (Carey 2011).

11. As I discussed in Section 3.2, this also leads to forms of speciation—new species (categories) of products.

12. Unfit organizations can survive for some time, but in the end even the mighty fall (Collins 2009).

13. The least we can say is that the small amount of supersocial species such as ants and humans have been very successful (Nowak 2011: 155–158, 165–168).

14. According to Samuel Bowles (2006), warfare could be an explanation for altruism and group selection. When you know that you will not be left on the battlefield when you're wounded, but taken home and cared for afterwards, you are probably prepared to take more risks in the fight. This, in turn, increases the chances of your group during the fight. (For a further discussion of group selection, see also Nowak 2011: 81–94.)

15. In order to be able to talk about group selection, different groups have to be distinguishable with enough differentiating characteristics.

16. Other animals also show forms of the cultural transference of skills within the group, which illustrates the fact that human learning is only a further development at a higher level of emergent learning, which is already present in other species (de Waal 1996: 210–212; Boyd & Richerson 2000: 150–152; Laland & Odling-Smee 2000: 128–130; Lenski 2005: 37–39). This is also the basis of Ulrich Witt's continuity hypothesis, which states that natural selection has 'shaped the ground, and still defines the constraints, for man-made, or cultural, evolution . . . not withstanding that the mechanisms and regularities of cultural evolution differ from those of natural evolution' (quoted in Hodgson & Knudsen 2010: 58). For this reason, I disagree with Bart Nooteboom, who tends to view the use of an evolutionary framework as being mainly metaphorical (in generalized Darwinism we are talking about ontology, not just analogy). For the same reason I see no necessary contradiction with the use of learning or complexity approaches which Nooteboom proposes (Nooteboom 2000: 77, 87–90).

17. Hodgson and Knudsen (2010: 26, 38–39) rightly state that generalized Darwinism only provides an overarching theoretical framework rather than a complete theory encompassing all the details in either the social or the biological sphere. In each case, concrete analysis of the data has to answer the question as to why certain innovations are selected.

18. This is one of the major themes of my book *Mapping Strategic Diversity* (Jacobs 2010). Generalized Darwinism and (related) complexity theory on the one hand make strategy makers more modest compared with voluntaristic strategists who believe in long-term planning based on the idea that 'where there is a will, there is way'; however, on the other hand they may highlight where there is possibly room for smart—and especially interactive—strategic initiatives (see also Beinhocker 2006: 323–325, 333–348). In addition, this book tries to show how understanding and mapping selection systems may help to increase chances for innovative success.

NOTES TO CHAPTER 5

1. Just like the term 'evolution' itself, 'survival of the fittest' was not Darwin's original formulation but Herbert Spencer's, as Darwin himself preferred 'decent with modification' and 'natural selection.' Alfred Russell Wallace, who developed a theory of natural selection independently from Darwin, convinced Darwin to adopt Spencer's formulations (Hodgson 1993: 81–82).
2. In Section 6.2, I will also talk about market failure related to valuing innovation without buying, for example, in the realm of the arts.
3. Relative advantage and compatibility with culture are further elaborated in Section 5.4.
4. The definition of what is rewarding again differs between individuals and sectors. In the cultural sphere, quite a few suppliers (e.g., amateur musicians) are already pleased with a small amount of attention (or a few glasses of beer).
5. 'Value system' is the term Michael Porter (1985: 34–35) uses for the chain of activities from raw materials to end products. In Section 6.5, I use Porter's visualization of value systems to map selection in fashion (Figures 6.3 and 6.4).
6. In marginal analysis, it is assumed that consumers equalise the marginal utility gained from spending money on the different goods they consume. Marginal utility is important because as a rule utility decreases with the amount of a good consumed. Consumers will spend their last bit of money on goods with the relatively highest utility at that moment.
7. In this sense, fashion is also about marginal differentiation (Section 3.1). I will come back to this in Section 6.3.
8. From my experience of doing sector analysis in a variety of industries, I know how difficult it is for managers in an industry to think outside that box. See also my discussion of different framing schools in Chapter 7 of my book on mapping strategic diversity (Jacobs 2010: 134–146).
9. In Section 2.3 (on process innovation), we have already seen that increasingly firms are involving customers directly in innovation processes (co-design). I will come back to this in Chapter 6.
10. For an overview, see, for example, Aunger (2000).
11. Sometimes people combine elements of conflicting ideologies, such as Catholicism and Marxism, which suggests that these ideologies can be split into smaller cultural variants.
12. See also Section 4.2 on gene-culture co-evolution.
13. Kenrick and others (2002: 348–349) in a similar way talk about six domains of social life associated with corresponding fundamental goals: (1) self-protection, (2) coalition formation, (3) status seeking, (4) mate choice, (5) relationship maintenance and (6) offspring care.
14. Buss also subsumes conflict between sexes (including jealousy and tactics of mate retention) under this heading and—surprisingly—not under the second one.

15. In other eusocial species, such as ants, bees or naked mole rats, large-scale cooperation remains restricted to genetically related individuals.

16. People usually see themselves as smarter and more handsome than the average. One commentator of the 2012 US elections summarized it as basically a fight between about half of the population feeling itself intellectually superior against the other half feeling itself ethically superior. For an elaborate analysis of this framing of high versus middle-brow culture, see Bourdieu (1979; 1993).

17. As we have already seen before, this applies to all products. No product can be isolated from continuous societal discussions through which they are continuously requalified (Callon et al. 2002).

18. According to the Darwinian art critic Denis Dutton and others, most people in different cultures prefer similar paintings of a landscape which apparently looks a bit like the savannah from which our species evolved—this is referred to as the 'Savannah hypothesis' (Dutton 2009: 13–28).

19. In Darwinian literary studies, it has been found that typical storylines which are recognizable in people's daily life, such as love, family, justice, adventure, overcoming adversity and death, are most popular (Carroll 2004; Dutton 2009: 127–134). However, many people in the realm or art will only speak of valuable art when these stories are not too easily recognizable (Bourdieu 1993; Rothenberg 2012: 122–131).

20. In Bourdieu's terms, such an innovation requires investment in new cultural capital.

21. In the Dutch study on design effectiveness (Candi et al. 2010) I discussed in Section 2.1, usability was indeed subsumed under the technical elements of design.

22. Some people (e.g., Candi et al. 2010) here refer to the experiential, symbolic or emotional aspects of design, but in my opinion these terms are not sufficiently clear or discriminating. Experience, emotion and symbols may also be related to usability or more functional aspects of design.

23. Communication with customers may be very productive, but listening too much to them may also be counterproductive, as we saw in Section 2.1.

NOTES TO CHAPTER 6

1. Many strategy textbooks neglect the internal side of strategizing, presenting organizations as one supposedly rational strategic unit. I have tried to correct this picture in the strategy textbook I wrote myself (Jacobs 2010).

2. Apparently, Wijnberg here makes a jump from the selection of an innovation to the selection of the producer. Of course, the consumer may select an innovation because of the reputation of the producer, but not necessarily.

3. From another article, it appears that Wijnberg (1995: 226) sees the selection of scientific papers as a good example of this.

4. The authoritative Office of Technology Assessment (OTA), related to the US Congress, which existed between 1972 and 1995, was a source inspiration for this. It was finally closed down by the Republican majority in Congress led by Newt Gingrich in 1995.

5. Fashion critics are probably more important for the initial recognition and valuation of new fashion designers than for that of specific fashion items. When the reputation of a designer has been established, this designer will have some credibility in the longer term, relatively independently of what he or she specifically designs (see also Section 6.3).

6. 'Paying' is, of course, not a very adequate term here.

7. They may, of course, pay a part of it, for instance, in the form of an entry ticket or a donation and in this way help to maintain the monument.

8. At least from the perspective of high culture.

9. See, for example, Throsby's discussion of non-use values and externalities related to cultural public goods, such as museums and monuments (Throsby 2001: 36–38, 78–83, 87–88).

10. See all discussions about the presumed necessity and legitimacy of public funding in the realm of the arts (e.g., van Klink 2005: 17–32). A recent contribution was Richard Florida's observation that the cultural infrastructure of a region plays an important role in attracting the most creative professionals and, as a consequence, the most attractive businesses in a creative or knowledge-based economy (Florida 2002; 2005). Therefore, art appears to even play a role in the selection and survival of regions. It is, however, difficult to draw conclusions from all these interesting arguments—even when they would be correct about a concrete level of necessary public spending in the realm of the arts.

11. In some cases this may also take the form of market selection, for example, when museums compete (perhaps with private buyers) to purchase a work of art. The buying is not by a private individual but by a hierarchy (and possibly is the result of a public discussion) established with a clear cultural function. In other cases, funding is conditional on one authority and one executor (e.g., a theatre company) and may require that this executor earn a certain percentage of its income on the market. This is then a form of hybrid selection.

12. Of course, in all spheres of life, nonmarket activities take place which are possibly very valuable, even from an economic perspective (from the raising of children and private gardening to the creation of art), without being rewarded in monetary terms. As a consequence, the economic development of countries or cultures in which there is a high degree of nonmonetary economic exchange is sometimes underestimated (and the wealth created by their subsequent replacement by monetary exchange, overestimated). I will come back to such nonmarket activities later on, for instance, in the discussion about cocreation with customers (Section 6.7).

13. In addition, Williamson later on (1991a) recognized hybrid modes of economic organization between markets and hierarchies, but these have a totally different meaning than what I call hybrid selection. Williamson's hybrids refer to forms of long-term relationships between organizations such as long-term contracting, franchising and reciprocal trading which nowadays are mostly subsumed under the heading of 'networks' or 'interfirm alliances.' In my approach, most of these can be seen as forms of market selection. Networks have also a social meaning. In this meaning, they may lead to peer or expert influence (Sections 6.3 and 6.8) or to cocreation with customers (Section 6.7).

14. Nowadays children, in many cases, decide on purchases, whereas the parents pay—a new form of hybrid expert selection?

15. Especially in man's professional clothing, the example of CEOs, managing directors or partners appears to be of utmost importance. Therefore, according to Michael Bregg of Thomas Pink, 'Men's designers have to dress CEOs of companies' (Tang 2006).

16. Neotribes, a concept coined by Michel Maffesoli (1996), are a kind of virtual communities characterized by similarity in style. With this, he reacted to previous conceptualisations in terms of subcultures, which had a more realistic connotation and tended to exaggerate similarity, even when Maffesoli also emphasizes similarity. 'This bond is without the rigidity of forms of organization with which we are familiar; it refers more to a certain ambiance, a state of mind, and is preferably to be expressed through lifestyles that favour appearance and "form" ' (Maffesoli 1996: 98).

17. 'Value system' is the term Michael Porter (1985: 34–35) uses for the chain of activities from raw materials to end products, such as those represented in Figures 6.3 and 6.4.

18. From 1998 onwards, Lego had already experimented with customer cocreation with its more sophisticated Mindstorm Robotics toys. One of its fans even developed an alternative operating system for it (Prahalad & Ramaswamy 2004: 52–53, 139–140).
19. In Section 3.4, we saw that many innovations only take off after winning over pragmatic customers in relatively small niches.
20. A few years ago, trend watchers introduced the term 'crowd clout' for this.
21. In this respect, Marco Mossinkoff developed the concept of 'glue value' of different brands.
22. As a rule, this is also the case in the sciences. However, from time to time a new paradigm emerges, such as generalized Darwinism discussed in Chapter 4, aiming at interaction and synthesis.
23. For an inspiring visualization, see the more than fifty tribes photographed by Ari Versluis and Ellie Uyttenbroek (2002).
24. In 2011, the American fashion firm Abercrombie & Fitch even paid Michael Sorrentino, part of the cast of the MTV reality series Jersey Shore, *not* to wear its apparel (*Financial Times,* 20–08–2011)! These could be examples of what Wipperfürth (2005) calls 'brand hijack.' Wipperfürth himself doesn't, however, give many examples of real customer-induced brand hijacks. As a genuine marketer, he is more interested in cocreated hijack.
25. In this way, they play the role of opinion leaders as we know them from traditional two-step-flow communication theory (Rogers 2003: 204–312).
26. Such bandwagon effects are forms of increasing returns to adoption which operate purely on the information side of demand, contrary to other forms which operate more on the supply side (scale economies, learning by using) or via the combination of both (network externalities, technological interrelatedness) (Arthur 1988: 590–591; van den Ende et al. 2003: 274–276).
27. From complexity theory, we learn that the dynamics of a network, consisting of a number (N) of entities, is determined by the number (K) and strength (P) of the connections between these entities (Stacey et al. 2000: 113–116).
28. As we saw in Section 3.3, for this reason Geoffrey Moore (1995) proposes that we should think more tactically and strategically about crossing the chasm from the early enthusiastic adopters of an innovation to more pragmatic consumers.
29. This constitutes the so-called A-list of different kinds of professionals (actors, writers, visual artists, musicians, consultants) which implicitly exists in many of the creative industries (Caves 2000: 7–8, 28, 33–34).
30. For similar reasons, many producers try to extend a successful brand to other products. Such line extensions, however, endanger the clear brain position of such a brand (Ries & Trout 1986: 101–125).

NOTES TO CHAPTER 7

1. See also my process approach in Chapters 7 and 8 of *Mapping Strategic Diversity* (Jacobs 2010).
2. In the systems approach, a black box is a system or subsystem that is not analysed further. For example, you draw a goods warehouse with input and output within a larger system. The way in which that warehouse is organised internally is not seen as relevant for understanding the larger system.
3. In Latour's conceptualization, nonhuman elements may play a kind of autonomous role. For this reason, he prefers the neutral term 'actant' to the more anthropomorphic 'actor' (Latour 1987: 84; 2005: 54–55).
4. Of course, we are also continuously trying to convince other people. A large part of all management endeavour, for example, boils down to talking and writing

in a persuasive way (Eccles & Nohria 1992: 9). McCloskey and Klamer once calculated that (in 1993) 26% of the American economy consisted of persuasion or sweet talk (i.e., the persuasive and judgemental part of transactions). At one end of the spectrum, they estimated that the work of lawyers, judges, public relations specialists and social, recreational and religious workers was 100% talking and persuasion. However, even at the other end of that same spectrum, they still thought the work of natural scientists was 25% talk (McCloskey & Klamer 1995). I come back to this in Section 6 of Chapter 10.

5. In Chapter 8, we will see that for this it is necessary to take both a myopic and a far-sighted perspective on customer needs.

6. If through this practice a station plays unpopular music and for this reason loses listeners, payola can be seen as a form of compensation for this loss. This does not deny the fact that payola is legally restricted in different countries, which may increase the likelihood of DJs or programme directors being bribed personally (Caves 2000: 286–287, 291).

7. Astroturf is artificial grass, so the wordplay comes from comparing this kind of stealth marketing with genuine grass-roots movements.

8. More examples can be found in the Wikipedia article on astroturfing.

9. Our species is so supersocial that people may be so glad to be part of a community that they are prepared to be free volunteers for commercial advertising networks, even for products they don't really know (Walker 2008: 172–194)!

10. In the realm of the arts, many museums nowadays ask for a few works from—especially not yet well-known—artists in exchange for organizing exhibitions about them, as these exhibitions add value to the other works of these artists.

NOTES TO CHAPTER 8

1. Stichting Management Studies, The Hague, the Netherlands.

2. I come back to this in Section 8.2.

3. Other authors call such organizations 'ambidextrous'—literally having two right hands—incorporating structures and management processes that are appropriate to both the creation and the exploitation of innovation or, to put it differently, to combine incremental learning and developing radically new concepts (Daft 2004: 407–408). What Nonaka and Takeuchi (1995: 166–171) propose with their 'hypertext organization,' in which a project-team layer has to be combined with a business-system and a knowledge-base layer, follows a similar logic.

4. See also the Sections 1.3 and 6.7.

5. In 2011, Liz Claiborne gave up its attempts to integrated MEXX and sold it again.

6. Think for example of Apple and Steve Jobs. In accounting terms, we could say that the difference in terms of valuation of the firm is that between liquidation value (an organization too dependent of its founder or leader) and going concern.

7. This confirms the point made earlier (in Section 2.2) that there is a lot of hidden innovation not covered by traditional R&D statistics.

8. In a recent study, Jim Collins (2009) found out that *the* important reason why previously successful organizations began a downward movement was their failure to recognize problems. They just found all kinds of reasons to deny the seriousness of their problems.

9. See also Section 6.7 on open innovation.

10. To be clear, we did our study just before the recent financial crisis.

11. See also the Sections 1.3 and 6.7.

12. A problem is, of course, that forms of short-term feedback may be misunderstood for long-term developments. Are we successful because of our smart strategies and routines, or just because of sheer luck in a growing market? See also Chapter 8 on co-evolutionary approaches in my strategic management book *Mapping Strategic Diversity* (Jacobs 2010).

NOTE TO CHAPTER 9

1. Fortunately, thanks to discussions about the creative economy, in recent years this one-sidedness of public discourse about innovation has decreased.

NOTES TO THE BONUS TRACK

1. See Section 1.7 of the main text.
2. This firm, Stage Entertainment, is one of the cases presented in Chapter 8 of the main text.
3. However, as we saw in Section 8.3 of the main text, this has to be combined with the other nine disciplines of successful innovation routines in order to become 'productive creativity.'
4. Cultural tourism represents about 15% of total tourism related employment (KEA 2006: 76).
5. KEA collected data for the twenty-seven countries which have been part of the EU since 2007, plus Norway, Iceland and Liechtenstein. With EU 25, the EU member states of 2006 are meant, the actual EU minus Bulgaria and Romania.
6. See Section 5.6 of the main text.
7. Nevertheless, even in Las Vegas, Florida is able to find interesting new developments (2012: 343–345).
8. See also Section 1.1 of the main text.
9. However, according to the World Bank's Knowledge Economy Index (for which a combination of indicators related to economic incentive regime, innovation, education and ICT indicators is used) the Netherlands comes fourth in 2012, behind Sweden, Finland and Denmark, whereas the United States only comes twelfth (http://siteresources.worldbank.org/INTUNIKAM/Resources/2012.pdf).
10. The essence of a fuzzy approach has been explained in a separate box in Section 3.3.
11. Standaard Beroepenclassifictie SBC 2000, i.e. SBC 1992, partially updated in 2001 (CBS 2001).
12. See also Section 2.2 of the main text.
13. Policymakers in the Netherlands, for example, have been very proud of this country's high rankings in the field of scientific publishing but at the same time are complaining about the low level of application of these fantastic insights. What they only slowly start to recognize is that, to a very large extent, they are the cause of this knowledge paradox with their unilateral publishing-oriented yardstick. Here government risks falling in the same 'management by one-sided objectives' trap as many managers in business.
14. In his recent *The Rise of the Creative Class, Revisited,* Florida (2012) is more worried about the increasing red-blue polarization in the United States, where conservatism has become 'the default ideology of the economically left behind.'
15. See also Section 6.2 of the main text.
16. See Chapter 8 of the main text.

Bibliography

Abrahamson, Eric (1991) 'Managerial Fads and Fashions: The Diffusion and Rejection of Innovations,' *The Academy of Management Review*, 16 (3): 586–612.

Acemoglu, Daron & James Robinson (2012) *Why Nations Fail: The Origins of Power, Prosperity, and Poverty*, New York: Crown.

Agins, Teri (1999) *The End of Fashion*, New York: Quill.

Akrich, Madeleine, Michel Callon & Bruno Latour (2002a) 'The Key to Success in Innovation Part I: The Art of Interessment,' *International Journal of Innovation Management*, 6 (2): 187–206.

—— (2002b) 'The Key to Success in Innovation Part II: The Art of Choosing Good Spokespersons,' *International Journal of Innovation Management*, 6 (2): 207–225.

Aldrich, Howard (1999) *Organizations Evolving*, London: Sage.

Anderson, Chris (2006) *The Long Tail: Why the Future of Business Is Selling Less of More*, New York: Hyperion.

Arthur, Brian (1988) 'Competing Technologies: An Overview,' in Giovanni Dosi, Christopher Freeman, Richard Nelson, Gerald Silverberg & Luc Soete (eds.), *Technical Change and Economic Theory*, London: Pinter, 590–607.

Aunger, Robert (ed.) (2000) *Darwinizing Culture: The State of Memetics as a Science*, Oxford: Oxford University Press.

AWT (Adviesraad voor het Wetenschaps- en Technologiebeleid) (2006a) *Open stellingen: Essays over Open Innovatie*. The Hague.

—— (2006b) *Opening van zaken: Beleid voor een open innovatie*. The Hague.

Barrett, Louise, Robin Dunbar & John Lycett (2002) *Human Evolutionary Psychology*, Hampshire: Palgrave.

Baum, Joel & Terry Amburgey (2002) 'Organizational Ecology,' in Joel Baum (ed.), *Companion to Organizations*, Oxford: Blackwell: 304–326.

Beinhocker, Eric (2006) *The Origin of Wealth: Evolution, Complexity, and the Radical Remaking of Economics*, Boston: Harvard Business School Press.

Benkler, Yochai (2006) *The Wealth of Networks: How Social Production Transforms Markets and Freedom*, New Haven: Yale University Press.

Bennett, Andy (1999) 'Subcultures or Neo-Tribes? Rethinking the Relationship between Youth, Style and Musical Taste,' *Sociology*, 33 (3): 599–517.

Bessant, John, Sarah Caffyn & Maeve Gallagher (2001) 'An Evolutionary Model of Continuous Improvement Behaviour,' *Technovation*, 21 (2): 67–77.

Bhidé, Amar (2006) 'Venturesome Consumption, Innovation and Globalization,' paper presented at the Joint Conference of CESIFO and the Centre on Capitalism and Society, Venice, 21–22 July.

Bijker, Wiebe, Thomas Hughes & Trevor Pinch (eds.) (1987) *The Social Construction of Techologocial Systems*, Cambridge, Mass.: MIT Press.

Black, C. & M. Baker (1987) 'Success through Design,' *Design Studies*, 8 (4): 207–216.

Bourdieu, Pierre (1979) *La distinction: critique sociale du jugement*, Paris: Minuit.

—— (1993) *The Field of Cultural Production*, Cambridge: Polity.

Bowker, Geoffrey & Susan Star (1999) *Sorting Things Out: Classification and Its Consequences*, Cambridge, Mass.: MIT Press.

Bowles, Samuel (1998) 'Edogenous Preferences: The Cultural Consequences of Markets and other Economic Institutions,' *Journal of Economic Literature*, 36 (1): 75–111.

—— (2006) 'Group Competition, Reproductive Leveling, and the Evolution of Human Altruism,' *Science*, 314 (5805) 8–12–2006: 1569–1572.

Bowles, Samuel & Herbert Gintis (2011) *A Cooperative Species: Human Reciprocity and Its Evolution*, Princeton, N.J.: Princeton University Press.

Boyd, Brian (2009) 'Art and Selection,' *Philosophy and Literature*, 33 (1): 204–220.

Boyd, Robert & Peter Richerson (2000) 'Memes: Universal Acid or a Better Mousetrap?' in Aunger (2000): 143–162.

Brand, Jan & José Teunissen (eds.) (2005) *Global Fashion, Local Tradition: Over de globalisering van mode*, Warnsveld: Terra.

Brown, Stephen (2003) *Free Gift Inside!!*, Chichester: Capstone.

Buss, David (2009) *Evolutionary Psychology: The New Science of the Mind*, 3rd edition, Boston: Pearson.

Callon, Michel, Cécile Méadel & Volonola Rabeharisoa (2002) 'The Economy of Qualities,' *Economy and Society*, 31 (2): 194–217.

Candi, Marina, Gerda Gemser & Jan van den Ende (2010) *Effectiviteit van Design*, Rotterdam: Rotterdam School of Management.

Carey, Nessa (2011) *The Epigenetics Revolution*, London: Icon.

Carroll, Joseph (2004) *Literary Darwinism: Evolution, Human Nature and Literature*, New York: Routledge.

Carson, Paula, Patricia Lanier, Kerry Carson & Brandi Guidry (2000) 'Clearing a Path through the Management Fashion Jungle: Preliminary Trailblazing,' *Academy of Management Journal*, 43 (6): 1143–1158.

Caves, Richard (2000) *Creative Industries: Contracts between Art and Commerce*, Cambridge, Mass.: Harvard University Press.

CBS (2001) *Standaard Beroepenclassifictie SBC 2000*. Netherlands.

CEC (Commission of the European Communities) (2009) *Design as a Driver of User-Centred Innovation*, Commission Staff Working Document, 7 April.

Chakravorti, Bhaskar (2003) *The Slow Pace of Fast Change*, Boston: Harvard Business School Press.

Chesbrough, Henry (2003) *Open Innovation*, Boston: Harvard Business School Press.

Christensen, Clayton (1997) *The Innovator's Dilemma*, Boston: Harvard Business School Press.

Christensen, Jens (1995) 'Asset Profiles for Technological Innovations,' *Research Policy*, 24 (5): 727–745.

Ciborra, Claudio (2002) *The Labyrinths of Information: Challenging the Wisdom of Systems*, Oxford: Oxford University Press.

Collins, Jim (2009) *How the Mighty Fall*, London: Random House Business Books.

Conran, Terence (1996) *Terence Conran on Design*, London: Conran Octopus.

Cova, Bernard & Véronique Cova (2002) 'Tribal Marketing,' *European Journal of Marketing*, 36 (5/6): 595–620.

Croonen, Evelien (2006) *Strategic Interaction in Franchise Relationships*, Ridderkerk: Labyrinth.

Daft, Richard (2004) *Organization Theory and Design*, 8th edition, Mason, Ohio: Thomson South-Western.

Davenport, Thomas & John Beck (2001) *The Attention Economy*, Boston: Harvard Business School Press.

David, Paul (1986) 'Understanding the Economics of QWERTY: The Necessity of History,' in William Parker (ed.), *Economic History and the Modern Economist,* Oxford: Blackwell, 30–49.

Debackere, Koen, Bart Clarysse, Nachoem Wijnberg & Michael Rappa (1994) 'Science and Industry: A Theory of Networks and Paradigm,' *Technology Analysis and Strategic Management,* 6 (1): 21–37.

de Bono, Edward (1992) *Sur/Petition: Creating Value Monopolies When Everyone Else Is Merely Competing,* London: HarperCollins.

de Bruijn, Micha (2005) 'Het wordt stil in Aalsmeer,' *Intermediair,* 29 January.

de Jong, Eelke (2009) *Culture and Economics,* London: Routledge.

den Butter, Frank, Jan Möhlmann & Paul Wit (2008) 'Trade and Product Innovations as Sources for Productivity Increases: An Empirical Analysis,' *Journal of Product Analysis,* 30: 201–211.

den Hertog, Pim (2000) 'Knowledge Intensive Business Services as Co-Producers of Innovation,' *International Journal of Innovation Management,* 4 (4): 491–528.

—— (2010) *Managing Service Innovation,* Utrecht: Dialogic.

de Sitter, L. U. (1994) *Synergetisch Produceren,* Assen: Van Gorcum.

de Soto, Hernando (2000) *The Mystery of Capital: Why Capitalism Triumphs in the West and Fails Everywhere Else,* New York: Basic Books.

de Vries, Jan (2008) *The Industrious Revolution,* Cambridge: Cambridge University Press.

de Vries, Leonard (1973) *De dolle entree van automobiel en velocipee,* Bussum: De Haan.

de Waal, Frans (1996) *Good Natured: The Origins of Right and Wrong in Humans and Other Animals,* Cambridge, Mass.: Harvard University Press.

Dodgson, Mark, David Gann & Ammon Salter (2002) 'The Intensification of Innovation,' *International Journal of Innovation Management,* 6 (1): 53–83.

—— (2005) *Think, Play, Do: Technology, Innovation, and Organization,* Oxford: Oxford University Press.

Dolfsma, Wilfred (2007) *Knowledge Economies: Innovation, Organization and Location,* London: Routledge.

Dosi, Giovanni, Christopher Freeman, Richard Nelson, Gerald Silverberg & Luc Soete (eds.) (1988) *Technical Change and Economic Theory,* London: Pinter.

Dunbar, Robin (2004) *The Human Story,* London: Faber and Faber.

Dunbar, Robin, Louise Barrett & John Lycett (2007) *Evolutionary Psychology,* Oxford: Oneworld.

Dutton, Denis (2009) *The Art Instinct,* Oxford: Oxford University Press.

Eccles, Robert & Nitin Nohria (1992) *Beyond the Hype: Rediscovering the Essence of Management,* Boston: Harvard Business School Press.

Edquist, Charles (ed.) (1997) *Systems of Innovation,* London: Pinter.

Eldredge, Niles (1985) *Unfinished Synthesis: Biological Hierarchies and Modern Evolutionary Thought,* New York: Oxford University Press.

—— (1997) 'Evolution in the Marketplace,' *Structural Change and Economic Dynamics,* 8 (4): 385–398.

Eldredge, Niles & Stephen Jay Gould (1972) 'Punctuated Equilibria: An Alternative to Phyletic Gradualism,' in T. Schopf (ed.), *Models in Paleobiology,* San Francisco: Freeman Cooper, 82–115.

Evans, Harold, Gail Buckland & David Lefer (2004) *They Made America,* New York: Little, Brown and Company.

Florida, Richard (2004) *The Rise of the Creative Class,* New York: Basic Books.

—— (2005) *The Flight of the Creative Class,* New York: HarperBusiness.

—— (2012) *The Rise of the Creative Class, Revisited,* New York: Basic Books.

Florida, Richard, Charlotta Mellander & Kevin Stolaric (2011) *Creativity and Prosperity: The Global Creativity Index,* Toronto: Martin Prosperity Institute.

Fonseca, José (2002) *Complexity and Innovation in Organizations,* London: Routledge.

Foray, Dominique (2004) *The Economics of Knowledge,* Cambridge, Mass.: MIT Press.

Freeman, Chris & Luc Soete (1997) *The Economics of Industrial Innovation,* 3rd edition, London: Pinter.

Freeman, Christopher & Carlota Perez (1988) 'Structural Crises of Adjustment, Business Cycles and Investment Behaviour,' in Dosi et al. (1988): 38–66.

Frijda, Nico (1986) *The Emotions,* Cambridge: Cambridge University Press.

Gale, Bradley (1994) *Managing Customer Value,* New York: Free Press.

Gaus, H., J. van Hoe, M. Breckeleire & P. Van der Voort (1991) *Mensen en mode: De relatie tussen kleding en konjunktuur,* Leuven: Garant.

Gemser, Gerda (1999) *Design Innovation and Value Appropriation,* PhD thesis, Rotterdam: Erasmus University.

Gemser, Gerda, Dany Jacobs & Ritzo ten Cate (2004) *Design in ICT: An Exploratory Study on the Value Added of Design in the Dutch ICT Sector,* Amsterdam: Premsela Dutch Design Foundation.

Gemser, Gerda, Dany Jacobs & Ritzo ten Cate (2006) 'Design and Competitive Advantage in Technology-Driven Sectors: The Role of Usability and Aesthetics in Dutch IT Companies,' *Technology Analysis & Strategic Management,* 18 (5): 561–580.

Gemser, Gerda, Marina Candi & Jan van den Ende (2011) 'How Design Can Improve Firm Performance,' *Design Management Review,* 22 (2): 72–77.

Gemser, Gerda & Mark Leenders (2001) 'How Integrating Industrial Design Impacts on Corporate Performance,' *Journal of Product Innovation Management,* 18 (1): 28–38.

Gemser, Gerda, Mark Leenders & Felix Janszen (1997) *Concurreren door investeren in industrieel ontwerpen,* Amsterdam: BNO.

Giddens, Anthony (1979) *Central Problems in Social Theory: Action, Structure and Contradiction in Social Analysis,* London: Macmillan.

Gladwell, Malcolm (2000) *The Tipping Point,* London: Abacus.

Gold, Bela (1983) 'On the Adoption of Technological Innovations in Industry: Superficial Models and Complex Decision Processes,' in Stuart MacDonald, D. Lamberton & Thomas Mandeville (eds.), *The Trouble with Technology: Explorations in the Process of Technological Change,* London: Pinter, 104–121.

Green, Hardy (2005) 'Why Oprah Opens Readers' Wallets,' *Business Week,* 10 October: 39.

Green, Stephen, Mark Gavin & Lynda Aiman-Smith (1995) 'Assessing a Multidimensional Measure of Radical Technological Innovation,' *IEEE Transactions on Engineering Management,* 42 (3): 203–214.

Grin, John, Jan Rotmans & Johan Schot (2010) *Transitions to Sustainable Development,* New York: Routledge.

Groupe Bernard Juilhet (1995) *French SMEs and Design.* Research ordered by the French Ministry of Industry, Paris.

Hamel, Gary & C.K. Prahalad (1994) *Competing for the Future,* Boston: Harvard Business School Press.

Hammer, Michael & James Champy (1993) *Reengineering the Corporation,* London: Brealey.

Hampden-Turner, Charles & Alfons Trompenaars (1993) *The Seven Cultures of Capitalism,* New York: Currency Doubleday.

Hannan, Michael & John Freeman (1977) 'The Population Ecology of Organizations,' *American Journal of Sociology,* 82 (4): 929–964.

——— (1989) *Organizational Ecology,* Cambridge, Mass.: Harvard University Press.

Hård, Mikael & Andrew Jamison (2005) *Hubris and Hybrids: A Cultural History of Technology and Science,* New York: Routledge.

Harkins, J. (1994) 'Is Design Doing Its Job?,' *Machine Design,* 7 February: 53–58.

Harris, Michael & Richard Halkett (2007) *Hidden Innovation: How Innovation Happens in Six "Low Innovation" Sectors*, London: NESTA.

Hertog, Pim den (2000) 'Knowledge-Intensive Business Services as Co-Producers of Innovation,' *International Journal of Innovation Management*, 4 (4): 491–528.

Hodgson, Geoffrey (1993) *Economics and Evolution: Bringing Life Back into Economics*, Ann Arbor: University of Michigan Press.

—— (1997) 'Economics and the Return to Mecca: The Recognition of Novelty and Emergence,' *Structural Change and Economic Dynamics*, 8 (4): 399–412.

Hodgson, Geoffrey & Thorbjørn Knudsen (2010) *Darwin's Conjecture. The Search for General Principles of Social and Economic Evolution*, Chicago: University of Chicago Press.

Hofstede, Geert (1991) *Cultures and Organizations*, London: HarperCollins.

Holbrook, Morris (ed.) (1999) *Consumer Value: A Framework for Analysis and Research*, London: Routledge.

Holland, John (1995) *Hidden Order: How Adaptation Builds Complexity*, New York: Basic Books.

Hrdy, Sarah Blaffer (2009) *Mothers and Others: The Evolutionary Origins of Mutual Understanding*, Cambridge, Mass.: Belknap Press of Harvard University Press.

Hulsman, Bernard (2005) *De krul en andere modes in de architectuur*, Amsterdam: Prometheus.

Jacobs, Dany (1988) *Gereguleerd staal: Nationale en internationale economische regulering in de Westeuropese staalindustrie 1750–1950*, PhD thesis, University of Nijmegen, Nijmegen.

—— (1990) *The Policy Relevance of Diffusion*, The Hague: Ministry of Economic Affairs.

—— (1999a) *Het Kennisoffensief: Slim concurreren in de kenniseconomie*, 2nd edition, Alphen a/d Rijn: Samsom.

—— (1999b) 'Internet versterkt de behoefte aan transport,' *Economisch Statistische Berichten*, 2 September: D14–D17.

—— (2004) 'Looking at Strategy: Fashion, Design and the Paradoxes of Strategic Vision,' in Dany Jacobs & Andreas Stockert (eds.), *Fashion ChaChaCha: Fashion Chained and UnChained: Chances and Changes in the Chain*, Amsterdam: HvA Publicaties, 13–38.

—— (2006a) 'The Promise of Demand Chain Management in Fashion,' *Journal of Fashion Marketing and Management*, 10 (1): 84–96.

—— (2006b) 'Creativiteit en de economie,' *Holland Management Review*, 107 (May–June): 17–27.

—— (2010) *Mapping Strategic Diversity*, London: Routledge.

—— (2012) 'Creatief ondernemerschap en het dubbel succescriterium,' *Holland Management Review*, 146 (November/December): 37–42.

—— (2013) 'Een co-evolutionair perspectief op het dubbel succescriterium,' *Holland Management Review*, 147 (January/February): 52–59.

Jacobs, Dany & Hendrik Snijders (2008) *Innovatieroutine*, Assen: Van Gorcum.

—— (2012) 'The Innovation Decathlon: Ten Commandments for Successful Innovation,' *GSTF Journal on Business Review*, 2 (2): 174–179.

Jacobs, Dany & Jan Waalkens (2001) *Innovatie²: Vernieuwingen in de innovatiefunctie van ondernemingen*, Deventer: Kluwer.

Jacobs, Dany & Marco Mossinkoff (2007) 'Pomo-Hypo: Fashion Marketing at Two Extremes,' paper presented at the Conference Extreme Fashion, IFFTI (International Foundation of Fashion Technology Institutes), Toronto, 12–15 April.

Jacobs, Dany, Mies Bernelot Moens & Sue Westerman (2008) 'Creativiteit in gradaties,' *Economisch Statitsche Berichten* (7 March): 151–153.

Jacobs, Jane (2000) *The Nature of Economies*, New York: Vintage.

Jaikumar, Ramchandran (1986) 'Postindustrial Manufacturing,' *Harvard Business Review,* 64 (6; November/December): 69–76.

Janssen, Marco & Wander Jager (2001) 'Fashions, Habits and Changing Preferences: Simulation of Psychological Factors Affecting Market Dynamics,' *Journal of Economic Psychology,* 22 (6): 745–772.

Jenkyn Jones, Sue (2002) *Fashion Design,* London: Laurence King.

Kazmierczak, Elzbieta (2003) 'Design as Meaning Making: From Making Things to the Design of Thinking,' *Design Issues,* 19 (2): 45–59.

KEA European Affairs (2007) *The Economy of Culture in Europe,* Brussels: KEA.

Kelley, Tom (2001) *The Art of Innovation,* London: HarperCollins.

Kenrick, Douglas, Jon Maner, Jon Butner, Norman Li, Vaughn Becker & Mark Schaller (2002) 'Dynamic Evolutionary Psychology: Mapping the Domains of the New Interactionist Paradigm,' *Personality and Social Psychology Review,* 6 (4): 347–356.

Kleiner, Art (1996) *The Age of Heretics,* London: Brealey.

Knudsen, Thorbjørn (2002) 'Economic Selection Theory,' *Journal of Evolutionary Economics,* 12 (3): 443–470.

Krugman, Paul (1991) *Geography and Trade,* Leuven and Cambridge, Mass.: Leuven University Press/MIT Press.

Laland, Kevin & John Odling-Smee (2000) 'The Evolution of the Meme,' in Aunger (2000): 121–141.

Lammers, Cor, A. Mijs & Wim van Noort (1997) *Organisaties vergelijkenderwijs,* Zevende druk, Utrecht: Spectrum.

Latour, Bruno (1987) *Science in Action,* Cambridge, Mass.: Harvard University Press.

——— (2005) *Reassembling the Social,* Oxford: Oxford University Press.

Laursen, Keld & Ammon Salter (2006) 'Open for Innovation: The Role of Openness in Explaining Innovation Performance among U.K. Manufacturing Firms,' *Strategic Management Journal,* 27 (2): 131–150.

Leadbeater, Charles (2004) *Britain's Creativity Challenge,* Creative & Cultural Skills.

Leifer, Richard, Christopher McDermott, Gina Colarelli O'Connor, Lois Peters, Mark Rice & Robert Veryzer (2000) *Radical Innovation,* Boston: Harvard Business School Press.

Lenski, Gerhard (2005) *Ecological-Evolutionary Theory,* Boulder, Colo.: Paradigm.

Leonard, Thomas (2009) 'Origins of the Myth of Social Darwinism: The Ambiguous Legacy of Richard Hofstadter's *Social Darwinism in American Thought*,' *Journal of Economic Behavior & Organization,* 71 (1): 37–51.

Lessig, Lawrence (2004) *Free Culture: The Nature and Future of Creativity,* New York: Penguin.

Lester, Richard & Michael Piore (2004) *Innovation: The Missing Dimension,* Cambridge, Mass.: Harvard University Press.

Levitt, Steven & Stephen Dubner (2005) *Freakonomics,* London: Allen Lane.

Levy, Steven (1984) *Hackers: Heroes of the Computer Revolution,* New York: Doubleday.

Lidwell, William, Kritina Holden & Jill Butler (2003) *Universal Principles of Design,* Gloucester, Mass.: Rockport.

Lipovetsky, Gilles (1994) *The Empire of Fashion,* Princeton, N.J.: Princeton University Press.

Lundvall, Bengt-Åle (ed.) (1992) *National Systems of Innovation,* London: Pinter.

Maffesoli, Michel (1996) *The Times of the Tribes: The Decline of Individualism in Mass Society,* London: Sage.

Magretta, Joan (2002) *What Management Is,* New York: Free Press.

Manshanden, Walter, Otto Raspe & Paul Rutten (2004) 'De waarde van creatieve industrie,' *Economisch-Statistische Berichten,* 89 (28 May): 252–254.

March, James (1991) 'Exploration and Exploitation in Organizational Learning,' *Organization Science,* 2 (1): 71–87.

Markides, Constantinos & Paul Geroski (2005) *Fast Second: How Smart Companies Bypass Radical Innovation to Enter and Dominate New Markets,* San Francisco: Jossey-Bass.

Marlet, Gerard & Clemens van Woerkens (2004) 'Het economisch belang van de creatieve klasse,' *Economisch-Statistische Berichten,* 89 (11 June): 280–283.

Marsh, Peter (2012) *The New Industrial Revolution,* New Haven, Conn.: Yale University Press.

McCloskey, Donald & Arjo Klamer (1995) 'One Quarter of GDP Is Persuasion,' *American Economic Review,* 85 (2): 191–195.

McDonough, Edward & Kenneth Kahn (1996) 'Using "Hard" and "Soft" Technologies for Global New Product Development,' *R&D Management,* 26 (3): 241–253.

Metcalfe, John Stanley (2008) 'Accounting for Economic Evolution: Fitness and the Population Method,' *Journal of Bioeconomics,* 10 (1): 23–49.

Metz, Tracy (2005) 'Creativiteit is geld waard,' *NRC Handelsblad,* 18.

Micklethwait, John & Adrian Wooldridge (1996) *The Witch Doctors,* London: Heinemann.

Miles, Ian (2007) 'Innovation in Services' in Jan Fagerberg, David Mowery & Richard Nelson (eds.), *The Oxford Handbook of Innovation,* Oxford: Oxford University Press, 433–458.

Mintzberg, Henry (1989) *Mintzberg on Management: Inside Our Strange World of Organizations,* New York: Free Press.

Mirowsky, Philip (1990) 'Learning the Meaning of a Dollar: Conversation Principles and the Social Theory of Value in Economic Theory,' *Social Research,* 57 (3): 689–717.

Misa, Thomas (1992) 'Theories of Technological Change: Parameters and Purposes,' *Science, Technology and Human Values,* 17 (1): 3–12.

——— (2003) 'The Compelling Tangle of Modernity and Technology,' in Thomas Misa, Philip Bray & Andrew Feenberg (ed.), *Modernity and Technology,* Cambridge, Mass.: MIT Press, 1–30.

——— (2004) *Leonardo to the Internet: Technology & Culture from the Renaissance to the Present,* Baltimore, Md.: The Johns Hopkins University Press.

Mokyr, Joel (2002) *The Gifts of Athena: Historical Origins of the Knowledge Economy,* Princeton, N.J.: Princeton University Press.

Moore, Geoffrey (1995) *Inside the Tornado,* New York: HarperBusiness.

——— (2005) *Dealing with Darwin. How Great Companies Innovate at Every Phase of Their Evolution,* New York: Penguin.

Mossinkoff, Marco (2012) *Modern Marketing in Disguise,* PhD thesis, University of Amsterdam, Amsterdam.

Mossinkoff, Marco & Dany Jacobs (2009) 'Kennis-, creatief en beleveniswerk,' *Economisch Statistische Berichten,* 94 (23 January): 58–60.

Muller, W. (1990) *Vormgeven: Ordening en Betekenisgeving,* Utrecht: Lemma.

Nederlands Forum voor Techniek en Wetenschap (1994) *Naar een betere benutting van kennis in de industrie,* Amsterdam: Author.

Nelson, Richard (ed.) (1993) *National Innovation Systems,* Oxford: Oxford University Press.

Nelson, Richard & Sidney Winter (1982) *An Evolutionary Theory of Economic Change,* Cambridge, Mass.: Belknap Press.

Nijs, Diane (2003) 'Imagineering: Engineering for Imagination in the Emotion Economy,' in *Creating a Fascinating World,* Breda, NHTV: 15–34.

Nijs, Diane & Frank Peters (2002) *Imagineering. Het creëren van belevingswerelden,* Amsterdam: Boom.

Nonaka, Ikujiro & Hirotaka Takeuchi (1995) *The Knowledge-Creating Company,* New York: Oxford University Press.

Nooteboom, Bart (2000) *Learning and Innovation in Organizations and Economies,* Oxford: Oxford University Press.

North, Douglass (1990) *Institutions, Institutional Change and Economic Performance,* Cambridge: Cambridge University Press.

––––––– (1991) 'Institutions,' *Journal of Economic Perspectives,* 1 (5): 97–112.

––––––– (1997) 'Transaction Costs through Time,' in Claude Menard (ed.), *Transaction Cost Economics: Recent Developments,* Cheltenham: Elgar, 149–160.

Nowak, Martin & Roger Highfiel (2011) *Supercooperators: Evolution, Altruism and Human Behaviour,* Edinburgh: Canongate.

OECD (1992) *Technology and the Economy. The Key Relationships,* Paris: OECD.

––––––– (2002) *Frascati Manual: Proposed Standard Practice for Surveys on Research and Development,* Paris: OECD.

––––––– (2005) *Oslo Manual: Guidelines for Collecting and Interpreting Innovation Data,* Paris: OECD.

Osterwalder, Alexander & Yves Pigneur (2009) *Business Model Generation,* Amsterdam: Author.

Parks, Don & Ivan Noer (1993) 'Southwest Airlines: Expanding beyond the Standard,' in Bob de Wit & Ron Meyer (eds.), *Strategy. Process, Content, Context,* London: Thomson, 1028–1037.

Perez, Carlota (2002) *Technological Revolutions and Financial Capital,* Cheltenham: Elgar.

Peters, Tom (1994) *The Pursuit of WOW!,* New York: Vintage.

Petroski, Henry (2006) *Success through Failure: The Paradox of Design,* Princeton, N.J.: Princeton University Press.

Pinault, Lewis (2000) *Consulting Demons: Inside the Unscrupulous World of Global Corporate Consultants,* New York: HarperBusiness.

Pinch, Trevor & Wiebe Bijker (1987) 'The Social Construction of Facts and Artifacts: Or How the Sociology of Science and the Sociology of Technology Might Benefit Each Other,' in Wiebe Bijker, Thomas Hughes & Trevor Pinch (eds.), *The Social Construction of Technological Systems,* Cambridge, Mass.: MIT Press, 17–50.

Pine, Joseph & James Gilmore (1999) *The Experience Economy: Work Is Theatre & Every Business a Stage,* Boston: Harvard Business School Press.

Pinker, Steven (1994) *The Language Instinct,* New York: William Morrow.

Porac, Joseph, Howard Thomas & Charles Baden-Fuller (1989) 'Competitive Groups as Cognitive Communities: The Case of Scottish Knitware Manufacturers,' *Journal of Management Studies,* 26 (4): 397–416.

Porter, Michael (1980) *Competitive Strategy,* New York: Free Press.

––––––– (1985) *Competitive Advantage,* New York: Free Press.

––––––– (1990) *The Competitive Advantage of Nations,* New York: Free Press.

Potter, S., R. Roy, C. H. Capon, M. Bruce, V. Walsh & J. Lewis (1991) *The Benefits and Costs of Investment in Design: Using Professional Design Expertise in Product, Engineering and Graphics Projects,* Open University/Umist, Milton Keynes.

Prahalad, C.K. & Venkat Ramaswamy (2004) *The Future of Competition: Co-Creating Unique Value with Customers,* Boston: Harvard Business School Press.

Press, Mike & Rachel Cooper (2003) *The Design Experience,* Aldershot: Ashgate.

Pruys, S. (1972) *Dingen vormen Mensen: een Studie over Produktie, Consumptie, en Cultuur,* Bilthoven: Ambo.

Regis, Ed (2003) *The Info Mesa,* New York: Norton.

Reich, Robert (1991) *The Work of Nations,* New York: Knopf.

Reynaert, Indira & Daphne Dijkerman (2011) *Basisboek crossmedia concepting,* 2nd edition, Den Haag: Boom Lemma.

Ricchetti, Marco (2005) 'Good Design Is Good Business: The Economic Valuation of Design,' in Giannino Malossi (ed.), *Designing Value*, Milan: MeesPierson, 4–30.

Richerson, Peter & Robert Boyd (2005) *Not by Genes Alone: How Culture Transformed Human Evolution*, Chicago: The University of Chicago Press.

Ries, Al & Jack Trout (1986) *Positioning: The Battle for Your Mind*, revised edition, New York: Warner.

Rijkenberg, Jan (1998) *Concepting*, Den Haag: Bzztôh.

Rogers, Everett (2003) *Diffusion of Innovation*, 5th edition, New York: Free Press.

Roothart, Hilde & Wim van der Pol (2001) *Van trends naar brands*, Deventer: Kluwer.

Rothenberg, David (2011) *Survival of the Beautiful*, London: Bloomsbury.

Rothenberg, Randall (1994) *Where the Suckers Moon: The Life and Death of an Advertising Campaign*, New York: Vintage.

Rowe, Noel (1996) *The Pictorial Guide to the Living Primates*, Charlestown: Pogonias.

Rutten, Paul, Olaf Koops & Ottilie Nieuwenhuis (2012) *Toekomst van het Nederlandse Cross Media Cluster: Cross Media Monitor 2012*, Hilversum: iMMovator.

Rutten, Paul, Walter Manshanden, Jos Muskens & Olaf Koops (2004) *De creatieve industrie in Amsterdam*, Delft: TNO-STB.

Saad, Gad (2007) *The Evolutionary Bases of Consumption*, Mahwah, N.J.: Lawrence Erlbaum.

Schot, Johan & Arie Rip (1997) 'The Past and Future of Constructive Technology Assessment,' *Technological Forecasting & Social Change*, 54 (2/3): 251–268.

Schumpeter, Joseph (1934/1983) *The Theory of Economic Development*, New Brunswick, N.J.: Transaction.

Scoble, Robert & Shel Israel (2006) *Naked Conversations*, Hoboken, N.J.: Wiley.

Shankar, Venkatesh, Leonard Berry & Thomas Dotzel (2009) 'A Practical Guide to Combining Products + Services,' *Harvard Business Review*, 87 (11; November): 95–99.

Shapiro, Carl & Hal Varian (1999) *Information Rules*, Boston: Harvard University Press.

Simmel, Georg (1904/1957) 'Fashion,' reprinted in *The American Journal of Sociology*, 62 (6): 541–558.

Simon, Herbert (1990) 'A Mechanism for Social Selection and Successful Altruism,' *Science*, 250 (December): 1665–1668.

Smits, Ruud & Jos Leyten (1991) *Technology Assessment: Waakhond of Speurhond?* Zeist: Kerkebosch.

Snijders, Hendrik (1997) *Eendimensionale wetenschap*, Den Haag: Creon.

——— (2008) 'Indicatoren voor innovatie zijn contraproductief,' *Economisch-Statistische Berichten*, (12 December): 749–750.

Solomon, Michael & Nancy Rabolt (2004) *Consumer Behavior in Fashion*, Upper Saddle River, N.J.: Prentice Hall.

Stacey, Ralph, Douglas Griffin & Patricia Shaw (2000) *Complexity and Management: Fad or Radical Challenge to Systems Thinking?* London: Routledge.

Stahl, Geoff (2003) 'Tastefully Renovating Subcultural Theory: Making Space for a New Model,' in David Muggleton & Rupert Weinzierl (eds.), *The Post-Subcultures Reader*, Oxford: Berg, 27–40.

Stam, Erik & Jeroen de Jong (2005) 'De creatieve klasse op de pijnbank,' *Economisch Statistische Berichten*, 90 (June): 257–259.

Stevenson, Angus & Maurice Waite (eds.) (2011) *Concise Oxford English Dictionary*, Oxford: Oxford University Press.

Sutton, Robert (2001) *Weird Ideas That Work: 11½ Ways to Promote, Manage, and Sustain Innovation*, London: Alan Lane/Penguin.

Tang, Syl (2006) 'The Tipping Point,' *Business of Fashion*, magazine supplement to *Financial Times*, 3 March: 12–13.

Tellis, Gerard & Peter Golder (1996) 'First to Market, First to Fail? Real Causes of Enduring Market Leadership,' *Sloan Management Review*, 37 (2; Winter): 65–75.

Thompson, Don (2008) *The $12 Million Stuffed Shark: The Curious Economics of Contemporary Art and Auction Houses*, London: Aurum.

Throsby, David (2001) *Economics and Culture*, Cambridge: Cambridge University Press.

Tidd, Joe, John Bessant & Keith Pavitt (2005) *Managing Innovation: Integrating Technological, Market and Organizational Change*, 3rd edition, Chichester: Wiley.

Tukker, Arnold (2004) 'Eight Types of Product-Service System: Eight Ways to Sustainability? Experiences from SusProNet,' *Business Strategy and the Environment*, 13 (4): 246–260.

Ulrich, K. & S. Eppinger (1995) *Product Design and Development*, New York: McGraw-Hill.

Utterback, James (1994) *Mastering the Dynamics of Innovation*, Boston: Harvard Business School Press.

van Ark, Bart & Gjalt de Jong (2004) *Productiviteit in dienstverlening*, Assen: Van Gorcum.

van den Berghe, Pierre (1990) 'Why Most Sociologists Don't (and Won't) Think Evolutionarily,' *Sociological Forum* 5 (2): 173–185.

van den Ende, Jan, Nachoem Wijnberg, Rianne Vogels & Michiel Kerstens (2003) 'Organizing Innovative Projects to Interact with Market Dynamics: A Coevolutionary Approach,' *European Management Journal*, 21 (3): 273–284.

van der Heyden, Kees (1996) *Scenarios: The Art of Strategic Conversation*, Chichester: Wiley.

van der Zwan, Arie (1987) 'Koplopers en achterblijvers in de bedrijvenwereld' in Arie van der Zwan (ed.), *Koplopers en achterblijvers: Effectiviteit in beleid en management*, Baarn: Anthos, 74–91.

van Klink, Pim (2005) *Kunsteconomie in nieuw perspectief*, Groningen: K's Concern.

van Leeuwen, Theo & Carey Jewitt (eds.) (2001) *Handbook of Visual Analysis*, London: Sage.

Versluis, Ari & Ellie Uyttenbroek (2002) *Exactitudes*, Rotterdam: 010 Publishers.

Veryzer, Robert (1998) 'Discontinuous Innovation and the New Product Development Process,' *Journal of Product Innovation Management*, 15 (4): 304–321.

von Hippel, Eric (1988) *The Sources of Innovation*, Oxford: Oxford University Press.

——— (2005) *Democratizing Innovation*, Cambridge, Mass.: MIT Press.

von Hippel, Eric & Georg von Krogh (2006) 'Free Revealing and the Private-Collective Model for Innovation Incentives,' *R&D Management*, 36 (3): 295–306.

von Stamm, Bettina (2003) *Managing Innovation, Design and Creativity*, Chichester: Wiley.

Waldrop, Mitchell (1992) *Complexity: The Emerging Science at the Edge or Order and Chaos*, London: Penguin.

Walker, Rob (2008) *I'm with the Brand*, London: Constable.

Walsh, V., R. Roy, M. Bruce & S. Potter (1992) *Winning by Design: Technology, Product Design and International Competitiveness*, Oxford: Blackwell.

Watts, Duncan (2003) *Six Degrees: The Science of a Connected Age*, London: Heinemann.

Weinzierl, Rupert & David Muggleton (2003) 'What Is "Post-subcultural Studies" Anyway?,' in David Muggleton & Rupert Weinzierl (eds.), *The Post-Subcultures Reader*, Oxford: Berg, 3–23.

Wheeler, Alina (2003) *Designing Brand Identity*, Hoboken, N.J.: Wiley.

Wijnberg, Nachoem (1995) 'Selection Processes and Appropriability in Art, Science and Technology,' *Journal of Cultural Economics*, 19: 221–235.

——— (2004) 'Innovation and Organization: Value and Competition in Selection Systems,' *Organization Studies*, 25 (8): 1469–1490.

Williamson, Oliver (1975) *Markets and Hierarchies: Analysis and Antitrust Implications*, New York: Free Press.

——— (1991a) 'Comparative Economic Organization: The Analysis of Discrete Structural Alternatives,' *Administrative Science Quarterly*, 36 (2): 269–296.

——— (1991b) 'Strategizing, Economizing, and Economic Organization,' *Strategic Management Journal*, 12 (Special Issue Winter): 75–94.

Wilson, Edward (1998) *Consilience: The Unity of Knowledge*, London: Abacus.

Wipperfürth, Alex (2005) *Brand Hijack*, New York: Penguin-Portfolio.

Witt, Ulricht (1991) 'Economics, Socio-Biology, and Behavioural Psychology on Preferences,' *Journal of Economic Psychology*, 557–573.

Womack, James, Daniel Jones & Daniel Roos (1990) *The Machine That Changed the World*, New York: HarperPerennial.

World Bank (2012) *Knowledge Economy Index*, Washington (http://siteresources.worldbank.org/INTUNIKAM/Resources/2012.pdf).

Wouters, Frank (2005) *De bedrijfsnar: Manifest voor een marketingrevolutie*, Roeselare: Roularta.

Zyman, Sergio (2004) *Renovate before You Innovate*, New York: Portfolio.

Index

For Product Safety Concerns and Information please contact our EU
representative GPSR@taylorandfrancis.com
Taylor & Francis Verlag GmbH, Kaufingerstraße 24, 80331 München, Germany